Securities and Obscurities
a case for reform of the law of company accounts

R J Chambers

SYDNEY UNIVERSITY PRESS

SYDNEY UNIVERSITY PRESS
SETIS at the University of Sydney Library
University of Sydney
www.sup.usyd.edu.au

Originally published in Melbourne by Gower Press, 1973.

The publication of this book is part of the University of Sydney Library's
Australian Studies electronic texts initiative. Further details are available at
www.sup.usyd.edu.au

ISBN 1 920898 30 1
      978-1-920898-30-4

For current information see http://purl.library.usyd.edu.au/sup/1920898301

Designed in Australia at the University Publishing Service University of
Sydney

CONTENTS

ACKNOWLEDGEMENTS

The conclusions reached from evidence presented in this book were given in *Accounting, Evaluation and Economic Behavior* (Prentice-Hall, 1966) and 'Second Thoughts on Continuously Contemporary Accounting' (*Abacus*, vol. 6, no. 1, September 1970). Some of the evidence has been used in lectures, articles and books over the past twenty years. A pilot exercise in consolidating the evidence was a paper, 'Evidence for a Market Selling Price Accounting System', given at a symposium in the University of Kansas in May 1970 (published in Robert R Sterling, ed., *Asset Valuation and Income Determination*, Scholars Book Co., Lawrence, Kansas, 1971). To all who have sponsored or published these earlier pieces I am indebted for opportunity and encouragement.

I am grateful to the many companies which over years have supplied their annual reports; and to friends, colleagues and the financial and professional press for examples which would not otherwise have come to my notice. I acknowledge with thanks the assistance of works cited in the List of References, and especially the permissions granted to use copyright material.

To Dorothy Simons I am in debt for mining the mountain of material which yielded the figures digested into such modest space in Chapter 6, and for other countless and varied bits of excavation which are the lot of a research assistant. Thanks to Barbara Brennan, numberless drafts of patchwork manuscript were at last turned into a presentable typescript.

The examples cited in the book are only a fraction of what could have been tendered. The omission of reference to your company, your article or your book is regretted; but enough is enough. Hold me accountable for these and other omissions, errors or obscurities.

RJC

FOREWORD TO SERIES

During the 1960s and 1970s a remarkable series of books were produced by academic staff in the field of accounting at the University of Sydney. All were out of print. The Accounting Foundation believed that they should be made available to a new generation of scholars and researchers.

First and foremost amongst these was *Accounting, Evaluation and Economic Behavior (AEEB)*, written by the University's foundation professor of accounting, R.J. Chambers and first published in 1966. Several distinguished scholars have acknowledged that *AEEB* was a pivotal contribution to the development of the 'decision usefulness' theme in accounting research. It presented a systematic argument for the clarification of the meaning of key accounting concepts (such as 'asset', 'liability', 'equity', 'revenue' and 'expense'). It argued that there was a need to identify the property of assets and liabilities to be measured in accounting—with Chambers proposing the use of current market prices, or contemporary cash equivalents. It also argued for the use of adjustments to the application of money as a measurement scale when there were changes in the purchasing power of money. Decades later, many (though not all) of these ideas were adopted by the international accounting profession, when profession-sponsored bodies published 'statements of accounting concepts' or statements of conceptual 'frameworks'.

Chambers was a prolific contributor to research journals and many of those journal contributions are now available in electronic form. Amongst his later contributions in book form was *Securities and Obscurities*. When first published Chambers freely acknowledged that it was a polemic. Readers are left in no doubt that the world would be a better place if there was widespread adoption of 'continuously contemporary accounting'. Suffice it to observe that during the 1960s, questioning of the 'historical cost' model of accounting was often regarded as a form of heresy. By 2006, a surprising proportion of accounting standards now prescribe the use of market values in asset or liability valuation.

But arguably Chambers' greatest legacy at the University of Sydney was his encouragement of scholarly endeavour by colleagues and students.

The other books re-published at this time were all initially based on research undertaken by academic staff during the 1970s and early 1980s. The topics reflect the diversity of interests of the 'Sydney school' at that time: Clarke (1980) on the history of price level accounting, Walker (1978) on the history of ideas about the preparation of consolidated statements, Wells (1978) on accounting for common costs, and Wolnizer (1987) on auditing as independent authentication.

It was a period when academic research was largely analytical rather than empirically-based; and when the interests of academics at Sydney were largely directed at questioning the status quo—whether that be expressed in the way accounting or auditing was practised, or in the conventional wisdom as expressed in text-books of the time.

The interests of accounting academics have changed over time. But this collection of works displays the heritage of the University of Sydney in scholarly research and advocacy of the 'decision usefulness' theme in accounting.

(Neil Wykes)
President, Accounting Foundation
University of Sydney

PREFACE

Atlantic Acceptance, Reid Murray, Pergamon, Continental Vending, Pacific Acceptance, Westec, BarChris, Yale Express—such companies as these have provided the 'spice' of commercial and financial journalism in the last decade or so. The affairs of these and other companies have been constantly under the notice of company directors, lawyers, accountants and auditors, and the rest of us. Investors and creditors have lost millions through some of them. Auditors and directors of some of them have been sued for millions. Legislators and regulators have been kept constantly on their toes amending the rules, patching up the loopholes in rules and devising new rules to curb the inventiveness of the unfortunate, the astute or the fraudulent officials of companies.

One thing common to all the companies mentioned is that the financial information they published was seriously deficient in quality. This book strikes at that common element. Not because of the failures, losses and litigation that have befallen a relatively small number of companies; rather because prevailing laws and practices under them give rise, almost universally, to distorted representations of the financial results and affairs of companies.

Drawing primarily on examples from the United Kingdom, the United States and Australia, the book shows that the existing practices, even of companies that are well esteemed, are inadequate, uninformative and often obscurantist. But often through no fault of their own. The practices that companies have adopted have generally been permissible under the statutes, regulations and technical rules of accounting of their time. The trouble has been that the laws, regulations and rules have been vague, toothless and often self-contradictory.

The financial information on company affairs which flows to the securities market is the product, principally, of accounting rules. But we do not hold that accountants or their professional associations are alone responsible for the state of the rules. Managers, directors, stock-brokers, financiers, lawyers and others have also played a part, consciously or unwittingly, in bending and stretching the rules. We consider the consequences of this and find it in the interest neither of companies and their officers, nor investors and creditors, nor of the business community at large.

Drawing on other examples from the same countries, on the opinions of analysts, jurists, investigators and others, and on remedial amendments of the statutes, the book establishes a case for the reform of present laws and practices. It proposes a set of rules on financial reporting which would reduce substantially the ignorance and guesswork that now interfere with the exercise of informed judgment by investors on the merits of corporate security investments. The proposals are not a panacea for all commercial ills. But the evidence adduced supports their value to investors and others as protection against misrepresentation, whether innocent or fraudulent.

The value of a well-informed securities market is almost universally acknowledged. But that today's securities markets are well informed is a myth. Uneasiness about the present state of practice is widespread. But the will to reform it is weak and fugitive. Old habits die hard, especially when they serve specific parties at concealed costs to others.

The remedy seems to lie in the hands of the legislators. This book, however, provides evidence of the necessity and direction of reform, no matter who, in the upshot, brings it about.

R J Chambers
University of Sydney
August 1972

1

COMPANY LIMITED

'Limited liability: paid up capital; perfect publicity.'
/ William Clay, 1836 /

'Some seven men form an Association
   (If possible, all Peers and Baronets),
They start off with a public declaration
   To what extent they mean to pay their debts.
That's called their Capital: if they are wary
   They will not quote it at a sum immense.
The figure's immaterial—it may vary
   From eighteen million down to eighteenpence.

They then proceed to trade with all who'll trust 'em,
   Quite irrespective of their capital
(It's shady, but it's sanctified by custom);
   Bank, Railway, Loan, or Panama Canal.
You can't embark on trading too tremendous—
   It's strictly fair, and based on common sense—
If you succeed, your profits are stupendous—
   And if you fail, pop goes your eighteenpence.'
/ W S Gilbert, *Utopia Limited*, 1893 /

'The economic historian of the future may assign to the nameless
inventor of the principle of limited liability, as applied to trading
corporations, a place of honour with Watt and Stephenson and
other pioneers of the Industrial Revolution.'
/ *The Economist*, 1926 /

The modern business corporation is a relatively recent creation
of statute law. Its antecedents were certain types of non-business
corporation and non-corporate forms of business. Its distinctive
feature is that it is a device for marshalling smaller quantities into
larger quantities of money and other resources, and putting them
to use at the risks of business.

It is similar to a partnership, insofar as it puts together the contributions of members. But it differs from a partnership in having

a legal existence independent of the identity of its members. It differs also inasmuch as its management is not directly in the hands of its members, and the liability of its members for its debts and obligations is limited. Its management is privy to details of its operations; its members are not necessarily technically skilled in some phase of its operations, as are the members of a partnership.

Promoters, members, managers and creditors—these are the parties most closely associated with the formation, survival and growth of companies. Their fortunes are linked, sufficiently loosely it seems, to allow them all some space to manoeuvre but, ideally, sufficiently tightly to prevent any group from taking undue advantage of another. There are many circumstances in which the interests of these parties may be at odds. Promoters may conceal from prospective investors information that is necessary to enable investors to judge fairly the merits of a proposal. Directors and managers may conceal information that is necessary to shareholders or creditors in deciding their courses of action. The limited liability of shareholders may encourage managers to borrow or otherwise to trade on margins too fine for the protection of creditors' interests. Creditors may seek to enforce their rights under conditions which threaten the existence of a company and the residual rights of its shareholders.

The company laws have attempted to regulate the behaviours of these parties in order to avoid abuse by any one of them of the position of power or privilege in which it may find itself. A crucial element of fair trading and negotiation is that the parties shall have knowledge of what is traded and of the conditions under which bargains are struck. This applies with special force to the trade in securities. Those who buy and sell shares, debentures, bonds and other paper titles cannot judge their merits in the same way as the merits of tangible goods may be judged. They must rely on information supplied by others. The law attempts to secure that they shall have it. It will be useful to sketch the origins of the present rules.

PROMOTERS

The marshalling of funds is done by promoters. (For present purposes, 'promoters' includes the directors of existing companies when they seek to raise new money.) They publish prospectuses or similar documents describing the ventures they propose and laying grounds for the confidence of investors or lenders in the outcomes of those ventures. Their claims of success may be modest or spectacular. But without some show of optimism and boldness, no flotation is likely to succeed. Therein lies the prospect of delusion.

In the eighteenth and early nineteenth centuries, the inventiveness and exuberance of promoters and the gullibility of investors were notorious. Their heirs and successors are still with us. One of the earliest and most persistent exercises of legislators on company affairs has been to attempt to restrain the flights of fancy and golden promises with which promoters might adorn their prospectuses. Through experience of frauds and exaggerated claims, the law on prospectuses has gradually been tightened. A great amount of circumstantial detail must now be given in documents that constitute invitations to the public to invest in companies.

Of course, promoters have, or are presumed to have, more technical knowledge of their projects that can be, or should be, disclosed in any prospectus. After all, they are offering participation in a venture with at least some unique elements. It would be folly to expose these to the risk of piracy by others. Hence the information required to be contained in a prospectus relates principally to the legal and financial aspects of the proposed venture. The publication of this information in no way protects investors from the risks of business. But it is designed to protect them from some of the risks of initial ignorance.

CREDITORS

One of the inducements to investors in the shares or stock of a company is the possibility of participation with limited liability for the debts and obligations of the company. The propriety of the limited liability principle was strongly contested in mid-nineteenth-century England, when the future style of the business corporation was being debated.

Some took the 'partnership' line. Members should not be relieved of full liability for the debts and obligations of their companies. Limited liability would encourage wanton disregard of the proper interests of creditors: ' . . . the stain which now attaches to bankruptcy would cease to exist', failure would not be accompanied by 'the degradation and guilt of having recklessly gambled with the interests of traders'.*

Others saw the matter differently. Shareholders would have no share, such as that of partners, in the ordinary conduct of company business. It would be unjust to saddle them with the same burden of liability as informed and active participants in the conduct of partnerships. Further, if joint stock companies were required to publish information on their financial affairs, that information would provide safeguards against unsupported borrowing and foolish lending.

The idea of compulsory financial publicity had been in the air for at least two decades. Its value as protection for creditors was now affirmed. A deputy governor of the Bank of England held:

> 'It is clear that the credit of a partnership of limited liability will be limited also, and will be governed by the security afforded by the known capital, and not by a vague estimate of property supposed to exist independently of the business, which in nine cases out of ten has no existence at all, or only a delusive existence.'

The Companies Act of 1862 established the right of incorporation with limited liability but did not make financial publicity obligatory. This produced the following observation of a writer to *The Times* in 1864:

> 'With an unlimited company the creditor looks to the solvency of the shareholders; with a limited company, his only reliance is the position of the business. If it were right that the public should have the means of ascertaining this in the case of a bank or an insurance company, it is, at least, equally important that it should be obtainable from other companies, especially where the creditors have no other securities than the actual assets, and to whom therefore a knowledge of the true position of affairs is essential. Balance sheets are not now required to be registered, nor is any power given to the public or creditors to inspect them. This is considered an extraordinary oversight, for the principle of limited

---

* Cited by Bishop Carleton Hunt, *The Development of the Business Corporation in England 1800–1867*, Cambridge, Mass., 1936. The words of William Clay at the head of the chapter and the quotations in the next two paragraphs are from the same source.

liability should be compulsory publicity. How can the public know whether to trust a company, if ignorant of the state of its position?'

Clearly the protection of the interests of creditors of companies was very much in the minds of supporters and opponents of the limited liability principle. The omission of the 1862 Act to make financial publicity obligatory was not remedied until much later. Even now it does not provide adequate information to enable creditors to protect themselves. At this stage, however, we merely wish to point out that financial publicity was thought to be a proper check on disregard for creditors' interests by limited liability companies and their directors.

SHAREHOLDERS AND DIRECTORS

The administration of the affairs of companies is in the hands of directors elected by the members. Shareholders as such take no part in day-to-day management. Directors, by their election, acquire command over much greater resources than they could have controlled as individuals or partners. And they have the benefit of technical advice and knowledge of the drift of company operations, knowledge that is not accessible to shareholders. They determine the style and scope of a company's operations and decide when and in what ways they shall be varied. That knowledge of the operational details of company affairs should be private is in the interests of shareholders. But how may shareholders be assured that the powers and privileged knowledge of directors (and appointed managers) are being exercised in shareholders' interests?

The primary device is the annual report of directors to members, the most important element of which is the financial statements of the company. It is customary in modern annual reports to deal descriptively with varied aspects of company operations. But the financial statements alone enable the outcome of all operations and events affecting the company to be represented in compact form. It may not seriously be supposed that investors could judge the operational efficiency of retailing, banking, oil-refining, steel-making or food-processing companies. However, as the interests of investors are financial, they may be assumed to be able to judge the financial outcome of whatever operations a company engages in.

As early as 1844 in the United Kingdom it was enacted that directors of registered companies should cause 'a full and fair balance sheet' to be made up periodically, should approve it, should have it audited and should file it together with the auditor's report with the registrar of companies, where it would be open to public inspection. However, the provision does not seem to have been followed or enforced. The 1862 Act relegated the financial publicity requirement to the optional articles of association of Table A of the Act. The regular publication of balance sheets did not become generally obligatory until 1928.

Meanwhile the relationship of directors to shareholders seems to have been regarded as one of paternalistic care. Directors would report to shareholders such information as they thought share-holders ought to have. They would do what seemed expedient. They would understate profits and assets, creating secret reserves. And they would be supported by the courts. In the course of his judgment in *Newton* v. *Birmingham Small Arms Ltd* [1906] 2 Ch. 378, Buckley J observed:

> 'If the balance sheet be so worded as to show there is an undisclosed asset, the existence of which makes the financial position better than shown, such a balance sheet will not, in my judgment, be necessarily inconsistent with the Act of Parliament ... The purpose of the balance sheet is primarily to show that the financial position of the company is at least as good as there stated, not to show that it is not or may not be better.'

This easy attitude towards secret reserves no longer prevails, as guide or doctrine, in explicit form. However, we shall later show that the old habit, acquired over decades, dies hard.

The law was vague. The courts could or would do little to clarify or give teeth to it. Said Lord Macnaghten in *Dovey* v. *Cory* [1901] AC 477: 'I do not think it is desirable for any tribunal to do that which Parliament has abstained from doing—that is, to formulate precise rules for the guidance or embarrassment of businessmen in the conduct of business affairs'.

Such dicta as these and the vagueness of the law have left the contents of the balance sheets of companies very much at the discretion of directors. Notwithstanding amplification of the statutory provisions on the contents of financial statements, there is still an enormous gap between the ideal that the law seems to envisage and the minimum disclosure tolerated under the law.

AUDITORS AND THE STOCK EXCHANGES

Two classes of person not directly involved in the administration of companies have come to have a close interest in the financial information published by companies. Since 1844, as we have seen, the audit of accounts has been regarded as a safeguard against abuse of the discretion of directors in making up financial reports. Stockbrokers and their associations have concerned themselves with the conduct of a fair market in securities. From their rules and stipulations it is clear that they regard adequate financial information as an essential element of a fair market.

No doubt, compulsory independent audit has reduced the possibilities of flagrant concealment or distortion of information, and the consequential misdirection of investors. But it has not provided as sure a safeguard as is often supposed. Under-and over-statement of assets and profits have occurred and do occur, on a large scale if out-of-date figures are published in accounts. Some of this has been fraudulent, and has remained long undiscovered. Some of it is deliberate—perhaps paternalistic, but not fraudulent. However, the greater part of it is not even deliberate. It is due to the mistaken respect accorded over many years to rules devised for purposes other than the full and fair reporting of financial positions and results.

In most cases auditors have lacked neither care nor diligence in doing what they do. But, since, legally, the financial statements are part of the report of the directors, auditors have generally accepted and relied on the decisions of directors on what shall be reported. What might have been expected to be independent authentication of what is reported has turned out to be authentication of what directors have decided to report. There can be no suggestion of connivance or of a conspiracy of silence. Indeed, an air of innocence, almost of naiveté, seems to breathe over all. Most directors believe they are reporting what's best in the interest of companies and shareholders. Auditors believe directors know best what's best. Each is buttressed by the assumed integrity of the other. At least that is how it appears. But the assumptions are sometimes ill-founded, to the cost of auditors and directors, and the much greater cost of the mass of inarticulate shareholders and creditors who have relied on the adequacy of the checks and balances of informed competition and an informed securities market.

These things have occurred notwithstanding the supervision exercised by the stock exchanges and other regulatory bodies. These organizations either have had only modest powers, or have chosen to exercise their powers only modestly, to supplement or implement the general provisions of the law.

All parties—directors, auditors and the exchanges—seem to have paid more regard to the minimum standard of disclosures permissible under the law than to the ideal expressed in the law. It is true that much of current practice is better than the bare minimum. But, as we shall show, little of it approaches the ideal. It seems that, as between the legislators, directors, auditors and the exchanges, each has shown a 'proper' regard for the integrity, competence and discretion of the other. But the network of powers and checks and balances is so loose that the system fails to provide the protection that reliable financial information should give. Reform of the law seems to be the only corrective, since the law occupies a pivotal position in the system.

THE COMPANY — A FINANCIAL DEVICE

The limited liability company has a legal form and legal rights, powers and obligations. It has economic functions—but these are not peculiar to companies. In principle, the company is a financial device. The interests of shareholders and creditors are financial interests in money flows. It is reasonable that security holders and prospective investors and lenders should want to judge from time to time whether their prospects of money flows—as interest, dividends, repayments or realizations—are affected by recent operations of a company and other events that impinge on it. Hence the statutory requirement that *financial* information on the positions and results of companies shall be published from time to time.

The law does not stipulate that technical information be published in periodical reports. It respects the right of privacy, the right of a company to exclusive benefit from inventiveness, research and ingenuity. It does not assume or imply that shareholders or creditors are or should be competent to form opinions on technical matters. If in practice some of them pay attention to technical matters, they do so only to obtain a general idea of the drift of a company's affairs.

It seems to be proper, therefore, to regard the provisions on disclosure of financial information as one of the key elements of the companies legislation. Financial information is the link between the investments and operations under the control of directors and managers and the different rights and interests of shareholders and creditors. The quality of that information determines whether the securities market is a fair market or a casino with loaded dice.

The 1963 Report of the Special Study of Securities Markets, sponsored by the US Securities and Exchange Commission, observed:

> 'Disclosure is the cornerstone of Federal securities regulation. It is the *sine qua non* of investment analysis and decision. It is the great safeguard that governs the conduct of corporate management in many of their activities. It is the best bulwark against reckless corporate publicity and irresponsible recommendation and sale of securities.'

Ideally, no doubt. But the 'great safeguard' is not as safe as it seems.

In the last twenty years the periodical financial statements of many companies have been found to be unreliable. Some companies have reported profits which bolstered the confidence of shareholders and creditors at the very time when they were heading for insolvency. Some have reported interim profits only to disclose final losses in a year. Some have juggled their reporting practices to give the impression of growth when, but for the juggling, their affairs would have looked far from auspicious and their prospects anything but rosy.

PROGRAMME

The generalizations of this chapter will be illustrated in what follows, from the practices of companies in the United Kingdom, the United States and Australia. The particular laws and commercial circumstances of these countries differ. But the general principles are substantially the same. Some of the examples and some of the arguments have previously been used by the author, but most of them have been collected for the present purpose. They are dated at various times during the past twenty or thirty years but most are of recent date. Different dates, types of anomaly, companies and locations have been used to demonstrate that the problems and defects we identify are not local or novel, but widespread and persistent.

The evidence—for this is substantially a book of evidence—points in one general direction: namely, that the financial statements of companies should and can be in up-to-date terms, based on the market prices of assets and on the discoverable shift in the purchasing power of money from time to time. At the end there is proposed a set of rules which, if adopted in the laws and regulations on corporate financial publicity, would remove the obscurities and the license to be obscure that at present are tolerated.

2

THE LOOSE REIN OF THE LAW

'The only way that the Legislature should interfere [with the conduct of limited companies] is by giving the greatest publicity to the affairs of such companies, that everyone may know on what grounds he is dealing.'
/ Robert Lowe, President of Board of Trade, 1856 /

'An Act to provide full and fair disclosure of the character of securities sold in interstate and foreign commerce and through the mails, and to prevent frauds in the sale thereof ...'
/ Title of US Securities Act of 1933 /

'The best laid schemes o' mice an' men
Gang aft a-gley.'
/ Robert Burns, *To a Mouse* /

PERIODICAL ACCOUNTING

All present laws relating to the public conduct of companies specify that statements of account, or balance sheets and income statements, shall be published periodically, generally annually. The rule is based, no doubt, on the fact that the fortunes of companies change from time to time, either through the aggressive initiative of companies themselves or through changes in the state of competition, technology and the markets in which companies buy and sell.

These classes of event may have many specific effects on a company. Its turnover may rise or fall. Its labour costs and material costs may rise or fall. It may be able to raise its prices, and it may be forced to lower them. It may increase or decrease the amounts or change the styles of its issued and outstanding securities. It may increase or decrease its inventories, its investment in buildings or in plant or in the securities of other companies. Growth in the demand for its products may increase the value of its plant and equipment; slackening of demand, increased competition and technical obsolescence may decrease the value of those assets. Regional developments may increase or decrease the value of its real estate. Stock market movements may increase or decrease the value of its portfolio investments.

Some of these changes arise from deliberate acts or choices of managers and directors. Some arise from events external to the company, over which the officers of the company have no control. But the job of managers and directors is to meet shifts in conditions, however they arise. The consequence of all these things is made apparent in the profit earned each year and the changes in the financial position of the company between the beginning and the end of the year. The terms 'perfect publicity' and 'full and fair disclosure' used in statements of broad principle seem to contemplate disclosure of the full consequences in a year of all acts and events that have affected a company's finances.

What specifically do the statutes say?

As we shall later be dealing with anomalies which are widespread, it will be useful to consider legislation and regulation of the kind found in jurisdictions on the pattern of the United Kingdom and the United States. The statutes and rules vary in many particulars. It will be sufficient, however, to deal descriptively with the clauses or sections that are germane. It is believed that our descriptions do no violence to the general purport of the current legislation.

LEGISLATION ON THE ENGLISH PATTERN

In most statutes based on or related to the UK Companies Act, the financial publicity provisions are distributed between the body of the act itself and a schedule to the act. In general, the act deals with the main governing principles and the schedule with detailed prescriptions of what shall appear in the financial statements.

A true and fair view: The directors of every company in which the investing public may become financially interested are required to prepare annually a balance sheet and profit and loss account which shall be laid before the annual general meeting and sent to all persons entitled to receive notice of general meetings. The balance sheet and profit and loss account shall give a true and fair

view of the state of affairs (or financial position) of the company
as at the end of its year, and of its profit or loss (or results) for
the year, respectively. What the statements report is expected to
be consistent with the books of account and other records of the
company.

There is required to be appended to the balance sheet and
profit and loss account a statement, on behalf of the directors and
signed by some of them, to the effect that the financial statements
give the required true and fair view. The financial statements are
to be audited and the auditors are required to state whether they
are in accordance with the act and are drawn up in such a way as
to give the required true and fair view.

These provisions seem to give ample assurance of the reliability
of the financial statements. They may be regarded as reasonably
straightforward expressions of the idea of perfect publicity or full
disclosure.

Now, if a true and fair view of the financial position of a company
(and hence of all companies) is to be given each year, it might
be presumed that there are some firm rules which should be
followed uniformly by all companies and consistently, year by year,
by all companies. And it might reasonably be supposed that a
true and fair view of a company's financial position at a stated
date would be a view given by reference to the market prices of
its assets at or about that date. The provisions of the acts and
their schedules, however, cut right across these presumptions of
uniformity, consistency and up-to-dateness at some points while
seeming to uphold them at others.

Fixed assets—alternative valuations: The schedule usually provides
that the amount to be shown in the balance sheet for any investment or fixed asset is to be its cost or the amount of a valuation
other than cost, reduced by the amount written off for depreciation or diminution in value since its purchase or subsequent
valuation. In effect this permits the directors to use a valuation as
out-of-date as the date of purchase of the asset or as up-to-date as
the balance sheet, and to deal with some assets in one way and
other assets in another. It allows any such asset to be shown at
a value from zero to whichever is the higher of cost and some
valuation other than cost. There is no constraint upon the mode

of valuation. Any value in the range just mentioned would apparently be consistent with the stipulation that a true and fair view be given.

In defence of the statute it must be said that the detailed rules of the schedule are made subordinate to the statute; notwithstanding anything contained in the schedule, a true and fair view must be given. But lacking explicit indication of the meaning of 'a true and fair view', it is understandable that directors might choose to value assets at any value within the range permitted by the schedule. We shall later show that the latitude permitted may influence materially the inferences that investors and others may draw from the financial statements.

Dating of revaluations: By the United Kingdom Companies Act 1967, an addition was made to the provisions of Schedule Eight of the 1948 Act (the 'accounts' schedule), in respect of revaluations of assets. In the case of fixed assets, other than unquoted investments, whose amount is arrived at by reference to a valuation, there shall be stated 'the years in which the assets were severally valued and the several values, and, in the case of assets that have been valued during the financial year, the names of the persons who valued them or particulars of their qualification for doing so and (whichever is stated) the basis of valuation used by them'. The information may be given by a note to the balance sheet, or in an annexed report or statement, if not on the face of the balance sheet itself.

The dating of revaluations may be regarded as a way of enabling users of balance sheets to see how up-to-date or how out-of-date are the reported asset values. But if it is necessary for investors to know this, the dates of purchase of all fixed assets not revalued should also be required to be stated, at least in summary form. In effect, the new provision secures the publication of additional information on assets that have been revalued while it does nothing to assist readers to judge the up-to-dateness of information on assets that have not been revalued. An additional burden of disclosure is imposed on companies which, on their own initiative, have given more up-to-date information than original costs; but companies that have taken no such steps to provide more relevant information to investors are excused. It seems not unlikely that such a discriminatory provision may reduce the willingness of companies to revalue assets, however important or relevant up-to-date values of assets may be to investors. Nevertheless, the provision is a step in the direction of enabling investors to form better assessments of some companies than they could otherwise form.

Market values of land: A further provision of the 1967 Act is even more pointed. By it, the directors' report is required to give particulars of significant changes in the fixed assets of a company or its subsidiaries in the year under report. For such of those assets as consist of interests in land, if the market value as at the end of the year differs substantially from the balance-sheet value, the difference shall be indicated 'with such degree of precision as is practicable', provided that 'the difference is, in the opinion of the directors, of such significance that the attention of members of the company or holders of the debentures thereof should be drawn thereto'.

As is the case with many local variants of a statute of generally common form, it is probable that this provision arose from locally observed anomalies. In fact during the preceding twenty years there were many cases in which, through ignorance of up-to-date asset values, shareholders accepted takeover offers that gave bidders substantial real property at far less than its value. The possibility is universal if the continued use of original costs is permitted. If indications of market prices must be given in the interest of members and debenture holders, it seems odd that the directors should be left to judge whether the difference between balance-sheet values and market values is significant to those other parties. And it seems odd that the information should be assigned to the directors' report—where it could be lost to sight—instead of requiring it to be shown in some way on the face of, or as a footnote to, the balance sheet.

In any case, the provision strongly suggests that whatever basis of valuation is adopted for interests in land, the market value of such interests is significant and relevant to the judgments of shareholders and creditors. Market value overrides, in significance, the cost price and any subsequent valuation incorporated in the accounts.

Borrowing companies: Other jurisdictions, other problems: In certain
Australian states it was found that companies had issued 'mortgage
debentures' which turned out to be far less secure than their
title suggested. Dealing with companies that engage in public
borrowing, the relevant companies acts now provide that the
term 'mortgage debenture' may be used of loan securities only
if, *inter alia*, the prospectus includes a competent, independent
valuation of land so mortgaged, made not more than six months
before the date of the prospectus. Although this provision relates
to prospectus information, up-to-date valuations can be of no less
significance to lenders after an issue than before. For if land falls in
value, as does happen, the security of a mortgage loan diminishes.
The safest way to provide that lenders shall have knowledge of
this happening is to require that up-to-date valuations be used as
a matter of course in annual financial statements.

Current assets: In at least some acts, it is provided that, where
the directors are of the opinion that the realizable value of any
current assets is below the amount at which they are shown in
the accounts, they shall give their opinion as to the amount which
those assets might reasonably be expected to realize in the ordinary
course of business. At least in some circumstances, therefore,
contemporary market prices of current assets are deemed to be
necessary information to users of balance sheets.

Now, by virtue of the overriding rule, the balance sheet is
required to give a true and fair view of the state of a company's
affairs. If it does so, there should be no reason for a 'corrective'
or supplementary statement by directors on the realizable values
of assets. If the balance sheet does not give a true and fair
view—as the very existence of the provision under discussion
implies—then no 'correction' by information in the directors'
report can be considered as removing the defect. The act or the
appropriate schedule could and should remove this anomaly by
plainly stating that current assets may not be shown at amounts
greater than their realizable values (selling prices) in the ordinary
course of business.

The provision we have cited applies where the balance-sheet
value exceeds the realizable value. But it is no barrier to understatement. Yet if a true and fair view is not given in the one case,

neither is it given in the other. It seems therefore that the act or the schedule should also provide that current assets may not be shown at amounts *less* than realizable values in the ordinary course of business.

Security investments: Some acts or their schedules require that the market values of quoted or listed securities be given by way of note if not shown on the face of the balance sheet. (The statutes of other jurisdictions imply that market values *may* be used for such assets but do not require market values to be shown, even by way of note.) A similar observation as before may be made. If a balance sheet gives a true and fair view, as it is supposed to do, there can be no need for supplementary information on the market values of securities. The rule stipulating that market values be given *somewhere* implies that knowledge of those values is generally useful and necessary; readers are more truly and fairly informed with this knowledge than without it. If that is the case, then market values should be shown on the face of the balance sheet and in its main columns, not in footnotes or elsewhere, where they may be overlooked.

Winding up provisions: Those sections of the legislation that deal with the winding up of companies offer some additional indications of the kind of financial information necessary. Dealing with creditors' voluntary winding up, it is provided that the directors shall present to the meeting of creditors a full statement of the company's affairs, showing the method and manner in which the valuation of the assets was arrived at, and giving a list of creditors and the estimated amount of their claims. It should be clear that at this point in a company's history the only appropriate method of valuing assets is at their market values, for only by the sale of assets can creditors be satisfied. It should be equally clear that, to avoid reaching such a point, the directors and managers of any company should be continuously aware of the market values of assets.

Further, in the general sections relating to every mode of winding up, it is provided that, with some exceptions, any floating charge on the undertaking or property of the company that is created within six months of the commencement of the winding up shall be invalid unless it is proved that the company, immediately after the creation of the charge, was solvent. Solvency, or ability to pay debts, can properly be assessed only if the market resale prices of assets are known at the relevant time. As a floating charge may extend to all assets, and as any asset or class of assets may be sold in the event of financial stringency to avoid insolvency, it follows that market values of all assets should be known to a company's directors at the time of the creation of a floating charge, and to the creditors in whose favour the charge is given, if their security is not to be lost in the event of winding up.

These inferences may seem to be dubious, the line of argument tenuous. But they do not stand alone. The are consistent with the drift of recent amendments to the legislation and with the conclusions to be drawn from the failures and near-failures of business firms.

LEGISLATION AND REGULATION IN THE UNITED STATES

Control of the incorporation of companies is, in the United States as in other federal systems, a power of the States. For reasons related to their own economic development and fiscal expectations, many of the States engaged in fierce competition with one another in the 'chartermongering business'. They wooed incorporators by reducing the formalities with which companies should comply, especially those relating to financial publicity. As recently as 1926 it could be said of the requirements of the State of Delaware: 'Simple annual reports are necessary, but they do not require disclosure of the corporation's financial affairs'.* Needless to say, this kind of laxity provided ample opportunity for stock watering, market rigging, fraud and other kinds of manipulation. Experience of these things, complaints during the twenties about the inadequacy of corporate financial information and the experiences of the stock market crash and the depression years prompted remedial action at the federal level. Hence the Securities Act of 1933 and the Securities Exchange Act of 1934

---

* Cited, with other examples, in William Z Ripley, *Main Street and Wall Street*, Boston, 1927, p. 30.

which now regulate the financial publicity of US corporations whose securities are traded on the national securities exchanges.

The Securities Act of 1933 was titled 'An Act to provide full and fair disclosure of the character of securities sold in interstate and foreign commerce and through the mails, and to prevent frauds in the sale thereof ... ' It provided for the registration of certain securities on the filing with the Commission (originally the Federal Trade Commission, later the Securities and Exchange Commission) of a registration statement. The contents of the statement were specified in Schedule A of the Act. Securities were not to be offered for sale without registration. Subject to certain exemptions and provisos, every prospectus was to contain the information in the registration statement. The Commission was empowered to require a prospectus to contain such other information as the Commission may require as being 'necessary or appropriate in the public interest or for the protection of investors'. In brief, the Act was concerned with the initial offering of securities for sale and with the representations to be made in registration documents and prospectuses.

The Securities Exchange Act of 1934 created the Securities and Exchange Commission and gave it authority to regulate the conduct of national securities exchanges and the trade in securities. The Act provided for the registration of certain kinds of securities on national securities exchanges prior to trading in those securities. Applications for registration were to include, *inter alia,* balance sheets and profit and loss statements for the previous three fiscal years. Issuers of securities were to file subsequently with the exchange (and to file duplicates with the Commission where required) such information and reports as the Commission may prescribe 'as necessary or appropriate for the proper protection of investors and to insure fair dealing in' securities. Specific reference was made to annual reports and 'such information and documents as the Commission may require *to keep reasonably current* the information and documents filed' on original registration (emphasis added).

In the early years of the Commission there was disagreement among the commissioners on the mode of determining what accounting or reporting practices should be permitted. Two commissioners, both lawyers, considered that the Commission should promulgate a set of accounting principles to be followed by registrants. The other commissioners were opposed to this. So also was the chief accountant of the Commission who argued that 'the development of accounting principles should be left to the accounting profession ... and that the Commission should co-operate'. This was to remain the general position of the Commission.

In a statement of policy in 1938, the Commission said:

> In cases where financial statements filed ... are prepared in accordance with accounting principles for which there is no substantial authoritative support, such financial statements will be presumed to be misleading or inaccurate despite disclosures contained in the certificate of the accountant or in footnotes to the statements provided the matters involved are material. / *Accounting Series Release*, no. 4 /

The test of 'substantial authoritative support' was not explained. Neither was there any reference to what was necessary or appropriate in the public interest or for the protection of investors.

In 1940 the SEC adopted 'a uniform set of accounting requirements'—styled *Regulation S-X*—which would apply to the majority of the registration and report forms provided for under the acts administered by the Commission. It may have been intended that the Regulation would apply uniformly; but, by the nature of its rules, it could not have secured and has not secured that reports of companies are uniform in material particulars.

Asset valuation: For determining the amounts at which assets should be shown there were generally no specific rules. The common prescription for indicating how the amounts were determined is: 'State the basis of determining the amount'. Referring to cost of goods sold (when it appears in profit and loss statements) the Regulation says: 'State the amount of cost of goods sold as regularly computed under the system of accounting followed'. With one exception (marketable securities, shortly to be mentioned), the Commission took no stand on the valuation basis necessary to keep previously filed information *reasonably current*, to protect investors, or to insure fair dealing in securities.

In effect, by accepting the systems of accounting followed by registrants, by accepting the pronouncements on principle of 'the accounting profession' and by its own administration of its powers, the Commission has secured that the method of accounting in terms of or on the basis of the original costs of assets is almost universally followed in the United States.

Security investments: Only in the case of holdings of marketable securities is any clear indication given of a basis to be used for valuing assets. For marketable securities reported to be 'current assets', for example, the Regulation says: 'State the basis of determining the amount at which carried. The aggregate cost, and the aggregate amount on the basis of current market quotations, shall be stated parenthetically or otherwise'. Which of the two amounts shall be shown parenthetically is not clear, so it cannot be said exactly what was intended. But it may be inferred, from the slightly different formula for marketable securities shown under 'Investments', that market value is to be shown parenthetically.

The article of the Regulation dealing with management investment companies makes different stipulations for different kinds of company. It requires that the balance sheets of 'open end' companies reflect all assets at value (market value or fair value as estimated by the directors), showing cost parenthetically. The balance sheets of 'closed end' companies may show either all assets at cost with value in parenthesis, or all assets at value with cost in parenthesis. In what way these varied rules contribute to the protection of investors is not clear. The options can have no effect other than to increase the difficulties of investors who may wish to compare the results and positions of companies.

Fair presentation: The Act of 1934 stipulated that financial statements should be certified by independent public accountants if the Commission so required. *Regulation S-X* requires that the accountant's certificate should state clearly:

'(i) the opinion of the accountant in respect of the financial statements ... and the accounting principles and practices reflected therein (ii) the opinion of the accountant as to any material changes in accounting principles or practices or method of applying [them], or adjustments of the accounts required to be set forth ...' / Rule 2–02 /

There is no statement to the effect that the financial statements shall give a true and fair view of results and position, as in legislation on the English pattern. We may, however, deduce the principle from the law and practice under it.

The reference to 'full and fair disclosure' in the 1933 Act, although referring to registration statements and prospectuses, may properly be supposed to apply to subsequent statements which were intended to keep 'reasonably current' the information on a company and its securities. By the same Act, where any part of a registration statement contained 'an untrue statement of a material fact or omitted to state a material fact required to be stated therein or necessary to make the statements therein not misleading', those responsible for the statement or omission were made actionable. Again, it seems that the sense of this section could properly be transferred to annual reporting.

Further, according to a standard work (Louis H Rappaport, *SEC Accounting Practice and Procedure,* New York, 1959), the form of words commonly used in audit reports will usually comply with the SEC requirements. The usual form of (unqualified) audit report includes the following:

> 'In our opinion, the accompanying balance sheet and statement of income and surplus present fairly the financial position of X Company at December 31, 19—, and the results of its operations for the year then ended, in conformity with generally accepted accounting principles applied on a basis consistent with that of the previous year.'

Finally, reference is made at various places in the Regulation to magnitudes, or changes in method causing variations, which are material. And the meaning of the term is specified:

> 'The term "material" when used to qualify a requirement for the furnishing of information as to any subject, limits the information required to those matters as to which an average prudent investor ought reasonably to be informed before purchasing the security registered.'

The average prudent investor seems entitled to suppose that financial statements will give him all material information.

These general indications of the spirit of the administration of the laws and regulations are fine as far as they go. But general indications do not necessarily lead to practice consistent with general principle. Clearly, much depends on the propriety of the accounting practices of companies, and the propriety of 'generally accepted accounting principles'. These matters are left in the hands of the accounting profession. We shall see presently with what effect.

GENERAL SUMMARY

The two kinds of legislation and regulation we have considered are substantially similar, both in what they require and in what they omit to specify.

(a) The statutes in themselves lay down what seem to be quite proper principles. The English requirement that every balance sheet and profit and loss account shall give a true and fair view of a company's state of affairs (or financial position) and results is substantially the same in effect as the US references to the public interest, the protection of investors and fair dealing in securities. True and fair, or full and fair, disclosure is the dominant principle.

(b) The reference to a true and fair view in auditors' reports, under laws on the English pattern, is substantially the same in objective or function as the reference to fair presentation in auditors' reports in US practice.

(c) The 'accounts' schedule to acts of the English type and the regulations under the US acts both leave in rather vague form the prescriptions for asset valuation. The dominant principle governing disclosure is enshrined in the statutes in both cases; but the freedom usually given in schedules to the acts to choose different methods for ascertaining the amounts shown, leaves open the question of exactly what the legislation intends.

(d) The requirement that the financial statements shall be consistent with the books of account under English-type statutes, and consistent with generally accepted accounting principles under US practice, also leaves the method and quality of disclosure to be determined otherwise than by reference to the dominant principle.

(e) In neither type of legislation or regulation is there given any explanation of the way in which 'true and fair' (UK) or 'fairly presents' (US) should be interpreted.

(f) In neither type of legislation or regulation is there given any definition of 'state of affairs', 'financial position', 'profits', 'results' or terms having similar purport.

Had the terms mentioned in (e) and (f) been defined, there may have been some litigated cases which would throw light on their general meaning, some opportunity to have them explored or explained in a sufficient variety of settings to establish more firmly the intention of the law. There may also have been occasion for the major text and reference books on company law and securities regulation to deal at some length with the interpretation of the terms.

COMMENT ON THE LAW

We know of no official elucidation of the intended meaning of these key words. Nor do we know of any attempt to elaborate upon them in commentaries or surveys or specialist writing on the matter. *Buckley on the Companies Acts* (13th edition, 1957) makes only passing reference to the requirements of the statute. Gower's *The Principles of Modern Company Law* gives no discussion of the meanings that have been or might be attributed to the terms. Loss's *Securities Regulation* (1961 edition) makes reference only to the conventional interpretation of the relevant sections of the laws and regulations. Sidney I Simon's *Accounting and the Law* (1965) has a chapter on 'Fraud in the Balance Sheet' but neither there nor elsewhere in the book is there any discussion of the meaning or practical significance of 'fair presentation'. A Duke University Symposium on 'Uniformity in Financial Accounting' (*Law and Contemporary Problems*, vol. xxx, no. 4, 1965) yielded no paper in which the specific kind of information useful to investors was explored. The papers of a Washington DC Symposium, published as *Economic Policy and the Regulation of Corporate Securities* (1969) contained no analysis of the way in which financial statement information is or may properly be linked with the choices or decisions of investors and others. In a lengthy article entitled ' "Truth in Securities" Revisited', Milton H Cohen, formerly director of the SEC's Special Study of Securities Markets, drew attention to the 'exceptionally strong statement' of the full disclosure obligation in the 1933 Securities Act. On the quality of published information, he said:

> 'It is the fate of all information originally filed under either Act to become stale sooner or later, in greater or lesser degree … for purposes of the continuing trading markets, the value of the original disclosures under the 1934 Act will gradually diminish to vanishing point unless stale information is constantly replaced by fresh. The process of replacing stale information with fresh, in a continuous reservoir, is accomplished through periodic and current reporting requirements.' / *Harvard Law Review*, vol. 79, 1966, pp. 1353–6 /

Though he described the requirements of the 1934 Act as a 'continuous disclosure system' and devoted ten pages to a discussion of ways and means of improving the quality of the information disclosed, Cohen raised no question about the original cost basis for reporting the amounts of assets. This basis of reporting, long endorsed and enforced by the SEC, ensures that much of the published information will remain 'stale' indefinitely, even though, by the new date that the financial statements bear each year, the information purports to be current and up-to-date.

CONCLUSION

The vagueness of the law may be attributed to the belief of legislators or of lawyers that the terms used in the statutes are terms or art, peculiar to accounting and accountants, which should properly be left to accountants to elucidate. But the literature of accounting, voluminous though it is, lacks any extended analysis of the key terms and ideas mentioned. It may also have been supposed that there was a firm framework which gave specificity to the general terms of the statutes: a clear and acknowledged set of connections between the information given in financial statements and calculations leading to proper judgments by investors and creditors. We shall show that there is such a framework but that it is shown scant respect in practice under the legislation.

In any event, although the key terms occur in the work of accountants, they are not peculiar to accounting and accountants. The ideas or things for which 'true', 'fair', 'balance sheet', 'financial position', 'state of affairs', and 'income account' stand, are the common concern of all who have financial dealings and relations, even at a purely personal level. Specialists such as accountants may have a more exacting, a more disciplined notion of each of them than do lay persons. In the same way physicists have a more exacting idea of 'atom' and lawyers a more exacting notion of 'crime' than the notions of laymen. But as non-specialists have financial relationships and transactions with others, often on the basis of what is represented in accounting statements, the notions of accountants should not be materially different from what people understand in ordinary commercial intercourse. That there are in fact material differences we shall show in what follows.

3

TRUTH IN ACCOUNTING

'Technical rules of accountancy are admirable things, but they are
the letter and not the spirit. It is no good observing merely the
letter; the fundamental object of the profession is to ensure that
in documents which are produced a true and accurate account of
the affairs of the company is given.'
/ The Attorney General, *Rex* v. *Kylsant* /

'There is a principle which binds society together, because without
it the individual would be helpless to tell the true from the false.
This principle is truthfulness. If we accept truth as an individual
criterion, then we have also to make it the cement to hold society
together.'
/ J Bronowski, *Science and Human Values* /

We concluded the previous chapter with the suggestion that legislators may have presumed the existence of a firm body of opinion on
the functions of accounting and financial statements. There were
perhaps plausible grounds for believing that accounting was a reasonably well-disciplined art. It had a long history. It had served feu-
dal households, ecclesiastical establishments, bankers and traders
and other entities. It was not improper to suppose that its principles
would have been beaten into shape by force of use and experience.

As the UK Act of 1844 was the first public act to make mention
of a full and fair balance sheet, it is of interest to see what general
principles were held as the reasons for, or as guides to, the keeping
of business accounts.

THE FUNCTION OF ACCOUNTS
PRIOR TO 1844

The general style of most arts and crafts is learned by novices
from craftsmen themselves or from the handbooks and guides
produced by teachers and practitioners. Practice may deviate from
the ideal but its style is conveyed by statements of the ideal. Here

are some selections from handbooks in the decades prior to 1844:

?□ 1777: / Wardhaugh Thompson, *The Accountant's Oracle, York* / 'Book-keeping by double entry ... is the art of keeping our accompts in such a manner, as will not only exhibit to us our neat gain or loss upon the whole, but our particular gain or loss upon each article we deal in, by which we are instructed what branches to pursue, and which to decline; a piece of knowledge so very essential to every man in business, that without it a person can only be said to deal at random, or at best can be called guess'd work.

'... from it ... we can in a few hours, and with very little trouble, at any time, know the *exact state of our affairs*, viz. what goods of every sort we have in hand; what payments we have to make, and what cash we can command; by which means we are timely apprized to prepare for any demands which can be made upon us, and can extend or curtail our trade as we find our capital will admit of, or the nature of our affairs require.' [Emphasis added in this and later quotations.] / vol. II, pp. 1–2 /

□ 1800: / J W Fulton, *British-Indian Book-keeping*, Bengal / '... the method [of book-keeping] by double entry ... is capable of constantly exhibiting the *correct balance* under every alteration the fluctuation of affairs may impose on it.' / p. 5 /

□ 1800: / John Mair, *Book-keeping Moderniz'd*, 8th ed., Edinburgh/ 'Book-keeping is an art, teaching how to record and dispose the accounts of business so as the *true state of every part, and of the whole*, may be easily and distinctly known ... The end aimed at in book-keeping is to represent distinctly the *true state of one's affairs*; that is, to record a man's dealings and transactions; and withal, to range and dispose the accounts in such order, that the books may exhibit a *plain, full and exact account* of the conditions and circumstances of each part of his business; and to put the man in case at all times to satisfy both himself and others with respect to the state and posture of his affairs.' / p. 1 /

□ 1801: / P Kelly, *The Elements of Book-keeping*, London / 'A merchant's books should exhibit the *true state of his affairs*; they should show the particular success of each transaction, the general result of the whole, and afford a correct and ready information upon every subject for which they might be consulted.' / p. 1 /

Patently these authors contemplated that merchants' accounts should inform them, in up-to-date terms, of the financial results and states of business from time to time. The references to 'true' and 'exact' state of affairs express the ideal character of the accounts. The function of knowledge of the state of affairs is clearly indicated by Thompson: 'We are timely apprized to prepare for any demands which can be made upon us, and can extend or curtail our trade as we find our capital will admit of, or the nature of our affairs require'. Here is a sense of the intimate connection between financial information and business operations—a causal connection: by knowing what we have and what we owe, we can work out what to do next.

Note that representation of the true state of affairs was an idea already embedded in the teachings of accountants well before the nineteenth-century legislation. It is reasonable to suppose that the draftsmen of the legislation had this in mind; that there was one kind of statement which represented the true state of affairs—a statement which, because it was true, was equally fair to companies themselves and to members and creditors. Mair's reference to satisfying 'both himself and others with respect to the state and posture of his affairs' implies that informed dealing between a merchant and others is fair dealing. And that, it seems, was the intention of the legislators in respect of companies. The law could not have intended that there could be more than one true state of affairs. There could not, for example be a *true* state of affairs 'for publication' and a *different but true* state of affairs for management purposes. Nor could there be two different states of affairs at the same time, one relevant to dealings with creditors and another relevant to dealings with shareholders—for the interests of both lie in the same collection of assets.

What rules then would lead to representation of the true state of affairs?

Most of the texts of the period present no discussion of the mode of valuing assets at the end of each period. This is understandable if merchants were not holders of trading assets over long periods—and this was more common before the Industrial Revolution than it has become since. There are indications, in Thompson, Mair and Kelly, that the balances of goods on hand should be valued at cost. But there is evidence, before and after-wards, that the market selling prices of assets were regarded as proper valuations.

Thus we find:

☐ 1735: / Hustcraft Stephens, *Italian Book-keeping*, London /

'By the assistance of this money, everyone might compare what he had with the things of his neighbour ... thus, such a thing of my own is worth £20, that is, *people will give so much for it*; and such a thing of another man's is worth £20, consequently mine is equal to his in value ... Now the uncertainty of the prices of things renders my share of their [worth] liable to increase or decrease with them ... Suppose I have 2000 lb weight of tobacco, which I value at first at £50 ... suppose when I come to calculate anew, I find the tobacco, at the present rate, *able to purchase* more than £50 ... then I am so much the richer ...' [Emphasis added.]

☐ 1741: / Richard Hayes, *The Gentleman's Complete Book-keeper*, London /

'It is usual with merchants, when they make a general balance of their books, to value the goods that they have by them at the market price they then go at, at the time of their balancing, but some do not so.'

☐ 1788: / Robert Hamilton, *An Introduction to Merchandise ...*, Edinburgh /

'It is much more proper to value the goods on hand in conformity to the current prices, than at prime cost: For the design of affixing any value is to point out the gain or loss; and the gain is in reality obtained as soon as the prices rise, or the loss suffered as soon as they fall.' [Hamilton differs from Stephens and Hayes in speaking of current prices as 'such a value as the owner would be willing at present to buy for', but all agree in stipulating 'current prices'.]

Closer to 1844 James Morrison (*The Elements of Book-Keeping by Single and Double Entry*, London, 1825) wrote of the value of the balance of goods and other property 'estimated at prime cost, or at the current prices'. Both Mair and Morrison gave glossaries in which appeared the term 'price current'. According to Morrison this was 'a list of the various articles of merchandize in the market, with the present prices annexed to each. In most of the great commercial cities and towns lists of this description are generally published once or twice a week'. Thus, not only did Morrison allow that current prices could be used; he also knew that such prices were discoverable.

The market prices of goods on hand is clearly recognized as relevant to measures of wealth, or well-offness, and to the capacity to pay one's debts or otherwise deal with other persons. It would seem, therefore, a proper basis for the representation of the true state of affairs of a merchant.

THE FUNCTION OF ACCOUNTS AFTER 1844

Since the mid-nineteenth century the growth of corporate investment and of the number of investors in and creditors of companies has increased rapidly. It is of interest to see whether any change occurred in statements of the ideal objective or function of accounts. Again we take examples from textbooks, handbooks and articles by teachers and practitioners. A number of extracts from the United States indicate that the same ideal function was supported there as in the United Kingdom.

☐ 1889: / F W Pixley (practitioner, London) *Auditors: Their Duties and Responsibilities* /

'The balance sheet ... if properly drawn ... shows the *exact financial position* of the company ... the auditor must ... satisfy himself that the liabilities have not been understated, nor the assets over-estimated ... it would be very unfair to themselves [the directors] and to the shareholders, as well as very impolitic, to either overstate the liabilities or to under-estimate the assets.

'This applies to Companies whose business depends on their periodically showing to their constituents and the public their sound and *unquestionable financial position*, for while, on the one hand, nothing could be more reprehensible than for the Directors of a Bank to deceive their shareholders, by stating its securities at a value they know they do not possess, yet they would naturally, as competitors for public patronage, desire to set forth the assets at their full market value, and to this the Auditor cannot raise any objection. As a matter of prudence, however, he might suggest the cost price being inserted in the balance sheet, supposing the securities have not depreciated in value, and it being stated, in a footnote, the actual market value at the date on which the balance sheet is made out.' / pp. 145–6 /

☐ 1909: / H R Hatfield (professor, California) *Modern Accounting* /

'... the fundamental principle of *truthfulness* in accounting ...' / p. 170 /

☐ 1910: / L R Dicksee (practitioner and professor, London) *Auditing* /

'As a general rule, the amount at which *all* assets are stated in the balance sheet—except where a special statutory provision to the contrary obtains—should be regulated by the realisable value of such assets on the basis of a going concern.' / p. 194 /

☐ 1914: / E E Spicer and E C Pegler (practitioners, London) *Practical Auditing* /

'[The balance sheet] should be a document setting out the *true position* of the business.' / p. 399 /

☐ 1915: / W M Cole (professor, Harvard) *Accounts, Their Construction and Interpretation* /

'Accounting is nothing but sublimated common sense applied to finding and *telling the truth* about business. ... truth lies in the ear of the hearer as much as in the mouth of the speaker, and truth-telling consists of using language which will make the listener know the *facts*—even though the speaker must change his own vocabulary to convey the truth ...' / p. vi /

☐ 1922: / W A Paton (professor, Michigan) *Accounting Theory* /

'It is coming to be clearly recognized that both the periodic statement of financial position and the report [of income figures] ... should consistently reflect *true pictures* of current business conditions and tendencies—as affecting the particular enterprise—if these statements are to form a basis for rational judgments on the part of the immediate management, the investor, and other parties concerned ...' / p. 425 /

☐ 1938: / T H Sanders, H R Hatfield and U Moore (professors, Harvard, California, Yale) *A Statement of Accounting Principles* /

'... since *reliable* information is the main objective of the income statement, for whatever purpose prepared, no considerations of policy should prevent a *true* showing of the *facts*.' / p. 26 /

☐ 1939: / K MacNeal (practitioner, Philadelphia) *Truth in Accounting* /

'Accounting is the language of business. Members of the accounting profession are interpreters upon whom the vast majority of people must rely for information relating to any business or project with which they are not intimately and personally familiar. If interpreters do not *tell the truth*, or do not tell the whole truth, or tell truths intermixed with half truths, many people may be deceived to their hurt.' / p. 1 /

☐ 1941: / E B Wilcox and R H Hassler (practitioners, Illinois) 'A Foundation for Accounting Principles', *Journal of Accountancy*, October 1941 /

'... no part of the function of accounting can be useful unless it is *truthful*.' / / p. 311 /

These passages make it plain that the function of financial statements was considered to be truthful representation of the financial facts of business. In all conscience, no writer could allow that financial statements may be used to mislead or confuse readers, or to enable managers to evade responsibility for the performances and states of companies. But it did happen that the particular rules which came to be developed and accepted over this period had just these effects.

How this occurred can only be sketched. In the first place, the writers did not follow up their statements of ideal function with rules for asset valuation which 'told the truth' about the financial position of a firm from time to time. Scarcely ever is there to be found a firm statement about the way in which managers, investors or creditors could use the figures in the financial statements to guide their actions. Secondly, as the financial statements were regarded as the responsibility of directors and managers, there was no determinate limit to the rules they could invent and justify in some way by reference to the good of the firm or the interests of shareholders. Many directors of companies in many different circumstances + freedom to judge what is true and fair representation = a wide variety of rules, and precedents for rules, which, as we shall see = confusion.

LEGAL NOTICE OF THE FUNCTION OF ACCOUNTS

It may be thought that 'ideal' statements of function can scarcely be expected to be effective in the hurly-burly of practical affairs; that allowances must be made for the fact that the commercial world is not an ideal world in which pertinent financial facts are discoverable. To put the matter on a surer footing we cite some dicta from judgments handed down by eminent jurists in the English courts.

The courts are expected to interpret the law as it relates to the specific conditions of parties to litigation. They take account of the circumstances and conditions of the less-than-ideal world. Their judgments may therefore be taken as stating the obligations of companies and their directors, bearing in mind the practical difficulties they may encounter. As it happens, the dicta in important cases coincide with the prescriptions of the writers on accounting that we have cited:

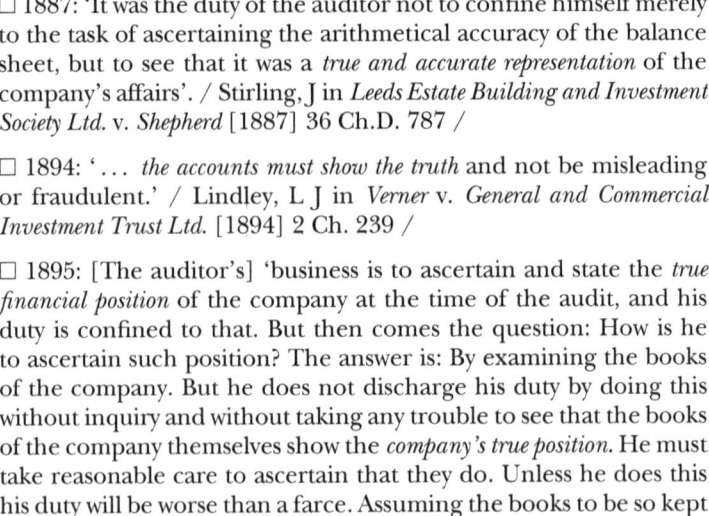

☐ 1887: 'It was the duty of the auditor not to confine himself merely to the task of ascertaining the arithmetical accuracy of the balance sheet, but to see that it was a *true and accurate representation* of the company's affairs'. / Stirling, J in *Leeds Estate Building and Investment Society Ltd.* v. *Shepherd* [1887] 36 Ch.D. 787 /

☐ 1894: '. . . *the accounts must show the truth* and not be misleading or fraudulent.' / Lindley, L J in *Verner* v. *General and Commercial Investment Trust Ltd.* [1894] 2 Ch. 239 /

☐ 1895: [The auditor's] 'business is to ascertain and state the *true financial position* of the company at the time of the audit, and his duty is confined to that. But then comes the question: How is he to ascertain such position? The answer is: By examining the books of the company. But he does not discharge his duty by doing this without inquiry and without taking any trouble to see that the books of the company themselves show the *company's true position*. He must take reasonable care to ascertain that they do. Unless he does this his duty will be worse than a farce. Assuming the books to be so kept as to show *the true position* of the company, the auditor has to frame a balance sheet showing that position according to the books, and to certify that the balance sheet is correct in that sense ... a *full and fair balance sheet* must be such a balance sheet as to convey a *truthful statement as to the company's position.*' / Lindley, L J and Rigby, L J in *Re London and General Bank Ltd., ex parte Theobald (No. 2)* [1895–9] All E R 953 /

□ 1926: '... an auditor who is instructed to make a full audit of business books is responsible not only for getting out such accounts as the books when properly made up appear to show, but they are also responsible for ascertaining *the true position* of the business, whether disclosed properly by the books or not.' / Astbury, J in *Trustees of the Property of Apfel (a bankrupt)* v. *Annan, Dexter & Co.* 70 *The Accountant* L R 57 /

□ 1931: 'Technical rules of accountancy are admirable things, but they are the letter and not the spirit. It is no good observing merely the letter; the fundamental object of the profession is to ensure that in documents which are produced a *true and accurate account* of the affairs of the company is given. If the documents convey to a reasonably intelligent person a false impression, all the technical rules of accountancy may be observed and at the same time the accountants' profession has failed to carry out its primary and obvious duty ... the law requires this, that the shareholders shall have put before them *true and accurate accounts.*' / The Attorney General, closing speech for the Prosecution, *Rex* v. *Lord Kylsant and another* (Collin Brooks, ed., *The Royal Mail Case*) /

These cases related to the interests of shareholders and creditors in specific circumstances. The courts did not lay down general rules on the meaning of a 'true and fair view'. But the accounts were clearly intended not to be misleading either to shareholders or to creditors. And there was no suggestion that diverse or divergent rules could give true and accurate accounts of the affairs of different companies.

CONCLUSION

Truth, accuracy, fairness, fullness and like terms occur in all these expositions or prescriptions. They are used frequently with reference to 'financial position' or 'state of affairs'. Undoubtedly the one thing that is absolutely necessary to the interpretation of a statement of financial affairs is its date. The 'true' state of affairs must consequently be the state of affairs at a specified date. The components of a statement of the true state of affairs must therefore be, themselves, true statements at the specified date. The amount of cash, the amount of receivables, the amount of liabilities must all be 'true' amounts at that date. True amounts would be financially significant amounts. The amounts of other assets and equities should also, it seems, be true or financially significant amounts at the same date. No out-of-date amounts and no expected amounts would be true amounts at that date. That at least seems to be a commonsense interpretation of what was said by the teachers, practitioners and jurists we have cited. How could there be any other interpretation? We shall see.

4

WHAT EVERY INTELLIGENT INVESTOR NEEDS TO KNOW

The proof of the pudding is in the eating.

In none of the laws, opinions and prescriptions cited in earlier chapters is there any indication of the ways in which financial figures may be used. Perhaps these should be obvious to anyone who has experience of commercial dealing. But if we wish to be specific about the meaning of a 'true and fair view' of the state of affairs of a company and its results, it will be instructive to consider the uses that could be made of information of the ideal kind. We begin with a sketch of the similarities of the financial affairs of private persons and companies.

THE FINANCIAL AFFAIRS OF PERSONS AND COMPANIES

A private person needing, for any purpose, to find his financial position would proceed in a fairly straightforward manner. He would find out the approximate prices he could obtain for his disposable assets—the market values of his house and land, car, securities and the surrender value of his insurance policies. He would find out how much he owed to creditors. The difference between the total market value of his assets and the total amount of his debts would be what he is 'worth'. A private person does not often have to calculate the whole of his worth. He may do so, for example, when thinking of going into business on his own account, or when thinking of moving to a distant place to live. But for any costly project he may wish to undertake, he may need to sell any combination of his assets less than the whole of them. To decide which combination to sell, he would need some idea of the market price of every asset, for this would help him to determine which assets he must sell to raise the amount of money he needs for the new project. As an alternative to selling some of his assets he may wish to borrow on the security of any part, up to the whole amount, of his assets. Because lenders on the security of assets base their loans on the market values of goods, he would need to know the market values of his assets to estimate how much he could borrow.

There is no reason whatever for regarding business firms or companies in any different light. They have assets; they owe money to creditors; the difference between the total amounts of assets and liabilities is net worth. The full statement of the values of assets and the amounts of liabilities and net worth is a statement of financial position. There is no reason for valuing assets in any way different from market values as in the case of a private person.

Both private persons and companies buy and sell, borrow and lend, commonly in the same or similar markets and by substantially the same kinds of contract and legal instruments. The financial affairs of a solvent individual are no more and no less those of a 'going concern' than the financial affairs of a solvent company. The obligations of individuals and companies to pay their debts and to meet recurrent expenses or outlays are, in principle, the same. And the tests of their capacity to do so are the same.

The rate at which private persons acquire the means of meeting their expenses and adding to their savings is of no less interest to them than the interest of company members and investors generally in the rate at which companies acquire means for similar purposes. The incomes of most private persons are cash incomes. If a private person wishes to know his total gains in a period, he will add to his cash income the gains he makes (or deduct the losses) due to changes in the market prices of his assets. If he incurs costs in earning those gains, he will deduct these to obtain his net income. So also should companies. The rate at which means are acquired is usually expressed as so much per period, so many dollars per year. If assets are used in earning income, whether by private persons or companies, we speak of the rate of return on the sum invested to earn that income; that is, the percentage of net income to the sum invested. Of course the sum invested at any time is the amount of cash the investor would have if he did not have the investment.

It is a common experience that some expenditures and investments do not turn out to be as satisfactory in some years as was expected, or as in other years. The attained net income of a period helps one to decide whether to change one's pattern of spending or one's holdings of assets—whether we refer to private persons, to private persons as investors in companies, or to companies themselves.

Private persons are well aware of the eroding effect on their purchasing power of rises in the general level of prices. Negotiations for increases in wages because of this erosion are a constant reminder of this common knowledge. Private persons also know that the prices of some things, such as houses and land in growing urban areas, tend to rise faster than the purchasing power of money falls. When they can, they borrow at fixed rates of interest to acquire such assets in the expectation that, while the prices of assets rise, they will be able to repay the amount borrowed in currency of lower purchasing power than its purchasing power at the time of borrowing. The managers of companies are equally aware of the eroding effect of rises in the general level of prices, if for no other reason than that they buy homes and land on borrowed money in their private capacities. In business, as in private affairs, they take steps to circumvent the effects of this erosion, and in ways similar to those used by private persons. They buy goods to hold when they expect prices to rise. They sell goods when they expect prices to fall. They also buy and sell for the immediate profit margins they can earn, but what they buy and sell is always influenced by present prices and expected price movements.

In the light of all these similarities, there seems to be no doubt that all the factors we have mentioned should be included in deliberate calculations of the states of affairs and the results of companies from time to time. The volume of business, the rates at which particular asset prices change, and the rates at which the purchasing power of money changes, in successive periods are always different. Their combined effects in any year represent the extent to which net worth has increased, the amount by which the residual interest of shareholders in the assets of a company has increased. The effects are of interest to shareholders, creditors, managers and other parties—as we shall proceed to show. We shall hold that it is necessary, in order to take account of all these effects, that assets be valued from time to time at their approximate market prices.

To make clear the principal elements of financial statements, consider a simple illustration. Suppose the balance sheet of a company at the end of its *third* year of operation were as follows:

Balance sheet at 31 December 19×3	$
Assets— *Current assets*	
Cash	1,000
Receivables (debtors)	4,000
Inventories (cost 5,000)	6,000
Marketable securities (cost 1,700)	2,000
Other assets (fixed)	
Plant (cost less depreciation 5,500)	5,000
Land and buildings (cost 6,000)	7,000
	25,000
Equities— *Creditors* (liabilities)	
Short term payables (current liabilities)	4,000
Loan due 19×6, at 7 per cent p.a.	6,000
Shareholders (ordinary)	
Paid in capital subscriptions	10,000
Undistributed past profits	2,000
Profit of the year 19×3	3,000
	25,000

The figures shown, in the main column, for inventories, marketable securities, plant, and land and buildings are the market prices of those assets at the end of the year. These are not the figures that usually appear in the balance sheets of companies. But the reason for their use will presently be explained. Note some of the general features of the balance sheet.

Firstly, the total amount of the assets is equal to the total amount of the equities. Secondly, the total amount of liabilities is the contractual amount of debts. Consequently, the amount of the shareholders' equity (equity, for short) is equal to the total amount of the assets less the total amount of the liabilities. This amount may also be described as the amount of the 'net assets'. Thirdly, the total amount of the increase in net assets in any year is an addition to the shareholders' equity at the beginning of the year. It is the amount of trading profits and other gains made (less dividends paid, if any) during the year. Of course, the increase in assets due to the profits of any year is not kept in the form of idle cash; it is used to pay dividends and to add to other assets. There is no necessary relationship between the profit of a year and the cash balance at its end.

These figures are obviously interlocked. If the amount of liabilities is correctly stated, the amount of shareholders' equity depends on the total amount of the assets. If the assets are under- or overstated, the shareholders' equity is correspondingly under- or overstated. If the change in the net assets in any year is under- or overstated, the net profit of that year is under- or overstated. It is possible to under- or overstate the amount of liabilities. But the contractual amount of debts owing is one of the more easily determined figures. The adequacy of the balance sheet as a statement of financial position therefore depends a great deal on the values assigned to the assets. For this reason much of the remainder of this book will concern itself with asset values.

Consider now the uses of this information.

INVESTORS AND MANAGERIAL STEWARDSHIP

It has long been held that one of the functions of annual financial statements is to give an account of the stewardship of the directors or managers who control the affairs and funds of a company. Some people interpret this very narrowly. They say that managers must account for the funds contributed by shareholders (and perhaps also by creditors). In the first year of the above company, the directors had the use of $10,000—the amount contributed by shareholders. How they laid out this money would be given by a statement of the things the company bought and their purchase prices. On this ground it is held that the use of purchase prices, or original costs, is a proper basis for the balance-sheet figures at the year's end. But this view is quite mistaken.

Investors and creditors no doubt need to be assured from time to time that the funds and other assets of a company have been employed in the proper exercise of the powers of directors and managers, and have not been used for unauthorized purposes. The proper mode of giving this assurance is by the independent audit of the accounts. The financial statements are highly condensed summaries. It is impossible for an outsider to detect from these summaries whether improper uses of funds or other assets have been made in any period. There have indeed been cases in which fraudulent managers and officers have concealed misappropriations for years, even from auditors. This could not have been possible if investors and creditors could themselves discover from the financial statements that assets had been diverted improperly.

The legal provisions requiring financial statements to be presented yearly to shareholders imply that if stewardship (or performance) is to be assessed, it is to be assessed yearly for the year just concluded, not for all years from the beginning of a company's existence to the latest balance date. Each year stands, in a sense, as a limited stage in the venture. If this is the case, the money equivalent of the assets as at the beginning of any year is the basic amount of money for which the directors and managers are accountable in that year. And this is the sum of the market prices of the assets at the beginning of the year. It is exactly analogous, for every subsequent year, to the amount of money put into the hands of the directors when the company was first launched.

The example we are using shows that the costs of inventories and marketable securities were in total $6,700, whereas their market prices at 31 December 19×3 were in total $8,000. The money amount for which the directors are accountable (in respect of these assets) in 19×4 is not $6,700 but $8,000. If the directors (or managers) were held accountable only for $6,700 and if willing collaborators could be found, some of these assets could be sold during 19×4 and some or all of the difference of $1,300 could be diverted to personal use or used to bolster the reported profits of 19×4, without the knowledge of outsiders. Only a proper audit will provide safeguards against diversion. But as long as the gain through the change in asset prices is not accounted for in the year in which it occurs, reported profits and other gains may be manipulated by the 'careful' choice of selling dates or by the choice of 'valuations other than cost' permitted under the laws.

To obtain a proper account of stewardship, even in the sense of an accounting for the money or money's worth with which any year began, it is necessary therefore to have non-cash assets valued at market prices.

SOLVENCY

Whatever financial arrangements a company may make with its creditors, it is expected to meet its debts as they fall due as well as to meet current outlays for wages and other expenses. If it cannot meet its debts it is insolvent. Creditors may then take steps to enforce their claims by legal process; arrangements to satisfy creditors may entail the sale of assets at prices below what could be obtained in the ordinary course of business; and the equity of shareholders may suffer as a result. Creditors, shareholders and managers alike are thus interested in the capacity of a company to pay its debts in the short run.

In the ordinary course of events, debts can be paid out of cash received from debtors or cash sales. But business does not always run so smoothly. Monetary and other fiscal policies may reduce customers' spending and lengthen the time they take to pay debts. Changes in demand for other reasons may similarly reduce a company's ability to pay its debts or to pay its ordinary running expenses. If expenses are cut back by retrenchment of workers, householders have less to spend; thus the difficulties of one company may spread to others. Cutbacks by the US government in 1970 affected seriously the large Lockheed and Boeing companies; it was also reported that the solvency of large numbers of smaller firms serving the West Coast population was seriously affected. Any firm may come under the adverse influence of other firms apparently quite different from and distant from it, at any time and unexpectedly.

When cash inflows diminish for any of these reasons, a company's second line of defence against insolvency is its assets. It may first try to collect its receivables, cut down its inventories or sell its security investments. But it could sell any asset or any combination of assets that would yield the cash it needs. Its managers will choose that asset or that combination which least disturbs the company's operations. Clearly then, if financial stringency may occur unexpectedly, managers must know at all times the approximate selling prices of *all* assets.

On the outside, investors and creditors are not concerned with this choice. They are concerned however with general indications of solvency, since insolvency will affect their prospects of income and other receipts.

The most commonly used test of solvency is the ratio of current assets to current liabilities, the *current ratio*. In the example the amount of current assets is $13,000; of current liabilities, $4,000. The ratio is in excess of 3 to 1. The current liabilities are very well 'covered'. Remember that these figures are based on the market selling prices of assets. The ratio is a proper one, since it compares the amount of money now owing with the money equivalent of current assets at present in hand. If we had taken the *costs* of inventories and marketable securities into the numerator of the ratio, the value of the ratio would be less than 3 to 1. And it would not be a proper ratio, for cost prices of assets do not indicate how well a company is able to meet its debts out of its readily available assets. Suppose, for example, that the selling price of the marketable securities had fallen to zero instead of rising to $2,000. A current ratio that included the cost figure among the current assets would be an entirely misleading indicator of the company's solvency.

Investors and creditors may wish to know the value of the current ratio each year and to know the direction in which it moves from year to year. If the ratio is low or falling, it may be considered to indicate imminent financial strain. In the light of other factors to be mentioned, this may presage new issues of securities or actual insolvency. Investors and creditors may then decide for themselves whether they wish to continue or to extend or to reduce their financial interest in the company.

BORROWING POWER AND GEARING
OR LEVERAGE

Consider now the negotiation of loans. Much borrowing is done on the security (by mortgage or lien) of particular assets, or on the security of a floating charge over all the assets of the borrowing company. Where assets are so pledged or charged, the lender usually lends some proportion of the current market selling value of the assets. He is not concerned with what the assets cost or with what the owner thinks they are worth. He is concerned only with market selling prices as they stand from time to time, for the market price indicates how well the lender is covered if the borrower defaults.

The manager of a company could make no reasonable estimate of the company's prospect of borrowing by reference to any asset valuations other than current market selling prices. He would be foolish to estimate borrowing power on the basis of prices paid for assets if the market prices of those assets have risen; he would be underestimating the company's borrowing power. He would be equally foolish to estimate borrowing power on the basis of cost prices if the market prices of assets have fallen below their cost prices; to negotiate from this footing would invite a lender's scornful refusal.

A company may not, at a given time, have borrowed up to the limit of its borrowing power. Nevertheless its manager may wish to know its 'reserve' borrowing power in case difficulties or new opportunities make it necessary or desirable to increase its borrowing. The market prices of assets are relevant in this case too. And if the market prices of pledged assets fall, the terms of the loan may require the borrower to give additional security, and of course the reserve borrowing power of the company will have fallen. No asset valuation other than market selling prices is useful in this direction.

What now of the shareholders and creditors of a company? They do not know when a new opportunity or other circumstances may give rise to a new issue of securities. A new issue of loan securities will increase the rate of return on shareholders' equity if the net cost of borrowing (interest less tax on that interest at company tax rates) falls short of the net return from the use of the additional funds. Shareholders in a company with reserve borrowing power could, therefore, expect that the rate of return, and perhaps the rate of dividend, may be sustained or raised by borrowing if new funds are required. If there seems to be no reserve borrowing power, shareholders could entertain no such expectations. On the other hand, existing creditors of a company with reserve borrowing power may expect the company to borrow further, reducing the asset coverage or safety margin of total debt. When a debtor company has little or no reserve borrowing power, it has no recourse but to additional issues of shares if it needs additional funds. This would increase the asset coverage or safety margin of existing creditors. It is reasonable to suppose that shareholders and creditors may think about their future prospects in these ways.

The indicator of the present security of creditors and the capacity of a company to borrow is the *debt-to-equity ratio*. In our example the total amount of debt is $10,000 and the total amount of shareholders' equity is $15,000. The debt-to-equity ratio is thus 2 to 3. Because the sum of the shareholders' equity and creditors' equities is equal to the sum of the amounts of all assets, we can also say that the asset coverage of creditors is $2.50 for each $1 of company debt.

Further, since the equity of a lender in the assets of a company is usually more secure than the equity of a shareholder, the cost to a company of borrowing is usually lower than the cost of equivalent new risk capital from shareholders or new investors. The earning capacity of a given risk capital is geared up by borrowing. The relationship of debt to equity may thus be briefly described as the gearing or leverage of shareholders' equity.

There are limits to what lenders will lend. The higher the debt-to-equity ratio becomes, the less ready will creditors be to give further credit. But the ratio is useless as an indicator unless the assets are valued at current market prices. If, in the example, we had used the cost figures given for certain assets, the total amount of assets would have been $23,200 and the debt-to-equity ratio would have been 10,000 to 13,200, or approximately 3 to 4. The company's prospect of borrowing therefore seems lower than if the market prices of assets are used.

The difference in this case is not great; but in many of the cases we shall consider later there are differences between cost and market value of a very large order. In some cases the reserve borrowing power is greatly understated, so that no outsider could know of the prospect of raising the rate of return by borrowing. In other cases the use of cost figures for assets when market values have fallen has enabled companies to borrow when they were already too heavily in debt; the consequence has been collapse, to the great disappointment and loss of creditors and shareholders.

Reporting assets at cost prices would not prevent a borrower from disclosing privately to a prospective lender the market values of assets to be charged as security for a loan. But privileged disclosure is unfair to others. Other creditors may have thought further borrowing was impossible—until, unexpectedly, they find the safety of their advances diluted by new borrowing.

In all these circumstances only the use of up-to-date market prices as asset values will give a true and fair view of a company's position.

EFFICIENCY AND RATE OF RETURN

It is generally held that one function of the securities market is to ration funds available for investment among those seeking their use. Other things being equal, an investor will prefer to invest for a higher rate of return than for a lower. This preference is expected to ensure that funds flow to the economically more efficient and are denied to the less efficient.

The *rate of return to a shareholder* by way of dividends is the dividend yield. It is the percentage of the amount of the dividend per share to the current buying price of a share. If an investor is about to buy a share he may calculate the dividend yields of several possible investments by reference to their purchase prices and make his choice on this basis. If he is already the holder of a share and is considering whether to hold it or to invest in some other way, he should do the same. Of course, in this case, the purchase price on the market of the share he holds is the selling price, to him, if he decides to switch. In general, all rates of return on asset holdings should be calculated on the basis of market selling prices to the holder, which are market buying prices to others (disregarding transfer costs, of course).

In the same way as an investor may judge the merits of his security holdings, he and others may judge the merits of the companies of which he holds or may hold securities. The appropriate indicator is *the company's achieved rate of return*: the percentage of the profit of a year to the amount of the ordinary shareholders' equity (or the amount of the net assets, which is the same figure) at the beginning of the year. As was suggested in the previous paragraph, the amount of ordinary shareholders' equity (or net assets) should be calculated by reference to the market selling prices of the assets. The example on p. 30 shows a profit for the year of $3,000. If we suppose there were no new share issues or reductions of shareholders' equity during the year, the opening amount of shareholders' equity would have been $12,000. The rate of return would be 25 per cent on an annual basis.

One of the things which prompt managers to seek to improve efficiency is comparison of the achieved rate of return of one company with those of others. One of the aids to the selection of a way to increase the rate of return is comparison of the achieved rate of return with the yields of alternative investments open to the company. The comparisons mentioned first are only legitimate if all companies prepare their financial statements on the same principles. And the comparisons mentioned second are only legitimate if assets are valued at market prices of the same or approximately the same vintage as the market prices of alternatives open to the company—that is to say, at current prices.

Out-of-date asset values will not do. If we had used the costs of assets in the example to calculate the amount of opening shareholders' equity, the calculated rate of return could have been much higher than 25 per cent if the market prices of assets had been rising, or much lower if the market prices of assets had been falling. Such a rate of return could not properly be compared with the current rate of return on any other investment.

Of course business assets are employed at varying risks from time to time. The rate of return will vary from year to year. Properly calculated rates of return are the only indicators that can be used to judge the relative efficiencies of different companies at any time, or to judge the changes in efficiency of any company from year to year. The rate of return is the one statistic that embraces the consequences of all the operations of the company and all the external events that may have impinged on it.

The 'total return to a shareholder' in a period includes not only his dividend receipts but also any rise or fall in the market price of his shares in that period. Similarly the 'total return to a company' in a period includes not only its trading profits but also any gains or losses from changes in the market prices of its assets during that period. Managers and others may wish to have separate knowledge of the effects of changes in market prices of some assets—separate, that is, from what may be considered as trading profits. But both are parts of the full gain or loss of a period. Both affect measures of solvency, measures of the relationship between debt and equity and measures of the full rate of return.

At a later point we shall show that if there has been a change in the purchasing power of money in an accounting period, the full gain or loss is computed only by taking this change into account. Rises in the market prices of assets may make a company better off, better able to spend or borrow, but only if those rises exceed in effect the rise in the general level of prices (or the fall in the general purchasing power of money). For present purposes we assume there has been no change in the general purchasing power of money. But when, later, we allude to the effects of 'inflation' or 'deflation', we shall be referring to shifts in the purchasing power of money, not to shifts in the specific prices of assets.

RISK

Business decisions must be made with knowledge only of the past and present. We can have only expectations, not knowledge, of the future. All business is therefore risky. Both investors and creditors assume some risks. Many of the causes of fluctuations or drifts in asset values and profits can be described in a general way: credit restriction or relaxation, changes in tax laws, tariff policy and other aids to specific industries, inflation, deflation, shifts in demand, and so on. But it is not possible to specify in advance when any one of these will occur or how it will affect any particular firm. If investors and creditors, when considering their investments, wish to assess the effects of these events, they may attempt to do so themselves. The signs of the imminence of such events and their extent when they occur are accessible public knowledge.

Events that are likely to influence the results or positions of *particular* firms, however, cannot easily be foreseen, even by managers. When a new product or a new advertising campaign will be launched by a competitor, when a new and more efficient machine will become available, when any class of workers will demand higher wages or strike and with what effects on the firm, cannot be foretold. One of the important strategies of competition is the secrecy with which each firm proceeds, designs, tests and negotiates before the time is considered ripe for revealing its plans. It is also important for each firm to keep to itself its hopes or fears about these and other events. It would be foolish indeed for a firm to disclose during the course of litigation that it expected to lose a lawsuit, or that it expected workers to strike, or that it expected to launch a specific new product, or that it expected its plant to become obsolete in a specified time. For the disclosure would be likely to put the firm at the mercy of its competitors, cause it to lose the advantage of surprise; in the case of expected detrimental events, disclosure may even hasten or bring about the detriment, converting what was only a possibility into a certainty. For these reasons it seems improper and contrary to the interests of shareholders and creditors to require companies to reveal expected consequences of events specific to them.

The assessment of risk must therefore be left in the hands of investors and creditors and their advisers and analysts. They may be expected, however, to want to make the best possible assessment in the light of past and present knowledge of a company, in the same way as managers base their decisions to a considerable extent on past and present knowledge.

The clearest and most reliable indicators of the risks of investments in particular companies are properly calculated current ratios, debt-to-equity ratios and rates of return. Each of these relates to a particular and important financial element of companies and each may vary independently of the others. A company may earn satisfactory profits and have a satisfactory debt-to-equity ratio, but have a low current ratio, due for example to the liberality of dividends or the rapidity of new investment in durable assets. A company may have a satisfactory current ratio, a satisfactory debt-to-equity ratio and a low rate of return. And so on. The main risks are: for a low current ratio, difficulties with short run payments and debts; for a high debt-to-equity ratio, difficulties of adaptation to change and difficulties with maturing debt and the high fixed costs of interest; for a low rate of return, difficulties in maintaining the confidence of investors and creditors.

There is no formula by which a meaningful 'risk factor' covering these different risks may be calculated and assigned to any company. But it is possible to see how these three ratios may be used to decide which of several companies is the least risky. Consider the following three cases:

	Current ratio		Debt to equity		Rate of return	
	Ratio	Rank	Ratio	Rank	%	Rank
Company *A*	3:1	1	2:3	1	25	2
Company *B*	2:1	2	1:1	3	30	1
Company *C*	1:1	3	4:5	2	15	3

The three companies would be ranked differently for each factor. For all factors, inclusively, *C* is clearly the greater risk. In any judgment, by managers or investors, there may be other factors. But the illustration shows how the figure-work helps to reduce to easily comprehensible terms the significance of quantifiable elements of positions and results. Any accounting practice that fails to disclose or that conceals the occurrence and extent of changes in the position of a company robs investors and creditors of the chance of fruitful speculation about the relative strengths and prospects of companies.

Trends and income smoothing: Managers and investors may take into account trends in the major ratios as well as their values at any date. For example, that the rate of return has been rising or falling may be as useful a piece of information as the rate of return for the latest year. But one is not a substitute for the other.

It is a mistake to assert, as some do, that trends are more important than reasonable exactitude in calculating the financial results and position each year. For, in the first place, no trend of a reliable kind can be obtained from raw figures which are themselves unreliable. And, in the second place, a reasonable user of financial statements and ratios will want to know whether the latest figures are above or below the trend of past figures. He will want to consider whether there are grounds for believing the deviation to be temporary and reversible, or whether he should change his expectations because the deviation seems to indicate a significant change in direction of the past trend.

Income smoothing, by occasionally changing asset valuation and other accounting rules, has been justified on the ground that investors are concerned with the normal performance of companies. But what the 'normal' performance is should be left to users of the statements to judge. It is conceivable that the trends of profits of two companies may be the same but while the annual profits of one may swing widely above and below the trend line, the profits of the other may vary only slightly from year to year. Given the possibility of income smoothing, investors could not distinguish between the two. Yet the company whose profits vary from year to year over a wide range is a more risky investment than the other. Income smoothing and other such devices thus prevent investors from making assessments of the relative risks of investment in different companies.

LIQUIDATIONS AND TAKEOVERS

When solvency is imperilled, when debt weighs heavily on equity or when the rate of return has fallen to a low level, a company may consider resolving its difficulties by liquidation or by sale of the undertaking and assets, lock, stock and barrel. Whether the members of the company would be better off by liquidation (or sale) than by continuing the company depends on the rate of return they could obtain by investing the proceeds otherwise. The magnitude of the income from an alternative investment depends on the amount invested. The amount available to be invested—in the case of orderly liquidation—is approximately the amount of the net assets of the company, calculated by reference to the resale prices of its assets.

If the whole undertaking were sold, it is possible that a buyer may pay more than the value of the net assets. However, when consideration is being given to the possibilities of continuation, liquidation or sale, the value of the net assets is the known minimum alternative investment. It is also the minimum price that should be demanded from any buyer of the whole undertaking and assets as a going concern, for the company could obtain that price by selling its assets at their several resale prices.

It follows that whether a company is a continuing venture (as was supposed in the greater part of this chapter) or whether it approaches the point of liquidation or sale, the market resale prices of assets are always the proper basis of calculations by managers or investors.

CONCLUSION

Analysts, investment advisers, investors, creditors and managers may make use of indicators other than those we have mentioned. But none can properly neglect the current ratio, the debt-to-equity ratio and the rate of return. For our purpose it is sufficient to examine these three, for it will be seen that they embrace every item in the balance sheet and the net profit of a year.

The analysis shows that proper indicators of the state of a company—its relationship with creditors and the rest of the world—and its full gains or losses in a period can only be derived if up-to-date market selling prices are used to obtain asset balances. It seems therefore that a true and fair view, or a fair presentation, of the state of affairs and of the results of a company is given only if its financial statements are based on the best possible approximations to the market selling prices of assets from time to time.

In revealing the need for up-to-date asset valuations, this chapter is consistent with the conclusions of the previous chapter. If all companies were to base their financial statements on this rule, the positions and results of different companies would be directly comparable. Investors would have a firm foundation for decisions to buy, sell or hold securities. And the securities market could be expected to ration available funds, on the basis of proven efficiency and financial administration, in the selective manner that is expected of it.

5

THE LORE OF FINANCIAL STATEMENTS

'Things are seldom what they seem,
Skim milk masquerades as cream;
Highlows pass as patent leathers;
Jackdaws strut in peacock's feathers.'
/ W S Gilbert, *HMS Pinafore* /

Chacun à son goût.

We have seen that the laws and regulations on corporate financial publicity have for over a century enunciated a sound principle — that financial statements shall give a true and fair view of financial position and results (Chapter 2). We have seen that this principle has been backed up by professional and legal opinion (Chapter 3). And we have considered the financial features of business firms on which managers, investors and creditors need information of the kind that financial statements could yield (Chapter 4).

We have also seen that the laws and regulations were and have remained vague on important matters. The sense of the laws on financial reporting was left to the interpretation of those whose actions the laws were intended to regulate.

At the outset this meant the interpretation of directors and managers. They were made responsible for giving the report of which the financial statements were a part. The guidance they could expect from accountants was minimal, for company accounting was a novelty in many respects. Perforce they relied on the slow clarification of the law by judicial process. Among the more important problems that confronted the courts was the legality of dividend payments in unusual circumstances. For the protection of creditors, the law forbade the payment of dividends otherwise than out of profits. But accountants had no firm notion of capital or of profits. The judgments or dicta of the courts served — in the absence of other principles. Generally, of course, litigated cases are highly specific. They may become precedents. But the courts have been far from satisfactory as generators of technical principles.

Companies and their directors were of course advised and aided by accountants. The antecedents of the modern professional associations of accountants arose in the latter half of the nineteenth century. But, as is the case with all such associations, they were concerned in their early years with status and ethics, not with technical problems. To what extent a professional association should or can effectively engage in the determination of technical principles is debatable. But, for better or worse, the associations did enter the field—within the last fifty or sixty years. They established their place so effectively that the SEC in the United States decided, as we have seen, to 'cooperate' with the professional institute on matters of technical principle; and more recently, in the United Kingdom, the Jenkins Committee expressed the view that 'it is primarily to the initiative of the professional associations that we must look if the general principles of the Act are to be effectively applied in practice' (para. 334). In this chapter we consider the interpretations of professional associations of the functions of financial statements.

PROFESSIONAL OPINION IN THE UNITED KINGDOM

We shall deal with professional opinion in the United Kingdom as illustrative of the views developed in jurisdictions which followed the English pattern of legislation and accounting practice. These views are substantially similar in purport to the views of associations in other similar jurisdictions, and generally they are more fully described than in the publications of other associations.

The Institute of Chartered Accountants in England and Wales has, over the past thirty years, published numerous statements or recommendations on particular accounting practices or problems. Of these statements it might have been expected that (a) they would be guided by the overriding rule of the statute: that a true and fair view be given and/or (b) they would be circumscribed by the practical uses (as up-to-date indicators of solvency, gearing and rate of return) to which those who receive accounting statements may apply them. There is no principal statement that establishes a framework in these terms for all or any of the recommendations made. But in the course of certain recommendations there are some allusions to general principles:

> 'The function of a balance sheet is to give a true and fair view of the state of affairs of the company as on a particular date. A true and fair view implies appropriate classification and grouping of the items and therefore the balance sheet needs to show in summary form the amounts of the share capital, reserves and liabilities as on the balance sheet date and the amounts of the assets representing them, together with sufficient information to indicate the general nature of the items. A true and fair view also implies the consistent application of generally-accepted principles.'
> / *Recommendation N18*, 'Presentation of balance sheet and profit and loss account', 1958 /

So far the statement seems reasonable. It does not elucidate the meaning of 'a true and fair view', nor the meaning of 'state of affairs'. But it does refer to the state of affairs at 'a particular date', which could be interpreted as requiring that the magnitudes of assets and equities should be up-to-date magnitudes. The Recommendation continues:

> 'Assets are normally shown at loss less amounts charged against revenues to amortise expenditure over the effective lives of the assets and to provide for diminution in their value.'

The Recommendation appears, then, to assert that a balance sheet in which assets are consistently valued at cost, less amounts written off to amortize expenditure, gives a true and fair view of the state of affairs of a company as on a particular date. Yet this is patently at odds with any ordinary interpretation of the meaning of 'the state of affairs' of a company. The cost prices of assets (less amounts, if any, written off) are not prices of assets as on the balancing date. They may be vastly greater or less than the market prices—the financially significant amounts—of the assets. If the market prices of assets are greater than their cost prices or costs less amortization, a balance sheet that conforms with the recommendation would overstate the then ratio of debt to equity; it would lead to understatement of the asset backing for shares and debt, to understatement of the extent of past gains, and possibly to overstatement of the rate of return of the year under report. If the market prices of assets were less than their cost prices, distortions in the opposite direction would occur. It is impossible to see how such a balance sheet could be said to give a true and fair view of a company's state of affairs.

What uses of the financial statement do the recommendations contemplate then?

> 'The primary purpose of the annual accounts of a business is to present information to the proprietors, showing how their funds have been utilised and the profits derived from such use. It has long been accepted in accounting practice that a balance sheet prepared for this purpose is an historical record and not a statement of current worth. Stated briefly its function is to show in monetary terms the capital, reserves and liabilities of a business at the date as at which it is prepared and the manner in which the total moneys representing them have been distributed over the several types of assets. Similarly a profit and loss account is an historical record.'
> / *Recommendation N15*, 'Accounting in relation to changes in the purchasing power of money', 1952 /

This is principally an allusion to the stewardship notion dealt with in the previous chapter. Taken together with the valuation of assets at unamortized costs it leads to the fault pointed out in that chapter (see pp. 31–2). Directors and managers are not held accountable year by year for the money and money's worth with which each year begins. If the assets at the beginning of a year are represented by amounts which differ from their money worth, the reserves (undistributed surpluses) are improperly stated.

Note also that the balance sheet is said to be 'an historical record and not a statement of current worth'. There is no necessary reason why a balance sheet should not be both an historical record and a statement of current worth. Any running account of a changing magnitude—the score in a game, the weight of a child, the size of a population—gives both a resultant of what has happened in the past up to specific points of time and a statement of the current magnitude at specific points of time. If a series of consecutive balance sheets does not give the current worth of assets from time to time, it can scarcely be said to be a full historical record. The growth in assets and in shareholders' equity would be improperly represented.

Caveats: Curiously, the recommendations explicitly acknowledge the defects of the style of accounting that they endorse:

> 'A balance sheet is therefore mainly an historical document which does not purport to show the realizable value of assets such as goodwill, land, buildings, plant and machinery; nor does it normally purport to show the realisable value of assets such as stock-in-trade. Thus a balance sheet is not a statement of the net worth of the undertaking and this is normally so even where there has been a revaluation of assets and the balance sheet amounts are based on the revaluation instead of on cost.' / *Recommendation N18* /

The mere mention of 'realizable value' and 'net worth of the undertaking' (i.e. the net value of assets) implies that some interested parties may or do find such information useful. The form of words seems to be a defence against charges that the balance sheet does not give this information. But how else those parties may come to know about realizable values and net worth when accountants decline to inform them is not made clear.

Further:

> ' ... the results shown by accounts prepared on the basis of historical cost are not a measure of increase or decrease in wealth in terms of purchasing power; nor do the results necessarily represent the amount which can prudently be regarded as available for distribution, having regard to the financial requirements of the business. Similarly the results shown by such accounts are not necessarily suitable for purposes such as price fixing, wage negotiation and taxation, unless in using them for these purposes due regard is paid to the amount of profit which has been retained in the business for its maintenance.' / *Recommendation N15* /

Here is stated a number of settings in which it might be expected that the reported profit figure would be useful to managers and shareholders and in negotiations with other parties. Yet the figure is said to be useless of itself for these purposes, and no indication is given of the way in which a useful figure may be obtained.

Subsequent to the 1963 case, *Hedley Byrne & Co. Ltd* v. *Heller & Partners Ltd*, the Institute sought Counsel's advice on the accountant's liability to third parties. In the course of the advice, as it was published in 1965 for the guidance of Institute members, there occurs the following:

> 'In Counsel's view the object of annual accounts is to assist share-holders in exercising their control of the company by enabling them to judge how its affairs have been conducted ... No claim by an individual shareholders [against an auditor] would succeed in respect of loss suffered through his own investment decisions made on the strength of misleading company accounts supported by an auditor's report containing negligent misrepresentations, since the purpose for which annual accounts are normally prepared is not to enable individual shareholders to take investment decisions.'

By what principles Counsel was guided we do not know. The law requires that a true and fair view of the state of affairs and the results of a company be given. If a true and fair view is given, it will be equally pertinent both to shareholders acting collectively in general meeting and to shareholders as individual investors. It would be fatuous to suppose that judgments on how a company's affairs have been conducted could be, or were thought by the draughtsmen of the company laws to be, entirely different from and separable from judgments made by individual shareholders in respect of their investments. The sweeping nature of the final observation in the passage quoted implies that the widespread practice of financial statement analysis is an absurd waste of time, that the financial community should take no notice of company accounts, and that, in all honesty, accountants should plainly state on the face of every set of financial statements that they are not intended to be used for the making of investment decisions!

Consider the several passages cited. It appears that a balance sheet prepared according to the endorsed, historical cost principle must *not* be taken as giving an indication of up-to-date, realizable values of assets, *nor* an indication of net worth; that the results are *not* a measure of increase or decrease in wealth in terms of purchasing power; that the results are *not* necessarily serviceable in price-fixing, wage negotiations or taxation; and that company accounts are *not* prepared with the object of assisting individual investors in decision-making. Instead of financial statements being the means by which all parties of interest may be reliably informed of the extent of their several interests, it seems that those who rely on such statements do so at their peril.

Official endorsement: In the light of these disclaimers, it is curious that neither the (Cohen) Committee on Company Law Amendment in 1945 nor the (Jenkins) Company Law Committee in 1962 found cause to question the propriety of the conventional mode of accounting. The Cohen Committee endorsed, by quotation without further discussion, a submission by the Institute in terms similar to those of *Recommendation N18* quoted above (Report, para. 98). The Jenkins Committee noticed part of the above quotation from *Recommendation N15*, and considered that 'this "historical cost" basis of accounting ... should continue to be the basis on which company accounts are prepared' (Report, para. 333).

The Jenkins Committee does not seem to have taken any notice of the following part of the same recommendation:

> 'Monetary profits [as calculated under traditional historical cost rules] do not therefore necessarily reflect an increase or decrease in wealth in terms of purchasing power; and in times of material change in prices this limitation upon the significance of monetary profits may be very important. *It would be a major development in the building up of a coherent and logical structure of accounting principles if the limitations of accounts based on historical cost could be eliminated or reduced by the adoption of new principles,* capable of practical application to all kinds of businesses in a manner which could be independent of personal opinion to a degree comparable with the existing principles based on historical cost.' [Emphasis added.] / *Recommendation N15* (para. 4) /

The reference to 'the building up of a coherent and logical structure of accounting principles' is tacit admission of the inadequacy of the present structure. Burdened as they were with review of the whole of the Companies Act, these Committees could not, perhaps, have been expected to question seriously the mode of accounting practice. But submissions critical of the existing mode were made to the Jenkins Committee which, together with the above statement, should have prompted closer examination of the utility of the information yielded by traditional accounting processes. There is no evidence in the Report of the Committee that such an examination was made of the general quality and usefulness of the accounting information made available by companies under the law as it stood at that time.

PROFESSIONAL OPINION IN THE UNITED STATES

As early as 1917 the American Institute of Accountants (later the American Institute of Certified Public Accountants—AICPA), published a statement entitled *Approved Methods for the Preparation of Balance Sheet Statements.* This was prepared at the instigation of the Federal Reserve Board and the Federal Trade Commission in the interest of improved standards of accounting for the protection of lenders, particularly bankers. The 1936 revision of this statement, published by the Institute under the title *Examination of Financial Statements by Independent Public Accountants,* pointed out that it related to financial statements 'prepared for credit purposes or for annual reports to stockholders'. The acknowledgment of a wider readership—creditors *and* stockholders—was consistent with the growth in private investment in corporate securities.

The 1936 statement affirmed that 'Financial statements are prepared for the purpose of presenting a periodical review or report on progress by the management and deal with the status of the investment in the business and the results achieved during the period under review'. No description or definition was given that clarified the meaning of 'status of the investment' or 'results achieved'. We are forced to rely on inferences from other parts of the statement. At one point it says:

> 'One of the most important accounting conventions is that the balance sheet of a going concern shall be prepared on the assumption that the concern will continue in business. Plant assets, permanent investments and intangibles are usually stated at cost or on some other historical basis without regard to present realizable or replacement value.'

Notice that the second sentence is not stated to be a consequence of what is said in the first. But their association suggests that 'cost or some other historical basis' is consistent with the going-concern assumption. Notice too that present selling prices and present purchase prices are to be disregarded for the classes of asset mentioned. It seems therefore that the 'status of the investment' was considered to be represented, in respect of the assets mentioned, by cost or some other historical basis of asset valuation.

That confronts us with a problem. The status of the investment in a company at a given date is the basis of its plans for the future, and the basis of investors' expectations of the future. The basis of all plans for and expectations of the future can properly be nothing else than the present prices of assets. Yet we are told that assets are usually stated at cost or on some other historical basis. The status of the investment is also the consequence of all past transactions and events that have affected the investment. Rises and falls in asset prices since their purchase are one class of such events. Yet we are told present prices are disregarded, and it is implied that they should be disregarded.

A statement published in 1936 by the American Accounting Association (an association primarily of university teachers) is substantially consistent with the view of the American Institute. It said, *inter alia*:

> '... the purpose of the [financial] statements is the expression, in financial terms, of the utilization of the economic resources of the enterprise and the resultant changes in and position of the interests of creditors and investors. Accounting is thus not essentially a process of valuation, but the allocation of historical costs and revenues to the current and succeeding fiscal periods.' / *A Tentative Statement of Accounting Principles* /

The statement made no attempt however to show how, from time to time, asset account balances resulting from allocations of historical costs represented in any significant way the 'position of the interests of creditors and investors'.

The history of the commerce of the United States (as of other countries) is full of examples of business failure and insolvency. From the experiences of 1929–31 especially, no one who thought seriously about the 'position of the interests of creditors and investors' could have been unaware of the relevance to survival of the market prices of company assets, nor unaware that asset prices may rise or fall to the joy or chagrin of their holders. Real estate prices, inventory prices, security prices—all had dropped spectacularly and for many companies fatally at some time during the seven years preceding 1936. Yet the original cost principle was endorsed as if price changes were irrelevant to the interests of creditors and investors.

From 1939 to 1953, the American Institute published a series of *Accounting Research Bulletins* on technical problems and other matters. The 'official' description of balance sheet is of interest:

'[A balance sheet is] a tabular statement or summary of balances (debit and credit) carried forward after an actual or constructive closing of books of account kept according to principles of accounting.'

The bulletin in which this appears quotes with disapproval a description which runs: 'A statement made by merchants and others to show the true state of a particular business'. Whereas this description gives some indication of the function of a balance sheet, the official description gives none. There was thus no connection between the uses to which balance sheets would be put and the 'principles of accounting' according to which they would be prepared.

Over time, 'principles of accounting' have come to be described as 'generally accepted accounting principles'. As many people have pointed out, this phrase does not mean—as it may be supposed to mean—that there is a fixed code of principles to which all companies adhere. It is used loosely of the vast range of rules, many of them having quite opposite consequences to others, which have come to be used by some companies under whatever pretext or circumstance. The consequences of this looseness are illustrated extensively later in this book.

There are good grounds for believing that this range of rules has come into use because of the inadequacy of the original cost basis of accounting. But notwithstanding the disputes, distortions and difficulties to which the historical cost idea has given rise, it still remains the basis of asset accounting avowed by the AICPA.

RECENT DEVELOPMENTS — UK AND USA

Both the English Institute and the American Institute have shown some awareness of the deficiencies of the established, conventional doctrine. In the late 1940s the American Institute and in the early 1950s the English Institute published statements on the 'limitations' of conventionally prepared financial statements in inflationary periods. But no firm step was taken to eliminate these limitations. The American Institute in the late 1960s and the English Institute in 1971 made further statements on the same matter. They have suggested that the traditional cost-based accounts should be varied by the application to original costs of general price level corrections. This is recognition of the existence of problems and difficulties, but it is an inadequate solution as we shall later show. In any case it seems quite clear that suggestion alone is insufficient to secure reform, for suggestions have been in the air for twenty years without any change in the respect accorded to the historical cost doctrine. Among the latest professional exercises on the valuation of assets is an inquiry, launched in 1971 by the American Institute, into the proper mode of valuing marketable securities. The question is whether such securities should be valued at market prices. Whether the inquiry will mark the first step in a break from the tradition of historical cost valuation remains to be seen.

SUMMARY

Several things are remarkable in the professional recommendations, bulletins, suggestions and opinions, and the discursive material that has accompanied them. We have noticed that the law is quite vague on the meaning of 'a true and fair view' or 'fair presentation', and that there is no clear specification of what is meant by 'state of affairs', 'financial position', 'profits', 'results' and so on. As these words appear in the laws or rules which govern published financial information, it might be expected that the professional bodies would have explored their meaning and have used some selected set of meanings as the basis for all their pronouncements, opinions and prescriptions. They have not done so, except in a very superficial way.

(a) In its recommendations the English Institute has made only the briefest reference to the giving of a true and fair view. No connection is established between the specific rules which the recommendations endorse and the measures of solvency, gearing and rate of return which are the main guides and indicators to investors and creditors. The technical terms mentioned above are not elucidated or defined. In the absence of links with the realities of commercial dealing and financial analysis, it should not be surprising that the recommendations are equivocal. For although they stipulate that 'normally' assets are valued at unamortized cost, they also contain rules that enable the same events and transactions to be represented by materially different magnitudes. The choice of rules from the battery permitted is left to directors and managers, for each company according to its taste or circumstances.

(b) Likewise the vast amount of material published by the American Institute lacks the cohesion that adoption of firm meanings for the most important ideas would give. The legislation of 1933 and 1934 has been called 'Truth in Securities' legislation. It was intended 'to provide full and fair disclosure of the character of securities sold'. There has been no professional analysis of the meaning of full and fair disclosure of the character of securities. It seems to be quite impossible to hold that the character of a security in 1971 is fully and fairly disclosed by financial statements in which assets are reported at, or on the basis of, prices paid for those assets in 1961 or 1951 or 1941. Yet the holding of this view is entailed in the practices endorsed by the Institute.

The section of the Securities Act that deals with defences of experts against legal actions by buyers of securities requires that there shall have been 'no omission to state a material fact required to be stated [in any expert statement] or necessary to make the statement therein not misleading'. There has been no professional analysis of and no position taken on the meaning of this provision.

We have seen that the Institute's 1936 statement makes reference to the 'status of the investment in the business and the results achieved'. But there is no amplification of 'status of the investment', no reference to solvency, leverage or rate of return. It seems to be quite impossible to hold that the status of the investment in a business is represented by figures derived by formal bookkeeping rules without regard for changes in the prices of assets and changes in the purchasing power of money. And it seems to be impossible to hold that the 'results achieved' can be represented by figures which, as we shall show, may be boosted or reduced simply by a change in bookkeeping rules.

(c) The verbal justifications that the professional bodies have adopted are likewise imprecise, indefinite and misleading. Thus, although the professional statements aver that financial statements are historical statements, based on historical costs, this is not strictly true. At best it is a half truth. The traditional mode disregards entirely the effects on position and results of past changes in asset prices and the purchasing power of money—events that are no less historical than the prices paid for assets. On the other hand, in the calculation of asset values and charges against revenues, expectations have as great an influence as original costs; expected realizable values of inventory and expected service lives of durable assets may influence substantially the reported figures. And these expectations are certainly not historical. There are other technical words and circumlocutions which are just as misleading or confused. But they need not be discussed here.

CONCLUSION

The failure of the legislative and regulatory bodies to specify the meaning of key terms and phrases is thus not remedied by the professional accounting associations, which might have been expected to interpret, in practical and fruitful detail, the general prescriptions of the law. Legislators and regulators have declined to clarify matters that are the special province of accountants. And the accounting profession has apparently declined to deduce from the law the limited set of rules which would satisfy the general principles that the law enunciates.

This tender respect, each for the other's field of influence or competence, has had two effects.

It has left the disclosure of financial information at the discretion of managers and directors: in the upshot, every man to his taste. The very parties whose effectiveness is expected to be judged from the published accounts are the final arbiters of what is published.

Consequentially, it has left investors and creditors without the protection which reliable knowledge of company positions and periodical results would give.

Under the circumstances, there can be no complaint or charge of misrepresentation against managers and directors and their advisers, except in the case of gross or obvious self-serving. But neither can there be any way of judging fairly which companies (and their managers and directors) are more efficient than others, for all are free to adopt accounting rules that mask their relative efficiency or inefficiency or conceal their wealth or poverty, as the case may be. 'Skim milk may masquerade as cream.'

These may seem to be wild and fanciful charges. We proceed to show how, and on what scale, concealment and misdirection can occur, and under what circumstantial pressures the doctrines avowed by the professional associations are disregarded.

6

WHAT IS IT WORTH?

'Following a revaluation of freehold property, the balance sheet should present a truer and fairer picture of our net worth.'
/ Chairman's Address, 1951 /

'It is proposed to write up the assets to a more realistic value.'
/ Memorandum to Stockholders, 1966 /

'Curiouser and curiouser.'
/ (Alice) *Through the Looking Glass* /

By reference to the information needed by investors and creditors, we have shown that assets should be shown in balance sheets at up-to-date market values. If there is merit in our argument, we should expect to find some tendency, in practice, to value assets on bases other than their original costs. We would not expect more than a tendency, since cost is widely and frequently affirmed to be the proper basis of valuation. In fact we find a substantial body of evidence of divergence from the professional doctrine in the direction of up-to-date valuation.

The evidence presented in this chapter is from Australian and United Kingdom practice. In a number of other countries, including Canada, India, Ireland, Mexico and New Zealand, the upward revaluation of assets is permissible. We have no reason to suppose that practice in these countries would not yield evidence of the kind given in this chapter. In the United States, upward revaluation is not permitted; in later chapters we shall show that this prohibition has spawned its own brood of inconsistencies.

REVALUATIONS IN AUSTRALIA

We present some evidence of the frequency and extent of asset revaluations in Australia. Of the total number of listed public companies in Australia a large number are listed on the Sydney Stock Exchange. About 35 per cent are not listed in Sydney. We have not been able to examine all the companies which, at some time over the last twenty years, were listed on one or more of the exchanges. The principal source of information has been the Sydney Stock Exchange Investment Service, but use has been made of company reports and circulars, press reports and other sources of information. The sources have been cross checked where possible. Only cases for which clear evidence was available have been included in the figures tabulated below.

The companies to which the summaries relate are companies registered in, operating in, and listed on one or more of the Australian exchanges. Only the larger well-established mining companies have been included. The asset revaluations here represented were made principally while the securities of the subject companies were listed. Some revaluations before listing are included, and revaluations by subsidiaries of listed companies are included where clear evidence is available. There have been quite a number of downward revaluations but the number is small in relation to the number of upward revaluations. The figures given relate to upward revaluations only. Our survey has been extensive but the figures given are not claimed to be exhaustive.

The Australian monetary unit was changed from the pound to the dollar in 1966; all money figures prior to the change have been converted to dollar equivalents in preparing the tables. We are concerned mainly with the number and frequency of departures from the avowed 'cost rule', rather than with the sizes of revaluations relative to pre-revaluation or other figures; but we shall notice some 'relative' figures.

Here, then, is the total number of upward revaluations of assets which have come under notice:

Asset revaluations, 1950–1970 inclusive

	Number of companies	Number of revaluations	Total amount of revaluations
			$m
Companies listed in 1970 on Australian Stock Exchanges	615	1,190	1,327
Companies formerly listed	151	220	89
Totals	766	1,410	1,416

The total amount of revaluations is, of course, a heterogeneous total: the money unit has steadily declined in purchasing power over the period. In terms of 1970 prices, the total amount would be of the order of $1,730 million.

Many of the companies made only one revaluation in the period, but a large number made more frequent revaluations:

Number of revaluations	Companies listed 1970	Companies formerly listed
1	294	107
2	175	30
3	84	10
4	37	—
5	15	2
6 or more	10	2
Total	615	151

Note firstly that the number of companies that made revaluations while listed is quite significant. The number of companies registered in, operating in and listed in Australia, according to *Jobson's Year Book of Public Companies* for 1970, was approximately 1,150. Of these about 53 per cent have revalued some assets at least once. It would be interesting to know the distribution of all revaluations according to size of company, but size is a variable over a twenty-year period. We therefore give a table showing the distribution of the sizes of individual revaluations and the distribution of the aggregate of the revaluations made by individual companies in respect of companies that were listed for the whole of the period 1950–70.

Revaluations by companies listed, 1950–70 inclusive

Size ($000)	Number of individual revaluations	Total revaluations by companies
Up to 100	171	29
101 to 500	303	117
501 to 2,000	171	111
2,001 to 5,000	57	36
5,001 to 10,000	15	21
10,001 to 20,000	8	11
Over 20,000	5	5
Total	730	330
Companies making no revaluations		155
Number of companies listed 1950–70 inclusive		485

Two-thirds of all companies listed throughout the period made revaluations. Many of those that did not were utilities or financial and investment companies whose business was such that revaluations would not be expected.

The sizes of many revaluations were significant in relation to the sizes of companies in the Australian securities market. In many cases the amount of the revaluation was sufficient to provide for 'bonus' share issues on the basis of one-for-one of all ordinary shares issued at the time. Some of the larger companies will illustrate the extent to which revaluations have augmented the reported figures for net assets:

Company	Number of revaluations	Total amount of revaluations	Date last revaluation	Net assets after last revaluation*
		$m		$m
Broken Hill Pty	5	352	1968	813
Burns Philp	11	15	1970	92
Coal & Allied Industries	3	12	1967	33
Imperial Chemical Industries A & NZ	7	27	1969	190
Mount Isa Mines	2	35	1963	66
Myer Emporium	7	53	1969	143
North Broken Hill	2	84	1970	125

*Figures from consolidated balance sheets.

Note secondly that there is no regularity in revaluation. About half the companies made only one revaluation in the period. The greatest number of individual revaluations occurred in the years 1951, 1959, 1960, 1969, 1970. However there is no way in which investors might guess when or whether any specific company will disclose previously unreported increments in asset values. Investors are therefore unable to know the full extent of gains made year by year, the extent of the assets in which shareholdings give them an equity, or the rate of return currently earned by companies. Further, when some companies make revaluations while others do not, investors have no common basis on which they can compare the financial characteristics of any two or more companies, with the object of choosing investments in a deliberate and well-informed manner.

Thirdly, the greater part of all revaluations were in respect of so-called 'fixed' assets: interests in land and buildings. Accountants have long distinguished between assets that are in the course of short-run circulation (cash, receivables and inventories) and those acquired for use in a business and not for early resale at a profit (land, buildings, equipment, investments in subsidiary companies). The former class—circulating or current assets—are usually valued at something approximating up-to-date cost prices. But the latter class—fixed assets—have been valued according to the traditional doctrine at cost or less than cost. The upward revaluation of land and buildings is contrary to the traditional doctrine; one will search in the traditional literature in vain for any justification of revaluation, notwithstanding that so many companies do it. As we shall presently see, company directors themselves have offered reasons for revaluation which seem to be consistent with commercial or financial reality and to cut sharply across the traditional doctrines of accountants.

Fourthly, the auditors of companies that made revaluations include all the larger and many of the not-so-large firms of public accountants. There is no record of any of these firms 'qualifying' their audit reports as a consequence of or in respect of a revaluation. This is of interest in two ways. On the one hand it signifies that practitioners are not averse to revaluations or to the principle of revaluation, notwithstanding the traditional doctrine of their associations. On the other hand it signifies that the phrase 'true and fair view of the state of affairs and results', which appears in auditors' reports, has a surprisingly lax or fluid meaning. Recall that there were some eighty-five individual revaluations of $2 million or more, often in respect of only some of the assets of the revalued class. The auditors' reports in these cases contained the same reference to a true and fair view in the year before as in the year after the revaluation, when for no externally apparent reason the same assets were represented by materially different figures. These rises in value certainly did not occur just in the year in which they were reported. It follows that if a true and fair view was given after the revaluation, something rather less than a true and fair view was being given for years before the revaluation. Further, these increments in value never find their way into the report of profits or results, even though they are the consequence of investments made and held in the course of, and for the purposes of, business. If this part of the consequences of company decisions is omitted from the report of results, that report cannot be said to give a true and fair view of results.

Fifthly, we regard the numbers of companies and the numbers and amounts of revaluations as significant. It is equally significant that there are long intervals between revaluations by any company and that, for a large number of presently listed companies, no revaluations have come to notice. Over the twenty-year period considered, no company could have escaped the impact of changes in the general level of prices and in the structure of prices of durable assets. It seems reasonable to conclude, therefore, that the majority of balance sheets do not give anything like an up-to-date view of the states of affairs of presently listed companies. By how much the reported values of assets diverge from up-to-date values, shareholders and investors have no means of knowing. We may note that all the auditors of companies that have revalued assets are also auditors of companies that have not revalued assets. This is further evidence of inconsistency of the practices and the ambivalence of the beliefs underlying the sole sources of information on company affairs available to shareholders, creditors and investors generally.

REASONS FOR REVALUATION

The directors of some companies have given reasons or justifications for the revaluation of assets. Additional reasons for these companies and reasons underlying the revaluations of other companies may be deduced.

A truer and fairer view: Some directors have stated explicitly that the object of revaluation has been to give shareholders a more up-to-date indication of the values of company assets, to give a fairer view of the states of affairs of their companies.

> □ '[Following a revaluation of freehold property] the balance sheet should present a truer and fairer picture of our net worth, even though such assets as plant and machinery will remain unaltered in the books at a figure substantially below replacement cost.' / Henry B Smith, Chairman's Address, Annual Meeting, 1951 /

☐ 'For some time your directors have been of opinion that the value of the company's assets is greatly in excess of the figures shown in the books of the company. The effect of this is that the equity of the shareholders has been understated and a more correct value of the shares [of the company] has not been disclosed.' / Hotel Metropole, Circular to Shareholders, 1954 /

The company increased the reported value of its freehold property by some £50,000, or about 20 per cent.

☐ In 1960 G E Crane Holdings revalued two of the company's properties to agree in the company's books with the Valuer General's most recent assessment. Some items of plant were revalued to bring them 'closer to present-day values after depreciation'. / Annual Report, 1960 /

☐ In 1965 preparatory to a bonus issue of shares (capitalization issue, or stock dividend), G & R Wills (Holdings) revalued the company's shares in two major subsidiaries by over £1 million 'to bring their worth in our books more into line both with their net tangible asset backing and with their earning capacity'.

/ Annual Report, 1965 /

☐ In 1966 on the occasion of a bonus share issue, Coal and Allied Industries referred to writing up assets 'to a more realistic value'. Shares in subsidiaries were revalued by $10 million. / Memorandum to Shareholders, 1966 /

☐ In 1970 North Broken Hill wrote up its investments by $56 million. The directors said: 'The company's investments, under current conditions, have been very conservatively valued and, as shown in previous balance sheets, gave little indication of the real value of these assets ... It is felt that to allow this situation to continue is not in the best interests of the company or its shareholders'.

Mainly as a consequence of this revaluation and the revaluation of mine property, the reported value of the company's net assets rose from $56 million in 1969 to $125 million in 1970.

/ Annual Report, 1970 /

The examples span the whole twenty-year period. Clearly, whatever impelled these companies to revalue assets may occur at any time, without warning to existing or prospective shareholders and creditors. That more 'realistic' or more up-to-date values should be shown at all is commendable. That this should occur only infrequently however entails unfair discrimination between shareholders at the time of such announcements and shareholders prior to announced revaluations; the latter clearly would have quite inadequate knowledge of the asset values represented by the shares they had bought and sold. Where the option of revaluing assets may be taken at the discretion of the management, there is at least the possibility that insiders may obtain privileged benefits; there is also the certainty the shareholders may, for long periods, be kept in ignorance of the financial characteristics of their companies. In neither respect can the market be a fair market in securities.

Correction of apparently excessive earnings: The association of many of the above revaluations with bonus share issues suggests that there is more to asset revaluation than the simple desire to give shareholders more up-to-date information on assets. Announcements of bonus share issues have in fact been the first and most easily accessible source of indications of asset revaluations. What is the connection?

In any period of inflation, the market selling prices of the products of most firms tend to rise and the absolute amounts of profits tend to rise. Out-of-pocket costs of course rise too, but the charges for depreciation, if based on original cost prices, do not rise. The rate of return—reported net profit on the reported value of net assets employed—will rise if assets continue to be reported at original, long out-of-date prices. The apparent rise in the rate of return is due in part to the out-of-date charge for depreciation (lower than if based on the current values of assets) and to the out-of-date value of net assets employed (lower in the same sense).

Dividend payments will tend to rise under the same kind of pressure from shareholders as workers bring to bear in wage negotiations during inflationary periods. Dividend rates calculated on nominal amounts of shareholders' paid in capital will consequently rise. Unusually high rates of return and dividend rates tend to attract claims from workers for higher wages, from customers for lower prices, from suppliers and financiers for better terms and conditions. Yet these higher profit rates are only higher by virtue of the continued use of out-of-date asset prices; and the higher dividend rates are only higher by virtue of the use (as a denominator) of the nominal value of shareholders' paid in capital, which itself is also an out-of-date price, namely the issue price of the securities. Company profits *appear* to be unusually high, anomalous or excessive simply because the method of accounting leads to the technically improper and practically misleading comparison of up-to-date and out-of-date money magnitudes.

Asset revaluation tends to improve the technical propriety of calculations of rates of return and debt-to-equity ratios. Bonus share issues, whether made out of the surpluses arising on asset revaluations or from other sources, tend to make more realistic the percentage of dividends to 'paid up' capital, where this percentage is used by investors or analysts. Both asset revaluations and bonus share issues tend to remove the anomalous appearance of excessive rates of profit, the anomalous appearance of under-capitalization. These steps may also relieve companies of misinformed pressure on the part of workers (for higher wages), shareholders (for higher dividends), and suppliers, financiers and customers (for better terms) — good enough reason, in a practical sense, for taking them. The case we are making is that they are steps that are correct in principle. We must regard these measures as perfectly proper devices for coping with some of the defects of forms of accounting that disregard shifts in the prices of assets while accounting for current income in up-to-date prices.

☐ Buckley and Nunn made a one-for-one bonus issue out of the surplus on revaluation of freehold properties in 1954. Its record before and after the event was as follows:

	Ordinary share capital	Ordinary shareholders' equity	Ordinary share earnings	Dividend rate on ordinary share capital
	$000	$000	$000	%
1950	344	614	61.4	9
1951	344	640	70.2	$11\frac{1}{2}$
1952	344	667	58.0	9
1953	344	697	60.9	9
1954	688	1,121	103.1	9
1955	688	1,169	131.9	$12\frac{1}{2}$
1956	688	1,204	136.8	15
1957	688	1,245	142.7	15

It seems probable that the company had calculated its earnings on a very conservative basis up to 1953. The revaluation of fixed assets in 1954 provided it with no more working capital than before, yet the reported profit rose in that year by 70 per cent. To have paid a dividend of 18 per cent, 25 per cent and finally 30 per cent on the 'old' share capital would have 'looked' anomalous, excessive; indeed the old nominal capital was an inadequate indication of the capital invested. The asset revaluation and bonus issue had the effect of reducing the margin between mere book values and the then current commercial values of the assets and of the total investment.

☐ In reply to a criticism of dividend policy by shareholders, the chairman of Myer Emporium in 1970 said that 'a bonus issue is simply a fiddle.' / *Australian Financial Review*, 6 November 1970 /

The group had an asset revaluation reserve of $40 million. In 1970 it paid a dividend of 22 per cent, or $6·7 million, out of ordinary share earnings of $15·3 million. In 1971 the company announced a one-for-one bonus issue.

Why engage in what the chairman still described as 'a fiddle'? Doubtless to bring the outdated amount of ordinary share capital to a figure more closely related to the current amount of the firm's investments, and to avoid the false appearance of excessive earnings and dividends when the dividend rate already appeared to be high. The necessity of the fiddle arises from the fact that the results of the accounting methods used fall out of step with the real events which the financial statements are expected to report.

Disclosure of borrowing power: Lenders on the security of specific assets tend to lend up to some proportion of the current market value of the assets pledged. Also loan contracts commonly stipulate that total borrowings, at any subsequent time during the currency of the loan, shall not exceed a stated proportion or multiple of shareholders' equity. Prospective and actual borrowers therefore need to have knowledge of up-to-date values of assets. So do shareholders and creditors, since the present gearing is indicative of further borrowing power, of the prospect of reducing creditors' safety margins, and of the prospect of maintaining or improving earnings and dividends (see Chapter 4).

Among the cases examined there are some where the connection between asset revaluation and subsequent borrowing is clear. In many other cases it is not clear, but that there was a connection seems plausible. The circumstances may be illustrated by press comment on a recent revaluation of assets.

□ Carlton and United Breweries, in the year ended in 1971, revalued its real estate by $8·8 million. 'The $19·1 million additional cash outlay on plant and real estate [during the year] appears to have stretched the group's liquidity. The revaluation, consequently, could represent a preliminary to new long-term borrowings.' / *Australian Financial Review*, 27 October 1971 /

There have of course been cases of the opposite kind—where borrowers have or seemed to have borrowed sums larger than the reported values of pledged assets would justify.

□ In 1970 McDowells sold for $9·2 million properties whose book value was said to be $2·9 million. The directors announced that $3·2 million of the proceeds would be set aside 'for repayment of the mortgages relating to the property, together with the various costs associated with the sale'.

The amount borrowed seems clearly to have been in excess of what would ordinarily have been loaned on the basis of the book values of the properties. It seems that the loans were negotiated on the basis of values known to the lenders and the directors but not known to the shareholders or other creditors. In such cases it would have been impossible for shareholders to guess the extent to which earnings could be improved by borrowing, impossible for them to form reasonable opinions of future earnings prospects. (In the United States where the original cost basis of asset accounting is the rule, a vast amount of borrowing must be done on a scale unjustified by reported asset values; investors can have little idea at all of the prospect of increasing earnings by borrowing.)

Defences against takeover bids: Asset revaluations have often been made to fend off the threat of, or to counteract, takeover bids.

Bids may be made for many reasons, but it seems certain that the object of many bids is to acquire assets for use or liquidation, on terms that provide a substantial bonus to the bidder. An inquisitive and diligent bidder (competitor or other outsider) can discover the approximate market values of important assets of a company, such as real estate, values of which shareholders generally are ignorant. He can then bid for the shares at a premium on the prevailing price, but at such a price that he acquires, as 'profit', some part of the undisclosed value of the assets.

Under the threat or the pressure of a bid, the incumbent management may revalue assets to put shareholders on notice of the current asset value per share; or revalue assets and make a bonus or 'capitalization' issue out of the surplus; or increase the dividends paid or promised. Any of these steps or a combination of them may raise the prices of the company's shares and reduce the attractiveness of the bid. But we are concerned here with revaluations. Some examples, therefore:

☐ In 1955, prior to a one-for-one bonus share issue out of a surplus on asset revaluations, Griffin Coal Mining Company informed its shareholders: 'Just recently a verbal offer was received to purchase the whole of the issued shares of the company at a figure considerably in excess of par value but well below the true value of the company's assets and profit earning potential'.

The company's action may reasonably be interpreted as defence against other possible takeover bids.

☐ 'It is dangerous to underestimate the value of fixed assets when takeovers are so prevalent. It is to shareholders' advantage to have assets shown at their correct value. I do not think for a moment that the company is likely to be taken over, but, should anyone try, shareholders would know what their assets were worth.' / London Stores, Chairman's Address, 1956 /

The company had revalued its assets.

☐ The directors of Brick Industries 'intended revaluing assets of various subsidiaries to something approaching their present-day value ... The chairman left little doubt that he was very conscious of a potential takeover bid in the near future'. / Australian Financial Review, 22 June 1961 /

We will consider the relation between up-to-date asset values and takeover bids at greater length in Chapter 10.

SUMMARY

These are only some of the circumstances under which companies have found it necessary to revalue assets. By comparison with valuation at up-to-date prices, valuations at cost are ancient history; important though they were when they were incurred, they are worthless as information when a company is confronted with hard bargaining. Then, the cost doctrine is abandoned and its defects are mitigated by recourse to more pertinent valuations.

REVALUATIONS IN UNITED KINGDOM

Revaluation of certain assets, mainly real property, seems to be at least as common in the United Kingdom as in Australia. A survey of the financial statements of 300 major companies for 1969–70 provides the following information:

Revaluation of:	Property	Other tangible fixed assets excluding investments
	Number of companies	
Latest year of revaluation		
Year of account	37	14
Previous year	24	9
Two to four years earlier	63	19
Five to nine years earlier	42	22
Ten or more years earlier	22	16
Year not specified	5	4
Total	193	84
Per cent of all companies (300)	64%	28%

Source: *Survey of Published Accounts*, 1969-70, Institute of Chartered Accountants in England and Wales

Although most of the companies in the sample have revalued property and included revaluations in their accounts, only 45 per cent made revaluations in the four years up to the date of the survey. In general, therefore, asset values are still in many cases out of date. In Chapter 7 an indication is given of the extent to which book values are different from current market values.

Yet even companies that have revalued their assets have done so only partially and irregularly. As an example:

☐ Guest, Keen and Nettlefolds in 1970 carried revalued assets of certain companies in the group at valuations made in 1946, 1950, 1951, 1952, 1953, 1960, 1965, 1966 and 1970. The total value of assets thus revalued was £11 million out of a total of £130 million, shown at 'cost or valuation', for the group. / Annual Report, 1970 /

Revaluations of assets prior to 1967 were, as in Australia, events which could not have been expected by shareholders and investors generally. Yet the amounts of revaluations were material, sufficiently large to enable it to be said that, prior to revaluation, shareholders could not have had a true and fair view of the states of companies' affairs. Here is a selection of companies that made revaluations, most of them before 1967:

Revaluations of land and buildings (freehold and leasehold) of UK companies
(All figures are from consolidated accounts and notes thereto and are expressed in £ million.)

Company	Year	Surplus on revaluation	Balance of asset values at end of year	Net equity of ordinaries at end of year
Associated Engineering	1965	3·5	26·7	24·2
Boots Pure Drug Company	1958	13·4	26·1	34·7
	1965	11·8	43·7	63·8
British Home Stores	1959	5·8	8·8	11·6
British Cocoa and Chocolate	1956	3·2	10·7	32·9
later Cadbury-Schweppes	1969	11·0	68·7	126·8
Brooke Bond and Liebig	1970	6·5	48·1	53·6
Electric and Musical Industries	1960	2·9	6·7	20·9
	1965	4·7	12·4	32·5

Company	Year	Surplus on revaluation	Balance of asset values at end of year	Net equity of ordinaries at end of year
F W Woolworth & Co.	1963	35·9	105·0	118·6
George Cohen 600 Group	1965	4·2	6·7	18·2
J Hepworth and Son	1969	9·0	17·5	14·2
J Lyons & Co.	1969	25·8	45·6	63·3
Lewis' Investment Trust	1966	27·1	64·0	58·9
Manders (Holdings)	1964	1·4	1·5	3·0
	1969*	1·4	3·8	5·8
Marks and Spencer	1964	33·4	97·5	102·2
Montague Burton	1961*	32·8	47·1	50·4
Rowntree Mackintosh	1968	6·0	17·5	31·1
Smiths Industries	1966	4·0	9·0	23·7

*Revaluation after close of year.

The surplus on revaluation is in most cases a significant proportion both of the balance of the property account and of the net equity of ordinary shareholders after the revaluation. For example, the asset balance of Boots Pure Drug Company after the revaluation in 1958 was over 100 per cent higher than it would have been without the revaluation, and the net equity of ordinaries was 60 per cent higher than it would have been without the revaluation. Differences of this or of an even lesser order would have a substantial effect on calculations of rates of return, borrowing power and asset backing.

The increments shown as 'surplus on revaluation' did not, of course, occur just in the year in which they were reported. They are the cumulative consequence of increases in value over long periods. It follows that prior to the revaluations, calculations of rates of return, borrowing power and asset backing would have been inconsistent with the real state of affairs for long periods. Of course the inconsistency—or distortion—is even greater in the case of companies that have not revalued assets.

We shall deal in the next chapter with the additional information which, under 1967 amendments to the Companies Act, must be given on the valuations of property and on revaluations of assets.

Investments in subsidiaries: The legal balance sheet of the parent company of a group carries the amount of the investment in subsidiary companies. Investments in subsidiaries may be carried at cost—and there may be a material difference between a current valuation and cost (or earlier valuations than the latest balance sheet date).

☐ In 1960 the equities of Associated Portland Cement Manufacturers in two wholly owned subsidiaries were revalued on the basis of the net tangible assets of those companies. The revaluation increased the parent company's book values of those equities by £24·5 million. The amount of the value of investments in subsidiaries reported at the end of the year was £47·4 million and the net equity of ordinary shareholders at that date was £32·8 million. / Annual Report, 1960 /

☐ John Brown & Co. revalued its shares in subsidiaries in the same way as the abovementioned company in 1962. The surplus on revaluation was £5·7 million, the value reported at the end of the year was £21·8 million and the net equity of ordinaries at the end of the year was £23·3 million. / Annual Report, 1962 /

☐ Gestetner Holdings in 1964 and in 1970 reported revaluations by the directors of shares in subsidiaries:

	1964	1970
Surplus on revaluation was	£2·0 million	£4·4 million
Value of investment at end of year	£2·5 million	£11·8 million
Net equity of ordinaries at end of year	£7·7 million	£15·9 million

In these cases the proportionate upwards revaluation was obviously material in relation to the previously reported values both of the investment itself and of the net equity of ordinary shareholders.

HISTORICAL COST RECONSIDERED

In the light of the widespread practice of revaluation, it is proper to consider some of the arguments in support of the use of historical costs.

CONSERVATIVE VALUATION?

It has often been held that the use of historical costs yields a conservative valuation of assets. The view that the use of historical cost is a conservative kind of accounting probably arises from the belief that, if prices generally have risen, it may be safely assumed that the prices of assets of any particular firm will also have risen. For example, commenting on some objections to his company's reluctance to give up-to-date valuations of its properties, the chairman of John McIlwraith Industries said:

> 'It seems to me that an investor reading a balance sheet showing land and buildings at cost would be well aware that the present day value is higher, and would be aware too that the longer it is since a revaluation was made, the greater the difference between cost and today's value.' / Letter, *Australian Financial Review*, 30 September 1970 /

The belief is not justified. We have concentrated on giving examples of upward revaluations because of the frequency of objections—objections that are not so strongly held against downward revaluations. But there have been undisclosed falls in asset values—falls due to obsolescence, changes in styles of trading and changes in urban and industrial property use.

□ 'Today's statement [by Garrison Industries] showed that assets with a book value of £794,467 were estimated by directors to realise £228,252.' / *Australian Financial Review*, 28 October 1963 /

□ E S Lazarus and Co. (WA), a wholesaler, decided to liquidate in 1965. 'Shareholders received 67c for each $2 share compared with the stated net asset backing of $1.09 when the company went into liquidation.' / Editorial material, *Australian Financial Review*, 28 March 1966 /

□ 'Marcus Clark, the Sydney credit retailer, recently sold its Railway Square store for $1,400,000–$600,000 less than the book value.' / Editorial material, *Australian Financial Review*, 28 March 1966 /

□ '... The Australian subsidiary [of Brunswick International] charged special depreciation of $2·4 million to reduce the net book value of plant, equipment and leasehold improvements at 31 December to directors' appraisal of the value at that date. This reduced the value of fixed assets from $2,893,872 a year earlier to $213,000 at 31 December last.' / *Australian Financial Review*, 22 July 1966 /

☐ 'Directors [of Anthony Hordern & Sons] have written $1,308,826 off the value of the Brickfield Hill store ... the value of the freehold land and buildings as shown in the balance sheet is some $2 million in excess of the improved capital values for statutory purposes.' / *Australian Financial Review*, 24 November 1966 /

☐ Chevron Sydney 'has made a special provision of $6·6 million for loss on the sale of its hotel at Potts Point. This is the margin between the book value of the hotel and the price received from Whitehouse Properties Pty Ltd'. / *Australian Financial Review*, 22 February 1967 /

☐ 'Directors of Mick Simmons (Holdings) announced that the company's Haymarket property had been sold for $425,000, at a loss of $223,000.' / *Sydney Morning Herald*, 18 July 1967 /

☐ Trafalgar House Investments in 1971 acquired for $65 million the Cunard Steamship Company which had assets with a net book value of 'close to $100 million'. / *Australian Financial Review*, 28 September 1971 /

Clearly there are cases in which the continued use of historical costs or out-of-date valuations is not conservative, and where reliance on the notion that all prices rise together may be utterly misleading.

Fixed assets—for use, not resale: The most common justification for not valuing fixed assets at some current valuation is the dictum that such assets are not bought for resale but for continued use in a business. It is said that, as continued use is intended, fixed assets should be valued on a going-concern basis, and that original cost (less depreciation based on cost, where appropriate) is a going-concern basis. We will show that the dictum is empty, or false.

Granted, durable goods (land, buildings, plant) may be bought for continued use. However no firm is committed irrevocably to an original intention. Any constructed asset (buildings, machines) may become obsolete or economically inefficient to a present owner and yet be of value in use, at some price, to another firm. Real property may become so valuable on the open market, that its owner may sell it and rebuild in a less costly area. With few exceptions, any asset whatever may be sold if a bidder makes a sufficiently attractive offer to its owner. The making of such an offer, the appearance of a new opportunity, a shift in the market prices of particular assets, may occur at any time and may at that time cause a firm to change its former intentions. To consider the feasibility and the possible consequences of any such change the market selling prices of assets individually are necessary information. Further, as an indication of the extent to which a firm may shift or manoeuvre, this information is just as relevant to shareholders. Shifts and manoeuvres are the very means by which a firm remains a going concern.

Sales and profits on sales of durables: Any reader of the financial press will know that companies, large and small, may and do sell off parts of their so-called fixed assets. We cite just a few cases which are indicative of the extent to which shareholders may be misled by out-of-date valuations.

□ 'The last balance sheet [of Brisbane Theatres] showed freehold land and buildings at cost at £56,172. Recently the company sold its main asset, the Tivoli Theatre property for £275,000.' / *Australian Financial Review*, 10 October 1963 /

□ '... the sales price of the Prince Edward Theatre ... will be in marked contrast to the £128,395 valuation of the property in the books [of Carroll Musgrove Theatres].' / *Australian Financial Review*, 27 May 1964 /

The theatre property was subsequently sold for £650,000 / *Australian Financial Review*, 26 June 1964 /

□ '... since the year end we have sold our Australian interest at a price of £2,060,000 which compares with a book value of £543,815.' / Associated Television, Annual Report, 1964 /

The consolidated profit after tax in 1964 was £2·6 million; the net tangible assets £10 million.

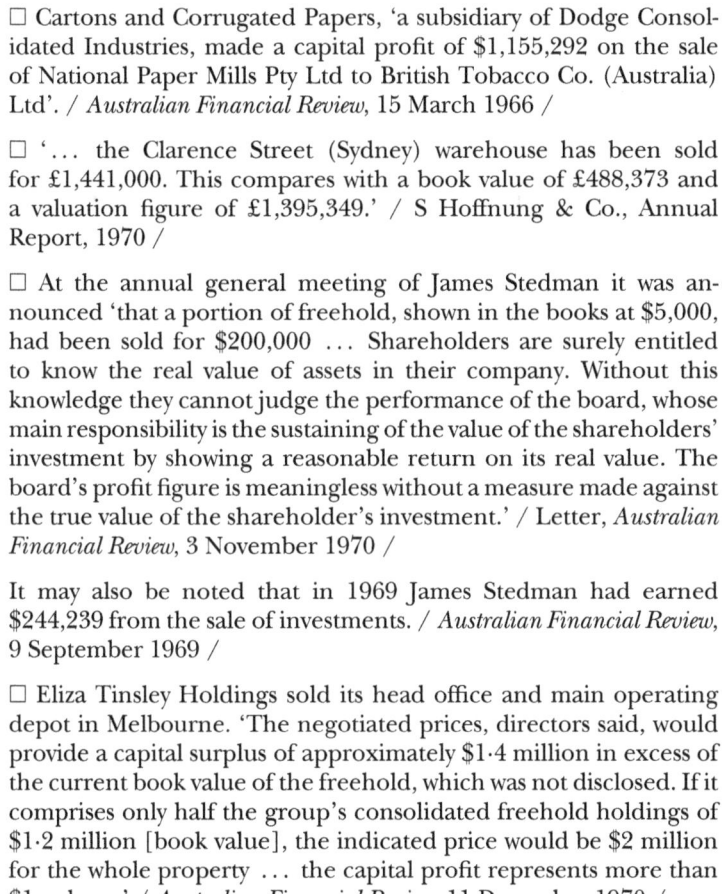

□ Cartons and Corrugated Papers, 'a subsidiary of Dodge Consolidated Industries, made a capital profit of $1,155,292 on the sale of National Paper Mills Pty Ltd to British Tobacco Co. (Australia) Ltd'. / *Australian Financial Review*, 15 March 1966 /

□ '... the Clarence Street (Sydney) warehouse has been sold for £1,441,000. This compares with a book value of £488,373 and a valuation figure of £1,395,349.' / S Hoffnung & Co., Annual Report, 1970 /

□ At the annual general meeting of James Stedman it was announced 'that a portion of freehold, shown in the books at $5,000, had been sold for $200,000 ... Shareholders are surely entitled to know the real value of assets in their company. Without this knowledge they cannot judge the performance of the board, whose main responsibility is the sustaining of the value of the shareholders' investment by showing a reasonable return on its real value. The board's profit figure is meaningless without a measure made against the true value of the shareholder's investment.' / Letter, *Australian Financial Review*, 3 November 1970 /

It may also be noted that in 1969 James Stedman had earned $244,239 from the sale of investments. / *Australian Financial Review*, 9 September 1969 /

□ Eliza Tinsley Holdings sold its head office and main operating depot in Melbourne. 'The negotiated prices, directors said, would provide a capital surplus of approximately $1·4 million in excess of the current book value of the freehold, which was not disclosed. If it comprises only half the group's consolidated freehold holdings of $1·2 million [book value], the indicated price would be $2 million for the whole property ... the capital profit represents more than $1 a share.' / *Australian Financial Review*, 11 December 1970 /

The borrowing base: A firm that owns durable goods (and even other goods) may 'use' them in two ways simultaneously: as working assets and as assets that may be pledged as security for loans. No out-of-date valuation is an indicator of what may be borrowed on the strength of assets owned. Further still, if a company has borrowed under rules restricting other borrowing or dividend payments, no out-of-date valuation is relevant to the question of whether the security of the lender remains within the contractual limits. The terms of the contract may in fact be breached if the values of particular assets fall subsequent to the making of the contract. If this happens and if the lender seeks to enforce his security, the borrower will not be able to rely on the 'intention' to hold the asset for use as a barrier to enforcement of the terms of the contract. The only precaution he can properly take against a creditor's action on the contract is to keep himself informed of the market value of the assets charged—and indeed of all other assets. To remain a going concern therefore the market prices of assets are continually necessary information to a borrowing company. There is no ground in these circumstances for the assertion that original costs (less depreciation, where appropriate) are going concern values of assets.

Supporters of the cost doctrine strongly deny the propriety of bringing into the accounts unrealized increases (appreciation) in asset values, but there seems to be no good reason why a mere form of accounting should deprive a firm of obtaining further commercial credit. Yet that is substantially the consequence of understating asset values, for it leads to understatement of the shareholders' equity and to a larger ratio of debt to equity than is really the case.

We have dealt in this chapter with examples and opinions on practice from jurisdictions in the UK tradition. It may be of interest to cite an opinion of two US legal scholars, written before upward revaluations were virtually outlawed in the United States. Dealing with unrealized appreciation of fixed assets, they observed:

'the increase may well be the result of the community's revaluation of the potential productivity and utility of the property, which, as it is not designed for sale, may escape record indefinitely. In such a case, the recognition on the balance sheet of an unrealized appreciation of a fixed asset ... presents a somewhat truer picture of the present worth of the company.' / A A Berle, Jr., and Frederick S Fisher, Jr., 'Elements of the Law of Business Accounting', *Columbia Law Review*, April 1932 /

SUMMARY AND CONCLUSION

Asset revaluation, though not universal, is very common in jurisdictions that do not forbid it.

'Generally accepted': Valuation of assets on the basis of their original costs—the professionally endorsed basis—seems to be rejected by almost as many companies as follow it. Certainly it cannot be described—as the professional bodies describe it—as the 'normal' basis, or the 'generally accepted' basis.

Consistency: Consistent use of the same valuation rules is conspicuously lacking, notwithstanding the high status accorded it, as a principle, by the professional associations. Every revaluation is a departure from the cost rule. But even those companies that revalue assets do so only partially and occasionally, which of course means inconsistency both at a given date and through consecutive years.

Relevance: The occurrence of revaluation is prompted by commercial or financial exigencies and circumstances in which out-of-date figures are of no service from any point of view, and which are in fact an embarrassment to directors and managers in their dealings with others. That revaluations are occasional and piecemeal can be due to no other reason than the wish, on the part of directors, to bring about some change in the 'appearance' of a company at a time and to the extent they consider desirable. We do not suggest that the wish is improper. It seems perfectly proper to reduce the margins between out-of-date and up-to-date values. There are enough different kinds or causes of exigency and enough examples of companies nudging their asset values towards up-to-date valuations to suggest that out-of-date figures are never useful in negotiations (except with the object of misleading other parties) or in the kinds of calculations investors or creditors must make for their purposes.

Materiality: If the sizes of the revaluations were modest, perhaps they could be dismissed as not 'material', a term widely used in laws and regulations to excuse disclosure of the trivial. However many of the rises in asset values far exceed the trivial or immaterial. Many asset revaluations have given rise to surpluses equal to or greater than the paid up capital of the company at the time. Many of them have been of the order of millions and tens of millions. Both in terms of relative and absolute size, they are large enough to have caused substantial errors in calculations of debt-to-equity ratios, asset-backing and rates of return, through the years before disclosure of the higher values.

Comparability: Taking all companies whose shares are traded in a given market, the apparently *random* or erratic occurrence of revaluations is due to the fact that the causes of embarrassment to companies and directors are many, and that cumulatively they become critical at different times for different companies. Comparisons of the financial features of companies, based on information that is subject to deliberate and discretionary variation, are hazardous and may be misleading. The risk that investors may be thus misled can only be averted if revaluation is regular and complete, rather than occasional, partial and unforeseeable.

'Lagged' disclosure of rises in asset values is better than no disclosure and better than the slavish use of the costs of assets, or of figures based on costs, in balance sheets. But only the uniform use of up-to-date valuations will ensure that investors' calculations are continuously consistent with the real states of affairs and results of companies. Nothing less will provide a serviceable foundation for a fair market in securities.

7

HIGGLEDY PIGGLEDY DISCLOSURE

From a company's balance sheet:
'Quoted securities (cost) $3 million
Properties (net book value) $55 million'
Footnote to its balance sheet:
'Market value of securities $17 million'
From its audit report:
'. . .a true and fair view of the state of the Company's affairs. . .'
From the report of its directors:
'. . .the present-day values of the Company's properties amount
to approximately $86 million.'
/ Collage from a company's annual report. /

'Who reads footnotes?'
/ Exasperated manager, when told he could put up-to-date asset
values in a footnote to his company's balance sheet.*

This chapter is concerned with supplementary financial information. By 'supplementary financial information' we mean information given in other ways than in the formal figures that appear in
the main columns of published financial statements. The form in
which the information is given may be footnotes or parenthetical
notes to financial statements, statements or comments in the body
of directors' reports or statements, or comments and explanations
deemed to be necessary by auditors and incorporated in their
reports.

We shall hold that some of this 'information' is *useless*, some
of it is *confusing*, and some of it is far *more valuable* than the
information given in the financial statements. There are good
reasons for the elimination of useless and confusing information and for the inclusion in the financial statements proper of
some information which is at present relegated to less noticeable
places.

---

* See Allan Landman, 'What's Wrong with Appraisal Values?'. *Journal of Accountancy*,
March 1971, p. 81.

DESCRIPTIVE NOTES

The schedules to acts on the English pattern and the SEC regulations in the USA both require certain information to be given, in financial statements and company reports, additional to the names and amounts of the main classes of asset and equity.

In some respects this information is strictly additional. The 'authorized' or registered capital of a company is not an element of its financial position; but as an indication of the limit to which directors may issue new shares without the sanction of shareholders it may be considered useful information to investors. That a loan or debenture is secured, and its maturity date, are pieces of information which may be of use. We shall be concerned primarily, however, with descriptive notes on the valuation of assets.

The laws and regulations require the bases of valuation to be stated in respect of most assets. The necessity for this arises from the facts that (a) there is no prescribed basis of valuation, (b) companies have chosen to use different methods for valuing similar assets, and (c) companies are to some extent free to vary the method used from time to time. The object of the note on the method of valuation is to enable users of financial statements 'to take account' of the effects of the methods used when attempting to interpret the financial statements.

Suppose an investor is comparing two companies, and that the balance sheets of the companies contain the following:

Company A	
Inventories, *at cost*	$3 million
Land and buildings, *at cost*	$5 million
Company B	
Inventories, *at lower of cost and market*	$3.5 million
Land and buildings, *at cost less depreciation*	$2.0 million

It is usually held that the descriptions 'at cost', 'at cost less depreciation', and so on, are useful information to readers of balance sheets. Certainly they put readers on notice that the figures were obtained in different ways. The notations indicate that the individual figures (and the totals to which they lead) are qualitatively different; and that the reported incomes of the companies are qualitatively different. The calculations of the current ratios, debt-to-equity ratios, rates of return and other indicators would consequently be qualitatively different—not comparable. Users of financial information might reasonably expect that they could evaluate the relative performances and positions of the companies by reference to the figures. But to state what basis was used merely serves to point out that there are differences; it gives users no information by which they could make the figures of the two companies comparable! In this context, therefore, the appended note on the method of valuation is *useless information.*

Take a simpler setting. Suppose Company *A* reported its inventories to be valued 'at cost—$3 million' in one year, and 'at lower of cost and market—$3.2 million' in the next year. Again the user of the information is put on notice that the figures of the two years are not comparable. Suppose that, in the second year, the company reported in a footnote that, if the cost basis had been used in that year, the value of the inventory would have been $3.3 million. The careful reader could adjust the figures so that the cost basis is used *consistently* for the two years. He should also add $0.1 million to the net profit reported in the second year, so that profits of the two years would be comparable; but unless he knows how inventory values affect net profit he will not do this. In any case he will not know which is the *proper* basis, and why it was *proper* in one year to use the cost basis and in the next year to use a different basis. The additional information is therefore confusing information.

We turn to some actual usages as evidence of the incomprehensible and confusing character of valuation notes.

INVENTORIES

The descriptions given for inventory valuation methods *seem* to suggest that practice is uniform for a substantial proportion of companies, but the appearance of uniformity conceals great diversity. We draw on some analyses of the valuation methods used in several countries. For certain years the methods reported were as follows:

Inventory Valuation Methods

	USA	Canada	Australia	UK
Year	1959	1958	1959	1969/70
Number of companies	600	300	300	300
Disclosed bases				
Cost	165	40	49	35
Market	10	9	2	
Mixed bases				
Lower of cost and market value or cost not in excess of market	524	257	67	258
Cost or less than cost	20	12	126	14
Other	4	4	39	43
Undisclosed bases				
Various	4	20	49	15

Sources
  USA: *Accounting Trends and Techniques 1960*, AICPA.
  Canada: *Financial Reporting in Canada, 1959*, Canadian Institute of Chartered
  Accountants
  Australia: present author's analysis
  UK: *Survey of Published Accounts, 1969–1970*, The Institute of Chartered
  Accountants in England and Wales

Consider the most commonly used bases. 'Cost' may be calculated in a great variety of different ways; for a manufactured good there are literally hundreds of possible values for 'cost'.* Where the word stands by itself, a reader of any two balance sheets could not know which method of calculation was used; there could thus be concealed differences in the method of valuation, for which, in the interest of comparison, the reader could make no allowance. Where there is an additional note indicating the name of the method used—average cost, first-in-first-out, standard cost, etc.—the reader is no better off. As between any two companies using the same method there could still be concealed differences, for each 'method' is really a whole family of different methods. And for two companies using different methods, there is no way of converting the asset values and results

---

* See Chambers, 'Financial Information and the Securities Market', *Abacus*, 1965.

of one so that the figures may be compared directly with those of the other company.

The basis most commonly used is clearly 'the lower of cost and market value'. The term 'mixed bases', used in the table, has reference to the alternatives implied by the description. A reader of such a note cannot tell whether, in any given case, 'cost' is used or 'market' is used. It is possible that one company using this rule may have valued its inventory in one year largely at 'cost', and in the next year largely at 'market'. The switch would not be disclosed because the same descriptive term could be used in both years. Further, for any *two* companies in a given year, the inventory of one could be valued largely at 'cost', and of the other largely at 'market', while the reader would suppose that the companies had used the same rule. As the purchase prices and selling prices of particular goods may move upwards or downwards and at different rates in any year, the effects of these movements may be completely obscured by the methods of accounting for inventories. The trend of the results of one company, and comparisons of the results in a given year of two or more companies, are thus open to distortion to an extent not disclosed.

Consider also some particular descriptions. The idea of disclosure seems in many cases to be pushed to ridiculous extremes. It may be worthwhile to give additional information—but only if there is a demonstrable way in which the reader could make use of it.

Here is a full descriptive note from the 1966 balance sheet of a US company, modified only to exclude references to the company's products:

'Finished goods have been stated at amounts (*less than cost*) based on selling prices *less allowances* for selling expenses, profits and possible losses from style changes. *Substantially* all of the raw materials and the raw material content of the work in process have been price at *cost* (*last-in-first-out method*) *not in excess of market*. All other inventories and supplies were priced at the *lower of cost* (*first-in-first-out method*) *or market*.' The inventory was stated as one figure.

It is impossible to understand from this statement what the published figure means. Every one of the italicized words or phrases (the italics have been added) can have a host of meanings. In any case there is a strong presumption that the sum of such a motley lot of figures derived by different means cannot possibly have a sensible meaning. The report showed a rise of 15 per cent in sales, a rise of less than 5 per cent in net profit before taxes and a fall of 15 per cent in inventory. Is there any possibility that the fall in the amount of the inventory and the relatively slight rise in profits for the rise in sales are due merely to the application of the above complex of rules (for the impact of each of the italicized phrases could have quite different, but unknowable, effects on reported profits in different periods)? This is a legitimate question for any analyst or investor to ask but we have no means of knowing the answer.

Here are some other examples:

☐ 'Inventories are stated at the lower of cost or market. Market for raw and packaging materials and stores and supplies is based on replacement cost and for other inventory classifications on net realizable value. Due to the diversified nature of the companies' operations, several bases of determining costs are used, including first-in-first-out, average and identified cost.' / W R Grace and Co., Annual Report, 1969 /

Total reported inventory was $348 million.

To what extent original cost, replacement cost and net realizable value were actually used in the valuation is unknowable.

☐ 'Products and materials inventories are generally valued at lower of average cost or market (net realizable value) except for steel products, certain food products and copper products which are valued at cost on the basis of ''last-in-first-out'', and certain meat products where costs are not ascertainable which are valued at market, less allowance for selling and distribution expenses.' / Ling-Temco-Vought, Annual Report, 1969 /

The reported value of the inventories mentioned was $449 million.

The reported figure is the sum of three kinds of figures—lower of cost and market, cost, and market. What this sum can mean in any form of financial calculation is beyond the imagination. It is not the amount of money laid out to acquire the inventory; it is not an amount of money that has an evident connection with any proper calculation of solvency, or the relationship between debt and equity, or net profit. It is an incomprehensible hybrid;

a fiction, notwithstanding the appearance of similarly described figures in the financial statements of other companies.

☐ 'The amounts included for stocks have been determined on bases and by methods of computation which have been applied consistently and which are considered appropriate in the circumstances of the business of each group subsidiary.' / Reed Paper, Annual Report, 1968 /

As an aid to understanding or interpreting the significance of a £60 million item, this note is useless. Whether the reported figure is an approximation to market value or cost no one can tell.

☐ 'Certain metal refining and fabricating subsidiaries value their base stocks permanently employed at fixed prices, reviewed periodically, which are below market prices of the metals concerned. Adjustments arising from variations in the quantities involved are dealt with through retained earnings.' / British Insulated Callender's Cables, Annual Report, 1968 /

The reported value of inventories was about £50 million, but how much this was below market value we are not told. The base stock method, like the last-in-first-out method in the USA, results in the assets being shown at long out-dated values. No idea is given of the interval since the last review was made of the prices of base stocks.

☐ 'Raw materials are valued at cost or average cost of purchase, and mined or quarried rock at the direct cost of mining. Finished goods are mainly valued at manufactured cost which includes direct works expenses. In certain subsidiaries, works, administration and selling overheads are included where considered appropriate.' / BPB Industries, Annual Report, 1968 /

Again, we have a cluster of different valuation methods, from the very conservative (direct cost only) to the very unconservative (direct cost and a whole range of overheads) — the lot represented by one figure in the balance sheet.

What does it matter? It may seem petty to complain about the obscurity of these descriptions and the impossibility of determining their significance. It would be petty if it was only a matter of one description against another. But the sheer incomprehensibility of many of these descriptions, and the diversity of the numbers which result from using different valuation methods, provide the most fertile conditions for misrepresentation, manipulation and fraud.

MARKETABLE SECURITIES

Of all assets, marketable securities are a class for which it is perhaps easiest to discover an up-to-date value. Dealing with security investments as assets, and citing two English cases, Berle and Fisher in 1932 concluded that the value on present liquidation, or net resale price, 'is apparently the only proper [value] the law recognizes in ascertaining the correctness of a balance sheet entry'.* As we have seen, the SEC regulations have long required market values to be shown in certain circumstances; and since 1948 the UK Companies Act has required the aggregate market values of quoted security investments to be shown by way of note if not otherwise.

The differences between the values shown in the main columns of balance sheets and the supplementary notes may be substantial. Here are some items selected from the balance sheets (and footnotes) of US companies:

Company	Year		Balance-sheet value	Quoted market value
			$000	$000
American Home Products	1969	Cost	4,064	20,753
Libbey-Owens-Ford Company	1969	Cost	11,745	32,700
Standard Oil Company (Indiana)	1968	Cost	14,860	115,678
Phillips Petroleum Company	1968	Cost	89,275	233,446
American Smelting and Refining Company	1969	Cost or less	4,223 / 45,296	92,729(a) / 171,453(b)

(a) shares in one company
(b) all named investments
Source: *Accounting Trends and Techniques*, 1969 and 1970.

---

* A A Berle, Jr., and Frederick S Fisher, Jr., 'Elements of the Law of Business Accounting', *Columbia Law Review*, April 1932. The cases were *Re London and General Bank (No. 2)* [1895] 2 Ch. 673 and *Dovey* v. *Cory* [1901] A.C. 481.

And here are some examples from the consolidated balance sheets of UK companies, for holdings of quoted securities:

Company	Year	Balance-sheet value	Market value
		£000	£000
Babcock & Wilcox	1968	3,422	16,676
John Brown & Co.	1968	918	8,567
House of Fraser	1968	933	2,803
British Insulated Callender's Cables	1968	1,296	4,853

The differences are material, taken by themselves. The amounts by which the balance-sheet values underestimate the current market values range from 83 per cent for John Brown to 67 per cent for House of Fraser. As a percentage of reported shareholders' equity there are marked differences in understatement: for Babcock & Wilcox the percentage is 40, for John Brown, 30; for House of Fraser, 5; for BICC, 4. In the case of the first two companies, the asset-backing per share would be materially understated, and the rate of return materially overstated by use of the figures given in the balance sheet proper.

Further, if any investor were to compare the asset-backing and rate of return of either of the former two companies with either of the latter two, the comparison would be seriously distorted if the main balance-sheet figures were used. Making adjustments only in respect of the net assets and the ordinary shareholders' equity, the figures are as follows:

	Rate of return		Net assets per £1 share	
	Published figures	Adjusted figures	Published figures	Adjusted figures
	%	%	£	£
Babcock & Wilcox	4·4	3·2	3·53	4·94
John Brown & Co.	4·8	3·7	2·02	2·60
House of Fraser	9·1	8·6	3·46	3·64
BICC	9·5	9·2	2·98	3·09

FIXED ASSETS — DISCLOSURE IN DIRECTORS' STATEMENTS

From time to time, some indication of up-to-date values of assets is given in the reports of directors and in the reviews and addresses of chairmen. The occasion and location of these comments are such that they are unlikely to be taken into account directly or at subsequent dates by analysts, reporters or investors when making calculations of asset-backing and other financial characteristics. Yet the margins between balance-sheet values and the values disclosed in these places are substantial.

☐ 'During the year we carried out a revaluation of the fixed assets of the company and its subsidiaries in the United Kingdom. The method adopted was to estimate the current cost of replacing the assets concerned and to reduce this amount to give effect to the expired life of the assets and an estimate of their future useful working life. Further adjustments were made for any known technical or commercial factors likely to affect their usefulness to the company in the future. The surplus on revaluation amounted to £6,981,000 for the group. It should be pointed out, however, that the estimated replacement cost of these assets at June 30, 1959, exceeded the revised value placed on them at that date by £11,471,000.' / Fisons, Chairman's Review, 1959 /

☐ 'Shareholders will recall that the chairman's statement in 1958 reported estimates of the then present-day values of the fixed assets based on their depreciated fire insurance values and up to date land values. The assessment has been repeated at the close of this financial year and shows that if land, buildings, plant and equipment appeared in the balance sheet at this estimated worth a surplus would arise of approximately £31,000,000, thus bringing the item to over £86,000,000. For the present it is not proposed to make any adjustments to the accounts in respect of this surplus.' / British Motor Corporation, Chairman's Statement, 1961 /

☐ A revaluation of fixed assets of Mather and Platt disclosed surpluses, over book values, for subsidiary companies £588,000, and for the parent company £3,283,000. 'The directors have decided that these revaluations will not, for the present, be reflected in the accounts of the company.' / Annual Report, 1961 /

☐ '... the freehold and leasehold properties with over ten years to run were professionally revalued as at the year end to show a surplus of more than £40 million over the book value. It is not intended to incorporate the new values in the balance sheet at the present time.' / Great Universal Stores, Statement by the Chairman, 1965 /

☐ The chairman of Windsor Hotels 'told nine shareholders at the annual meeting in Melbourne yesterday that value of the

Windsor property was about $4 million—more than 42 per cent above balance sheet book values.' / *Australian Financial Review*, 24 September 1970 /

☐ 'While we do not wish to incur the cost of having a valuation by a sworn valuer made of all the properties owned by the company, we do think you should know that the balance sheet value of $7,317,681 is, in the opinion of your directors, understated by at least $4,000,000, representing nearly 30 cents per share in assets backing.' / John McIlwraith Industries, Annual Report, 1970 /

UK REAL PROPERTY VALUES SINCE 1967

The 1967 amendment to the United Kingdom Companies Act, which required directors to comment on the relationship between book values and current market values of real property, is of interest in several respects.

Firstly, whatever basis of valuation is used in the balance sheet, and whatever changes are made in the basis used, shareholders are provided yearly with the market prices, instead of only occasionally and only by those companies that choose to make or disclose revaluations. There is thus an increase in the qualitative similarity of information available on all companies that hold real property, even though that information does not appear on the face of the balance sheet.

Secondly, the legislature apparently considered that information of the kind prescribed was necessary or in the interest of shareholders. It is not easy to understand why, then, the permissive provision of the Eighth Schedule was allowed to stand. If the financial statements are the responsibility of directors, there seems to be no reason why market values of real property should not be the values required to be shown as the main figures of the balance sheet.

Thirdly, accountants have often protested that the market values of durable assets are not accessible, or are of dubious value because they are likely to change. But the new provision seems to have given rise to no protest on the ground of availability of the information. The market value of any asset is no more or less a variable piece of information than the cash balance—which, of all account balances, is the most likely to change from day to day.

The protests against using market values of assets thus seem to be obstructionist or to be nullified by the readiness with which directors have complied with the amendment.

Here, then, are some statements made in accordance with the provisions of the amendment:

□ 'The directors consider that the market value of the freehold and leasehold properties at 31st August 1968 was approximately £71 million, which is £19 million in excess of their net book amount of £52 million.' / Montague Burton, Annual Report, 1968 /

□ 'In the directors' opinion, the value of properties exceeds their book value by £8 million.' / Allied Suppliers, Annual Report, 1969 /

The book value of properties in the consolidated balance sheet was £24·4 million; net tangible assets £40·7 million. The understatement in the balance sheet, amounting to 20 per cent of the reported net tangible assets, seems material.

□ 'It is considered that the market value of land and buildings is in excess of the value included in the balance sheet by about £4,000,000.' / The Associated Biscuit Manufacturers, Annual Report, 1969 /

The net book amount of land and buildings in the consolidated balance sheet was £5·5 million; net tangible assets were £10 million approximately. Again, the understatement in the balance sheet, amounting to 40 per cent of the reported net tangible assets, seems to be a material understatement.

□ The 1969 report of The Weyburn Engineering Co. included the following note to its balance sheet in which freehold properties were reported at £113,310: 'The directors are of the opinion that the present value of the company's freehold properties is likely to be significantly greater than the book value. It has been the company's practice for some years past to recalculate the value of fixed assets by reference to specially prepared indexes. The customary statement ... indicates that the recalculated value of the freehold properties is some £300,000 greater than the book value. (It must be emphasised that this figure is not based on a professional valuation and should be taken only as an indication of the excess of the present value over the book value.)'

☐ The 1969 report of Rolls-Royce noted: 'Based on advice from the company's professional advisers, the directors are of the opinion that the land and buildings of the company and its subsidiaries had a value, based on continuation of the existing uses of the properties, of approximately £18 million in excess of book values at 31st December 1969'.

The reported net value of land and buildings was £18·6 million; ordinary shareholders' equity on the basis of tangible assets was £119·7 million.

☐ 'The directors consider the market value of the land and buildings owned by companies in the group is in excess of the value included in the accounts. Whilst no precise figures are available the directors estimate that the surplus is about £16 million.' / Debenhams, Annual Report, 1970 /

The net book value reported for the group for these assets was £58·5 million; the issued share capital was £18·8 million in 10s. shares. The 'surplus' not included in the accounts would thus represent an additional 8s. 6d. worth of assets per 10s. share.

☐ 'In the opinion of the directors, the market value at the end of the year of all the fixed assets of the company and its subsidiaries consisting of interests in land was approximately £9,000,000 in excess of the net amount at which they are included in the con-solidated balance sheet (£51,285,000).' / J Lyons & Co., Annual Report, 1970 /

Note that this is additional to the revaluation surplus in 1969 referred to on p. 61 above.

☐ 'In the opinion of the directors, the market value of the land and buildings owned by the company and its subsidiaries is in excess of the value included in the balance sheet by approximately £12 million.' / Metal Box Company, Annual Report, 1970 /

The value of land and buildings, 'at cost or valuation', was reported to be £27·9 million in the consolidated balance sheet.

Notwithstanding the provisions of the Act, some companies remain secretive.

☐ 'The directors are of the opinion that the group's land and buildings have a market value materially in excess of their balance sheet value but that the amount of the excess is not significant in

relation to the value of the group's assets as a whole.' / Associated
Engineering, Annual Report, 1969 /

The book value of land and buildings in the consolidated
balance sheet was £17·8 million; net tangible assets £33·3 million.
About two-thirds of the group's property was revalued in 1964–66,
so that valuations are reasonably up to date. But the juxtaposition
of 'materially in excess' and 'not significant ... as a whole' leaves
some doubt about the facts that underlie the statement.

 □ 'Due to the upward trend in the value of property, and the high
 standard of maintenance, the current market value of land and
 buildings ... is in excess of book value. In view of the fact that all
 the group's property is used for normal manufacturing and trading
 purposes the excess has not been estimated because the directors
 consider that it would have little significance nor would the cost
 of valuation be justified.' / British Insulated Callender's Cables,
 Annual Report, 1969 /

Total group property, mostly valued at cost less depreciation,
was reported to be £36·8 million. The company's offhand response
to the amendment does not seem to be tolerable. The two factors
mentioned in the first sentence quoted might be supposed to have
created a margin between 'cost less depreciation' and current
market value which could be quite significant. The fact that
the group's property is used for normal business purposes is
no excuse for non-disclosure. The difference between the book
value and the market value of the property may be indicative of
'reserve' borrowing power, a matter that may be quite significant to
investors. (See, for example, the case of Stock Conversion, p. 131).

INSURANCE VALUATIONS

The common mode of reporting the values of plant, machinery
and equipment is to show its cost (or a valuation) less depreciation.
Such formal calculations may yield figures that differ materially
from the current values of assets of these kinds, for the prices of
equivalent or substitute goods may rise or fall and the depreciation
calculation may exceed or fall short of the change in value of the
assets. However, if for no other reason than insurance against

insurable risks, business firms need to have up-to-date valuations of plant from time to time. Some companies have supplemented the balance-sheet figures with notes on insurance values.

☐ Reference to insurance values by British Motor Corporation has already been noticed (p. 100).

☐ 'The fixed assets (excluding freehold land and motor vehicles) are insured as to buildings for £12,338,000 and plant machinery, etc. for £21,127,000 making a total of £33,465,000. The balance sheet values of fixed assets including freehold land and motor vehicles are £23,082,688.' / Wiggins, Teape, Directors' Review, 1961 /

The figures cannot be more closely analyzed; but clearly the balance-sheet values materially understate the then current values of the assets.

☐ General Aniline and Film Corporation gave the following figures in its 1948 report:

	Book values	Replacement values for insurance purposes
Gross	$58,327,282	$92,000,000
Net after depreciation	$37,537,898	$72,000,000

☐ In 1949, Equitable Office Building and Diamond T Motor Company gave insurance values for assets which were substantially in excess of balance sheet figures (for details see p. 111).

☐ 'In a table at the front of the annual report [of Softwoods Holdings], directors inform shareholders how way out of line the balance sheet values are with the insurance valuations. For example, the company's freehold forests are valued for insurance at £891,533 in excess of book value ... The excess value of the insurance valuation over book value on plant and machinery is £2·2 million. This means that the combined excess insurance value over book value is £3·1 million. Book value of the items appears to be about £1·7 million.' / *Australian Financial Review*, 14 October 1965 /

The practice of giving insurance valuations is indeed prescribed in Switzerland. The Swiss Federal Code of Obligations (Sect. 665) provides that durable assets shall not be valued in a balance sheet at a higher figure than cost price; that appropriate depreciation must be written off; but that, if such assets are insured, their insurance value as well as their book value must be mentioned in the balance sheet. By way of example, the 1966 balance sheet of J R Geigy AG showed fixed assets valued at 60·5 million Swiss francs (including 'land', 'office buildings' and 'dwelling houses', at 1 Swiss franc each) with a footnote showing insurance values for the whole group of assets to be 190 million Swiss francs.* The 1970 report of Nestlé Alimentana SA showed fixed assets at 1 Swiss franc; a parenthetical note gave the fire insurance value of buildings, office furniture and equipment as 6·7 million francs.

The measurement of wealth is of interest in other connections than the analysis of the financial affairs of individual companies. In the light of the known failure of company reports generally to give up-to-date asset valuations, insurance values have been used and recommended for use in estimating national wealth and income.[†]

The appearance of notes on insurance values is infrequent. But the fact that such values are or should be up-to-date values for the protection of the company's assets and the shareholders' equity in them, is just another example of the relevance and availability of up-to-date information.

NON-DISCLOSURE OF KNOWN VALUES

Some companies have indicated in rather vague terms that asset values are significantly greater than those shown in their balance sheets.

□ 'The value of our freehold properties in the centre of Birmingham was considered at the time of the issue of the prospectus, when it became demonstrably clear to your directors that the properties were worth considerably more than the figure at which they appeared in our accounts. We resisted however the temptation to re-value them, as has been quite rightly done by so many companies possessing freehold properties which have appreciated

---

* See Marcel F Kohler and Adolph Matz, 'Swiss Financial Reporting and Auditing Practices', *Abacus*, August 1968, pp. 3–16 at p. 8.
† See *Measuring the Nation's Wealth*, Papers from the Wealth Inventory Planning Study, George Washington University, National Bureau of Economic Research, Columbia University Press, New York, 1964, p. 334.

in value, but it is, your directors feel, unrealistic to continue to depreciate these buildings each year and no further depreciation is therefore charged against this year's profits.' / *Birmingham Post and Mail*, Chairman's Statement, November 1955 /

☐ In 1950 Ballarat Brewing revalued its hotel properties by £588,000, approximately doubling the previously reported value. But it was also pointed out that the new book value was still well below the valuations made of the properties by an independent valuer. / Annual Report, 1951 /

☐ In 1959 John Martin & Co. 'after consultation with competent real-estate valuators' increased the book value of the company's fixed assets by over £500,000. The resulting valuation of land and buildings was said to be 'more realistic, though still conservative'. The book value of listed shares was also increased, but to a figure 'still considerably below market value'. / Annual Report, 1960 /

☐ The 1962 address of the chairman of Australian United Investment pointed out that 'the book value of our shareholdings in Australian United Corporation Ltd is still very materially below the valuation based upon current market price for that Company's shares'. / *Australian Financial Review*, 25 October 1962 /

☐ The 1968 annual report of Australian Paper Manufacturers showed 'Land at Directors' Valuation 1962, $6,125,000'. The footnote explained: 'During the 1962 financial year the Company's land holdings were independently valued by Sworn Valuers. As these assets were not written up to the full amount of the valuation, they are shown as "Land at Directors' Valuation 1962".' There was a similar note on shares in subsidiary companies.

In all these cases it seems clear that the directors knew either the market values or the independently appraised values of the assets mentioned. That reference should have been made to these values at all indicates that directors regard market values and appraised values as significant types of value, significant in some way to shareholders. When these valuations were not reported, clearly there remained some 'inside' information, information to which shareholders and investors generally could not react.

It may be some comfort to shareholders and creditors to learn that the asset backing of shares and debt is really greater than it is shown on the balance sheet to be. But no firm calculations can be made in respect of undisclosed margins. 'Worth considerably more' than book value, 'very materially below' market value, and 'still considerably below market value'—all are suggestive of margins that investors might wish to have quantified, if they are to judge knowledgeably the rates of return, asset backing, and debt-to-equity ratios of companies or to compare these features of one company and of others.

BANKING AND INSURANCE COMPANIES

Bankers and insurance companies have long been coy about their asset values and results. The laws or regulations governing financial disclosures by companies have explicitly exempted these institutions from certain of the provisions applicable to other companies. In arriving at reported profits, UK companies so exempted (banks and discount companies) could make undisclosed transfers, to and from reserves and provisions, out of revenue; could value their investments 'at or under cost' without stating their market values; and could state the values of fixed assets without indicating the basis of the values reported.* In effect there was no possibility that shareholders would be given a true and fair view of the results and positions of these companies.

In appearances before the Cohen and Jenkins Committees, the representatives of banks urged the necessity of these exemptions. The drift of one line of argument was that although values of investments may sometimes decline sharply, the effect on any bank of the decline should not be generally known since it might destroy the confidence of depositors. For the same reason secret reserves were justified, since only by having secret reserves could the effects of falls in the values of investments be masked. These and other arguments were described by one (not unfriendly) observer in 1961 as 'sheer sophistry'.† The banks were in effect holding a blank cheque on the confidence of the public.

Like the Cohen Committee in 1945, the Jenkins Committee recommended continuation of the exemptions of banks and insurance companies from disclosing information required to be disclosed by other companies. Its report did remark that many

---

* *Report of the Company Law Committee*, Cmnd 1749, 1962, para. 400.
† Sir Oscar Hobson, 'As I See It ...', *Banker*, June 1961.

regarded the exemptions enjoyed by the banks 'as an anachronism'; and five members of the Committee entered a lengthy dissent in respect of the banks. The Companies Act of 1967 left the decision to continue the exemption or abolish it to the Board of Trade. Meanwhile the Prices and Incomes Board had thought it desirable that there should be 'full disclosure as soon as is practicable'. And in 1968, commenting on the proposed merger of Barclays, Lloyds and Martins, the Monopolies Commission observed:

☐ 'Because the banks have been permitted to conceal their true profits and their true reserves they have escaped the stimulus to efficiency and competitiveness that informed comparison of performances and profitability might have been expected to produce.'

In late 1969 the clearing banks, perhaps responding to a hint from the government, decided to disclose their 'true' profits and reserves. The 1969 figures were released in February 1970. The figures given below are from or based on the report in the *Financial Times* of 21 February.

	Reported 1968	profits 1969	Inner reserves disclosed in 1969	Shareholders' equity 1969	Rise in equity through inner reserves
	£m	£m	£m	£m	%
Barclays	19·7	32·7	137·4	364·8	60
Lloyds	13·0	24·1	98·0	265·5	59
Midland	14·4	19·1	60·2	192·8	45
National and Commercial	7·2	9·8	34·1	92·3	59
National Westminster	25·8	34·3	118·0	344·9	52

The profits for 1968 and 1969 are not comparable since there was a change in the method of calculation. But before publication of the above figures National and Commercial had already published its 1969 profit on the old basis—£6·6m. The main interest in the table however is the size of the previously undisclosed assets and reserves. The rise in shareholders' net equity due to disclosure of these alone was up to 60 per cent. The different percentages in the last column indicate that it would previously have been impossible to calculate comparable rates of return for these banks.

Other disclosures were made at the same time. It appears that, for all security investments of the banks, book values fell short of market values (or directors' valuations) by: Barclays £29m; Lloyds £20m; National and Commercial £15m; National Westminster £21m; and for Midland, book values exceeded market values by £8m.

Premises of the parent bank of the Barclays group were written up by £45m. Lloyds wrote back £10m in respect of fixtures and equipment previously written off. Lloyds directors considered that the current market value of the group's properties exceeded the book value but not by a significant proportion of total shareholders' equity. Midland directors were of the opinion that the current value of land and buildings was considerably in excess of book value. The estimated market value of the premises of National and Commercial exceeded book value by £21m; for National Westminster the excess was estimated to be not less than £80m. These differences in reporting practices still make it impossible to make comparisons on the same basis between the banks, but they are a vast improvement on previous practice.

In Australia banks and insurance companies are still exempt from the general disclosure provisions, but some have responded to the 'change in public opinion' which the Jenkins Committee noticed as a spur to changes in disclosure.

☐ Since 1969 the Bank of New South Wales has given footnote indications of the market values of some of its assets. Its 1970 report indicated that the estimated market value of certain land and buildings exceeded the balance-sheet value by $53 million. The consolidated balance sheet showed 'Bank premises, sites, furniture and equipment' at $77 million, but to what part of this total the above market valuation refers is not specified. Shares in listed companies, shown in the balance sheet 'at or under cost—$23 million', had a market value of $61 million. Market values of governmental security holdings are also given—$37 million lower than balance-sheet values. The total disclosed amount of these differences between book values and market values was thus $54 million, over one-third of the net equity of ordinary shareholders.

☐ In 1968 Australian Mutual Provident Society wrote up the book value of its investment portfolio by $13·56 million, to 'finance' a new terminal bonus scheme. It also reported that the market value of its portfolio was $327·7 million compared with the book value of $238·8 million (after the modest revaluation mentioned above). The chairman said that the Society should maintain an adequate margin between book and market values as a buffer against fluctuations in security prices. / *Australian Financial Review*, 15 May 1969 /

☐ Colonial Mutual Life Assurance Society also wrote up its portfolio by $1·8 million for a terminal bonus scheme. It reported that the market value of its portfolio was $189·3 million, whereas the book value (i.e. balance-sheet value) was $105·5 million. / *Australian Financial Review*, 4 June 1969 /

☐ City Mutual Life Assurance Society in the same year reported that the market value of its portfolio was $72·7 million compared with a book value of $45·8 million. / *Australian Financial Review*, 4 June 1969 /

☐ Mutual Life and Citizens Assurance Company declined to disclose the market value of its portfolio; the book value was $107·9 million.

The reasons given by MLC for not indicating market values were that market values are transient; that their disclosure implies that current market values are realizable values; and that 'market values capitalize the future and bring the implication that what is to be received, perhaps in perpetuity, is available for immediate distribution' (*Australian Financial Review*, 13 June 1970). It is open to serious doubt whether any shareholder or policy holder entertains such notions as these. We comment only on the 'transience' of market values, since the chairman of CML also observed that 'market values are impermanent and are liable to misinterpretation'.

Market values may be transient, but so is the amount shown in any balance sheet for any asset. No attempt is ever made to report a 'permanent' or 'non-transient' amount for the cash balance, for example. Asset values may be impermanent but they are nonetheless relevant to assessments, from time to time, of results and position. Presumably the directors of life insurance companies attempt to buy securities which they expect will increase in market value (at least on the average) in the interest of policy-holders. By how much and how consistently those values do increase would seem to be some indication to policy-holders of the skill and judgment of directors and of the safety of the financial interests of policy-holders. If market values are misinterpreted, insurance companies, or any other kind of company surely can correct mis-interpretations. But book values, which have no current financial significance whatever, give a sham appearance of permanence which thwarts interpretation and judgment altogether. It seems odd that insurers represent that there has been some kind of 'permanence' in the values of their assets, when in other aspects of insurance business the rule of 'utmost good faith' is supposed to prevail.

REFLECTIONS ON REVALUATION
IN THE UK

We have noticed that, since 1967, companies operating under the United Kingdom Companies Act have been required to give the dates of valuations and the amounts of valuations of fixed assets where the amounts reported in the balance sheet are valuations (i.e. not original costs). The provision is progressive. It should enable readers to see how up-to-date or how out-of-date are the reported balance-sheet values. How well does the idea work out?

We give below certain figures, taken from footnotes to the balance sheets of Brooke Bond Liebig for three years, for the fixed assets carried at valuations and at cost. 'Fixed assets' include freeholds, leaseholds and plant, vehicles and equipment.

The company seems to revalue regularly; it wrote in £12·7 million in surpluses on revaluation over the three years. And it seems that some of the older valuations have been up-dated. Nevertheless over 60 per cent of the total valuation before depreciation represents assets valued at cost. The figures shown for 'Additions during the year' may suggest that a large part of the items shown at cost are at quite recent costs—but we cannot be sure. Even to discover this the reader would have to have access to the footnotes of past years. In what years the assets still shown at cost were purchased, and how out-of-date these cost figures are, cannot be deduced

Balance date 30 June

	1968	1969	1970
Balance remaining of valuation in	£000	£000	£000
1945	105	—	—
1947	128	—	—
1955	1,015	1,116	96
1960	174	160	168
1961	459	217	216
1962	348	318	—
1964	3,928	3,321	3,451
1965	—	—	63
1966	20	22	—
1968	10,967	11,010	10,512
1969	—	420	420
1970	—	—	11,156
	17,144	16,584	26,082
Cost	39,214	42,030	43,160
	56,358	58,614	69,242
Less accumulated depreciation	18,894	20,199	21,129
Net book value	37,464	38,415	48,113
Additions during the year	14,222	4,637	7,171

in spite of the details given. For instance, in the present case we do not know whether a large part of the 'cost' was incurred before 1945 or after.

A much more satisfactory rule for giving readers an idea of the relative up-to-dateness of valuations would be one that required all assets to be classed by date of purchase or most recent valuation. Such a rule would catch both the companies that have revalued partially and those that have not revalued at all. It would certainly be a fairer rule than the present rule, which leaves shareholders of companies that have not revalued in abysmal ignorance. Of course, it would also lead to footnotes of extraordinary length.

Even then, if it is supposed that dates of purchase or revaluation would enable shareholders to deduce approximate current valuations, the supposition is in error. The current values of the particular assets of a company cannot be calculated by the application of any price index to past purchase prices or valuations, for particular asset prices change neither in unison, nor in the same direction over time.

The only solution to the problem, which the 1967 UK amendment seems to tackle, is to relieve the users of balance sheets of the task of applying their imagination and statistical skills to out-of-date figures by requiring up-to-date valuations to be used in balance sheets. This would also reduce considerably the size and complexity of footnotes.

CONCLUSIONS

Much of the supplementary information now given serves, at best, only to put readers on notice that direct comparisons of the financial features of two or more companies cannot be made. It provides no means of converting reported figures to up-to-date or comparable figures. It is useless except as a warning. But in the absence of a means of making figures comparable the warning itself is useless and in practice it must be just disregarded.

Much supplementary information now given in footnotes and directors' reports is useless because it cannot be interpreted. Technical descriptions of accounting methods and valuation rules used are meaningless to lay persons. Even independent expert accountants who may know what technical terms mean cannot say to what extent and in what ways the reported results of any company have been 'influenced' by the accounting rules it used.

It may be said in respect of these kinds of information that inquisitive persons may be prompted to demand further information. However, in one of the important cases on disclosure of financial information it was held to be insufficient to give information that might prompt readers to ask for more. 'Information and means of information are by no means equivalent terms' (Lindley L J, in *Re London and General Bank*, 1895). In any case many users of financial statements do not know that information of better quality can be provided. Many who have sought additional information have been rebuffed, as readers of reports of company annual meetings will know.

Useless warnings and useless descriptions should be proscribed. They have the appearance of better disclosure but they lack its substance. They are delusive. If uniform rules were prescribed, financial information on different companies would be comparable and there would be no occasion for 'amplifications' which are either empty or unusable.

Higgledy-piggledy disclosure is better than no disclosure at all. But when different, and sometimes contradictory, information can be spread over balance sheets, footnotes, auditors' reports and directors' reports, much of what is relevant will often be lost to sight. Some is virtually lost for ever; for the tabulations of balance sheet and other information made by the investment advisory services cannot and do not cope with possible variations on the main balance sheet figures. They have no space for the caveats, provisos, addenda and corrigenda found in the reports of any company over the five to ten-year spans covered by their tabulations. Which is all the more reason for putting the best, most up-to-date and relevant information on the face of the financial statements.

On the brighter side, in numerous cases directors have given supplementary up-to-date information, beyond the requirements of the law. Some have done so under pressure but some, no doubt, from conviction that out-of-date valuations and inferences from them are misleading to investors and contrary to the interests of their companies.

In the light of the evidence it cannot be held that up-to-date valuations are inaccessible. Nor, since directors are made responsible for the contents of the financial statements, can it be held that up-to-date valuations should appear as supplementary information only, outside the main figures of the financial statements. Nor can it be held that auditors could not properly give 'clean' reports on accounts containing up-to-date valuations; they already do so.

There is thus no reason why the laws on company financial statements should not be amended to make obligatory the use of up-to-date figures in balance sheets, and the calculation of annual results on that basis. If the cost prices of assets are deemed to be useful information for any purpose, let *them* be put in footnotes or directors' comments. The present rules are just the reverse of what should be prescribed if their objective is to give a true and fair view of financial positions and results. They give prominence to what is useless and allow what is useful to be scattered, if not buried.

8

COOKING THE BOOKS

Headlines:
Cooking the Books to Fatten Profits
/ *Time* /

Time to Clean up the Accounts Chaos
/ *Sunday Times,* UK /

Conglomerate Earnings: Credibility Gap
/ *Wall Street Journal* /

Depreciation Manipulation for Fun and Profits
/ *Financial Analysts Journal* /

In the previous two chapters attention was directed to asset valuation practices. The greater part of the illustrative evidence was drawn from the practices of companies in jurisdictions where asset revaluation is permitted. Revaluation introduces inconsistency in reporting and prevents proper comparisons being made of the reported figures of one company in successive years and of the figures of different companies. We held that this inconsistency is a consequence of the fact that out-of-date values are useless as a basis for negotiation and fair representation of financial position. One kind of mistake—insistence on the use of original costs in accounting—is patched up by recourse to practices that contravene the avowed principle of consistency. To overcome one error, it is necessary to make (what is described as) another!

In this chapter we consider more of the same, but with a different twist.

NET PROFIT AND ITS DISTORTION

In the United States, as we have seen, the upward revaluation of assets is not acceptable as a rule. Yet if original costs become useless as indicators of financial position in, say, the United Kingdom or Australia, they must be no less useless in any other developed community. There must therefore be other ways of coping with the consequences, if revaluation of assets is not acceptable. There are.

Firstly, it has become a well-established doctrine among accountants that the balance sheet is not to be taken seriously as a statement of financial position. There are some who have spoken of it as an appendage, or a footnote, to the income account. It is regarded merely as a repository of (as yet) unamortized costs of assets. Clearly, this viewpoint pays no regard to the contents of the balance sheet as indicators of solvency, effective leverage and rate of return.

Secondly, for most purposes connected with the day to day securities market, pride of place is given to the income figure—in the form of earnings per share or the price-to-earnings ratio. Let it be noted that neither of these provides a guide to achieved efficiency. They do not relate earnings to net assets employed. It seems reasonable to forgo the calculation of a rate of return if the net assets figure is irrelevant; and the sum of the unamortized balances of asset costs *is* irrelevant. But the market would then be left without an indicator of the relative economic efficiencies of companies. For the moment, let that pass.

Given the emphasis on income, and because income (change in wealth) depends on asset values, any failure to take account of changes in asset values will produce distortions in the amount of income reported. Just as deviations of reported asset values from up-to-date values produce embarrassment and prevent proper comparisons from being made, so also will distortions in reported income. If it is the prerogative of directors to choose the rules by which income shall be calculated, it may seem unduly harsh to describe the consequence as distortion. However, the examples will show that there is ample opportunity for deliberate manipulation as well as unwitting distortion. We shall refer principally to United States practices in this chapter—to 'even up' the evidence, so to speak—but we shall also make use of examples from other jurisdictions.

DIVERGENT CONSEQUENCES
OF PERMISSIBLE RULES

There is an extensive array of specific rules for charging against the total gains of a company the costs and expenses of a year.

For almost every item of expenses there are at least several such rules, each having different effects; and all these rules are equally acceptable to accountants and auditors as a group. It is therefore possible, by selection from the range of rules available, to boost or to 'dampen' the profits reported in any year. The extent of the possible variations in reported net income has been indicated by several analysts of the state of accounting.

☐ A study, reported in 1938, of a group of US companies over an eight-year period showed that, by the application of a conservative set of rules, aggregate net profit would have been $125 million, whereas the application of a liberal set of rules would have shown an aggregate net profit of $275 million. The difference arose exclusively from the choice of different rules from the range of equally acceptable rules. / Howard C Greer, 'What are Accepted Principles of Accounting?', *Accounting Review*, 1938, p. 29 /

☐ A calculation tendered in the course of a debate between two eminent practitioners at the 1960 meeting of the American Institute of Certified Public Accountants showed that, from the same data relating to a hypothetical firm, there could be derived financial statements which reported net incomes per share as different as $0.80 and $1.79, the difference being due solely to the specific accounting rules chosen from the battery of generally accepted rules. / See T A Wise, *The Insiders*, New York 1962, pp. 37–8, 203–36 /

☐ In 1963 Leonard M Savoie (until 1972 Executive Vice President of the American Institute of Certified Public Accountants) showed that, by the use of different sets of accounting rules the same basic events could be shown to have yielded a net profit as different as $624,000 and $28,000. / 'Accounting Improvement: How Fast, How Far?', *Harvard Business Review*, July-August 1963 /

☐ A table tendered at a 1966 conference on corporate accounting problems showed the difference in net income that can arise from the use of different but equally 'acceptable' methods of accounting. The figures were said to be based on an actual company. For ten items a 'liberal' and a 'conservative' rule was chosen. The application of the liberal rules gave a net income 58 per cent greater than the application of the conservative rules; income per share for the two methods was $3.14 and $1.99. / *Forbes*, May 1967 /

The three examples last mentioned were demonstrations in respect of one particular year. They illustrate the wide margins within which calculated net incomes may fall, given that any combination of rules could be chosen. But, because the closing account balances of one period necessarily become the opening account balances of the next period, under- or overstatement in one year may influence the reports of successive years in the opposite direction. If, for example, a company charges very high rates of depreciation—rates higher than the actual diminution in value of assets—the balance of an asset account will be exhausted long before the asset itself is exhausted. Net income will have been understated in early years and overstated in the later years when no further charge for depreciation can be made. It follows that distortion in one year may lead to distortion in subsequent years, and that comparison of the performance of any company in successive years may, for this reason, be utterly misleading.

INTER-FIRM COMPARISONS

If the decisions of investors entail choices between the securities of different companies, the freedom of each company to choose its own rules and to vary the rules it uses at its discretion may abort any attempt to benefit from comparisons of the financial features of companies. There is an almost limitless variety of combinations of rules that a company may use.

☐ The Institute of Chartered Accountants in England and Wales has set out in several of its recommendations the rules permissible for asset valuation. For the valuation of *inventories*, one of three bases may be used: cost, net realizable value and replacement price. At least four 'principal' methods of calculating costs are permissible. There are three possible ways of dealing with overheads in the calculation of inventory costs. There are four permissible methods of calculating the depreciation component of overhead costs; in practice each of these methods will yield different depreciation charges for the same asset according to the auxiliary assumptions made about the economic life and scrap value of the asset. In choosing which of the three bases (cost, net realizable value or replacement price) shall be used, the total inventory may be treated as single items, as classes of items or as a whole. For the valuation of *durable or fixed assets*, cost or a revaluation may be used as the basic figure and, as we have said, there are four permissible methods of providing for depreciation. Different methods of calculating the depreciation charge may be used for different assets. For *investments*, there are four methods of deriving the amount of trade investments, four methods for quoted investments and three methods for shares in subsidiaries.

A little exercise on the combinations of these and other permissible rules and methods will show there are over one million *sets* of rules, each of which could be said by managers and auditors to give a true and fair view of a company's state of affairs and its results. The odds against the financial statements of any two or more firms being comparable are enormous.*

□ Among the Research Studies published by the American Institute of Certified Public Accountants is *Inventory of Generally Accepted Accounting Principles for Business Enterprises*. Among these 'principles' there are apparently four methods for determining the amount of revenue, four methods for determining pension payment charges and eight methods for determining the taxes chargeable against a given year's income. There seem to be 72 ways of determining the amount to be charged by way of depreciation and 122 methods for determining the amount of inventory. There are five named classes of item, each of which may be represented by figures obtained in either of two ways. Thus, for any company that has in its accounts instances of all the above classes of item, there are 30 million possible ways of representing financial position and results.†

Again, the odds against finding any two companies whose financial statements are comparable are astronomical. It should not need emphasizing that, where there are so many generally accepted or permissible rules, it is impossible to say what the reported income of any company really means. And the diversity of rules provides almost unlimited opportunity for varying the rules to match the impression company officials wish to convey.

*The Recommendations on which the analysis is based, and the calculations on which the conclusion is based, are given in Chambers, 'Financial Information and the Securities Market', *Abacus*, September 1965, reproduced in *Accounting Finance and Management*, 1969, pp. 174–203.
†The argument is given in greater detail in Chambers, 'A Matter of Principle', *Accounting Review*, July 1966. An earlier exercise similar in kind appears in Chambers, 'Financial Information and the Securities Market'. Robert R Sterling subsequently pointed out that by distinguishing further varieties of accounting the number of sets of accounting rules could be in the region of 3,000 million. 'In Defence of Accounting in the United States', *Abacus*, December 1966.

Both the examples of potential differences in calculated results and the computations of the sets of permissible rules, however, indicate what *might* happen. What has in fact happened?

VARIETY OF CHANGES — US AND CANADA

The most numerous and most striking examples of changes in accounting methods which have come to notice are of United States companies. If accounting practices generally lead to financial statements which, with the passage of time, deviate from reasonable approximations to actual positions and results, the forces of conflict and competition are likely to compel some change in those practices. We have seen that many United Kingdom and Australian companies have revalued assets. This type of change is denied to US companies. They must react in other ways. They have generally reacted by changing the ways in which income is calculated.

There is some collated evidence of the extent to which companies have varied their methods of accounting.

United States: Accounting Trends and Techniques, 1967, reported that in 1960, 1965 and 1966 there were 54, 43 and 29 cases, respectively, of 'changes in consistent application of generally accepted principles of accounting'. The publication summarizes the features of the accounts of some 600 companies. The 1970 edition reported 142 changes made by 121 companies. The changes were made in respect of depreciation (35 cases) consolidation and valuation of investments (34), deferred taxes (17), capitalization of expenditures (16), inventory valuation (15), other (25). No attempt is made in *Accounting Trends and Techniques* to interpret the changes as evidence of the scope available for the manipulation of reported profits.

Canada: A study by Blaine of switches in accounting methods by Canadian companies supports the view that the available alternatives enable 'managers to change … methods in order to present financial statements more closely in line with the image of corporate success that the managers wish to communicate.'*

The raw material consisted of 459 annual reports of a random sample of 104 Canadian companies listed on the Toronto Stock Exchange for the fiscal years ended in 1963 to 1967. Blaine found 143 changes in accounting method. They were distributed over ten categories of reported items. The changes were made in respect of depreciation (25 cases) consolidation and valuation of investments (19), deferred taxes (22), intangible assets (20), other (57). Only 33 companies made no change; 23 companies made 3 to 5 changes. There were 44 changes that had the effect of increasing the amount of reported income and 35 that reduced reported income.

Changes that increased reported income were made by 16 companies whose income would have been higher than in the previous year, and by 23 companies whose income would have been lower than in the previous year, but for the change. Changes that decreased reported income were made by 26 companies whose income would have been higher than in the previous year, and by 6 companies whose income would have been lower than in the previous year, but for the change.

There were thus 49 cases in which the change either boosted profits that were lower than those of the previous year or reduced profits that were higher than those of the previous year. In other words, almost half the sample of companies took action consistent with the hypothesis that managers may smooth out variations in reported income from time to time by changing the methods of accounting used. The objections to income smoothing have already been indicated (pp. 51–2).

DEPRECIATION ACCOUNTING

Depreciation—the fall in value of machinery and other assets due to use and obsolescence—is a charge against the trading results of a year in calculating net income. The usual way of calculating the annual charge is to take the cost of the asset, reduce it by the

*Earl Blaine, *Reported Accounting Changes and Financial Statement Manipulation*, University of British Columbia, January 1970 (mimeograph).

expected selling price at the end of its expected life and to spread this net cost over the expected life. The net cost may be spread equally over the expected life; thus the asset value falls by equal amounts each year. The method is called the straight-line method. There are other ways of spreading the net cost; we shall be concerned with a class of methods by which the whole or the greater part of the net cost is charged in a much shorter period than under the straight-line method. These methods are described as 'accelerated depreciation' methods. Accelerated depreciation burdens the results of the earlier years in the life of an asset with higher charges than the straight-line method. If the trade of a company is buoyant in the years in which new assets are bought, its revenues may be able to stand the additional burden of accelerated depreciation. If the amount of accelerated depreciation is an allowable deduction in calculating taxable income, the burden of accelerated depreciation is relieved to some extent.

However if, after choosing to use accelerated depreciation the company's prices or sales volume come under strain, the additional burden may become too great. Earnings per share, if calculated on the same basis as before, would fall. The company's credit rating may fall, its share prices may fall and it may become exposed to the possibility of takeovers by other companies. To switch the method of depreciation accounting to the straight line method would, by a stroke of the pen, so to speak, enable the company to boost its reported net income and to avoid these 'unpleasant' consequences.

The first example will be United States Steel Corporation. The case is of particular interest because it shows that the inadequacy of accounting for depreciation on the original cost basis has long been known, and because the company was thwarted by the conventional wisdom in its attempt to account for depreciation on a more realistic basis.

In the late forties, rising replacement costs and high rates of taxation affected US Steel as they did many other companies. In notes to its 1947 financial statements, the company explained its depreciation charges for that year:

☐ 'Wear and exhaustion of facilities of $114,045,483 includes $87,745,483 based on original cost of such facilities and $26,300,000 added to cover replacement cost. The added amount is 30 per cent of provisions based on original cost, and is a step towards stating wear and exhaustion in an amount which will recover in current dollars of diminished buying power the same purchasing power as the original expenditure. Because it is necessary to recover the purchasing power of sums originally invested in tools so that they may be replaced as they wear out, this added amount is carried to a reserve for replacement of properties. The 30 per cent was determined partly through experienced cost increases and partly through study of construction cost index numbers.'

Although of the same opinion in 1948, the company was obliged to abandon the method used in 1947 'in view of the disagreement existing among accountants' and in view of the opinion of the American Institute of Accountants and the SEC that original cost was the proper basis for calculating depreciation, regardless of the change in the purchasing power of the dollar. The company adopted a form of accelerated depreciation.

In its 1968 Report US Steel describes the pressure under which it was again obliged to change its method of accounting. The tax laws had been modified in 1954 to permit accelerated depreciation charges. Most companies in the steel industry, including US Steel, had adopted this in their financial reporting. However, the Report stated, during 1968, a number of these companies announced a change in method of calculating depreciation for annual report purposes from the accelerated basis to the straight-line basis. The effect of this, as we have said, is to boost the reported net income of the year. Any company that did not run with the tide would appear to have done less satisfactorily than others.

There was another thing.

'The Revenue Act of 1962, as amended in 1964, provided for an investment credit against Federal income tax of a portion of the cost of certain depreciable property. US Steel adopted the accounting method by which it deferred this credit and amortized it over the lives of the properties acquired. All other major steel companies now flow the full investment credit to income as realized.' / US Steel, Annual Report, 1968 /

The 'flow-through' practice also would show up companies that used it to advantage in comparison with companies that spread the effect of the credit over the lives of the assets acquired—at least in the short run. The 1968 Report continues, linking the two matters referred to above:

□ 'US Steel considered the procedures it previously followed in connection with depreciation and the investment credit to be preferable to other methods in the reporting of results of operations. However, to enhance the comparability of financial statements in the steel industry and to bring depreciation and investment credit accounting policies more in line with methods followed by US businesses in general, US Steel, for financial reporting purposes, revised the lives of certain properties and changed its methods of recording depreciation and investment credit for the year 1968 to a straight-line basis and a flow-through basis, respectively. The effect of these changes was to increase reported income for the year 1968 by $94·0 million or $1·74 per share of common stock.'

The resulting income per share of common stock was $4.69.

We have some sympathy with a company that endeavoured in 1947 to determine depreciation charges on the basis of 'experienced cost increases and ... construction cost index numbers'; this was an attempt at realistic reporting. The events since that time show that even very large companies are sensitive to comparisons between their own performance and the performances of others. If, for whatever reasons, other companies use accounting methods that show them to advantage, no single company can be expected to forgo the use of the same methods. We are less concerned with the fact that US Steel could boost its reported earnings by $94 million or its earnings per share by almost 60 per cent, by a book entry, than with the system of practice that makes such unexpected moves possible. The freedom to switch methods is subversive of the whole idea of fair representation of results and trends in the results of companies.

Just switching? or manipulating? A study by Archibald in 1967 provides figures for 53 companies that switched from accelerated to straight-line depreciation between 1956 and 1966.* In 13 cases

---

*T Ross Archibald, 'The Return to Straight Line Depreciation: An Analysis of a Change in Accounting Method', *Empirical Research in Accounting: Selected Studies 1967*, The Institute of Professional Accounting, University of Chicago.

the absolute amount of the 'improvement' due to the change exceeded $1 million; the highest was $6·5 million. The ratio of the 'improvement' to the figure exclusive of the improvement was in 12 cases greater than 20 per cent and in 30 cases greater than 10 per cent. In 18 cases the reported income in the year of the switch was less than the reported income of the previous year, in spite of the boost from the change. In 4 cases the reported income in the year of the switch would have been lower than the reported income of the previous year, had it not been for the change.

The following table, from another study, gives some indication of the consequences of switching for 19 companies that made the change in 1965 and 1966. (Eleven of the companies were included in the Archibald study previously mentioned.)

Earnings per share on change from accelerated to straight-line depreciation (dollars)

Changed in 1965	Old basis		New basis	
	1964	1965	1965	1966
Diamond International Corp.	2·10	2·73	2·61	3·07
Divco-Wayne Corp.	2·55	3·10	3·14	3·41
Endicott Johnson Corp.	·96	·69	1·01	2·36
Eversharp Inc.	1·86	1·52	1·66	1·43
General Cigar Company Inc.	1·75	1·44	1·60	2·07
Ideal Cement Company	1·38	1·33	1·52	1·27
Owens-Illinois, Inc.	2·65	3·01	3·29	3·51
Riegel Paper Corp.	1·78	1·67	1·95	1·95
St Regis Paper Company	2·06	2·45	2·75	2·99
West Virginia Paper and Pulp Company	2·59	3·02	3·71	4·39
Weyerhaeuser Company	2·21	2·51	2·72	2·60

Changed in 1966	Old basis		New basis
	1965	1966	1966
American Seating Company	1·52	·89	2·03
Armco Steel Corp.	6·32	6·32	5·86
Beech-Nut Life Savers Inc.	2·44	2·49	2·59
Dana Corp.	3·73	4·77	4·86
International Paper Company	2·02	2·28	2·40
Lily-Tulip Cup Corp.	2·10	2·20	2·44
National Biscuit Company	2·80	2·91	2·99
Youngstown Steel & Tube Company	4·85	3·97	4·01

Source: John H Myers, 'Depreciation Manipulation for Fun and Profits', *Financial Analysts Journal*, November–December 1967.

In 17 cases the change in the method enabled the company to report higher earnings per share than if it had continued to use the accelerated method. If we suppose that directors set value on the appearance of improved earnings in successive years, the change in method may be attributed to nothing more substantial than window-dressing. In 7 cases, continued use of accelerated depreciation would have yielded a drop in earnings per share from the previous year; in 4 of these cases, indeed, the change enabled the company to report higher earnings per share than in the previous year.

Three companies in the paper and packaging industry (Diamond, Lily-Tulip and St Regis) gave as reason for the change the desire to report consistently with other companies in the industry, a motive already noticed in the case of US Steel. Beech-Nut gave as the reason 'to evaluate better the performance'; General Cigar, 'to give a better picture of the company's earnings'; Weyerhaeuser described the change as 'to the more suitable straight-line method'. Whether, in the light of the 'improved' results, these are reasons or rationalizations, the reader may judge. If they are reasons, we are left to wonder why, suddenly, shareholders should be given a *better* picture of a company's earnings, a *better* basis for evaluating performance; and why, if the straight line method was *more suitable*, it had not been used before.

There was a rash of switches in 1968, accompanied now and then by acidulous headlines in the press.

☐ Trans-World Airlines changed its method of accounting for depreciation of airplanes, from writing off over eleven years to writing off over twelve to fourteen years, for 60 per cent of its fleet. The effect was to raise its net income before tax by over $20 million and its income after tax by about $14 million. The company also changed its basis of computing deferred income taxes; the effect was to increase its 1968 net income by $18 million. It reported a preliminary net income of $21·2 million or $1.94 per share compared with $40·8 million or $3.97 per share in 1967. / Digested from *Wall Street Journal*, 22 January 1969 /

☐ From 1 January 1968, National Steel Corporation 'adopted the straight-line method of computing depreciation for financial reporting purposes; however, it will continue to use accelerated methods for tax purposes. Provision has been made for the deferred federal income taxes applicable to this change. The effect of this change was to reduce depreciation expense by $21,158,822 and to increase income for 1968 by $10,000,780 or $0.61 per share.' / Annual Report, 1968 /

☐ Bethlehem Steel changed its method of accounting for depreciation in a manner similar to National Steel Corporation. The effect of the change was reported to be 'a 3 per cent increase in the company's earnings for 1968 as against 1967'. / *Australian Financial Review*, 26 March 1969 /

☐ Allegheny Ludlum Steel Corporation changed its method of accounting for depreciation, 'increasing' its net income by $2·6 million or about $0.56 per share. Reported earnings were $3.65 per share. / Annual Report, 1968 /

☐ Westinghouse Electric Corporation similarly increased its net income by $2·4 million or $0.06 per share. Reported earnings were $3.49 per share. / Annual Report, 1968 /

☐ In the same year B F Goodrich changed to depreciation on a straight-line basis and changed the method of presenting its earnings. Without the changes Goodrich would have reported earnings of $2.76 per share; with the changes it reported earnings of $3.25 per share. / *Australian Financial Review*, 26 March 1969; also *Time*, 11 April 1969, 'Cooking the Books to Fatten Profits' /

☐ Writing in *Fortune* (15 May 1969) under the title 'A Bit of Rouge for Allis-Chalmers', HBM said: 'The accounting that appears in annual reports sometimes serves a cosmetic purpose—it is there not so much to inform stockholders as to help management keep them happy, or at least quiet, by touching up blemishes and brightening beauty spots ... Quite a number of companies in this year's [*Fortune* directory of the 500 largest US corporations] used bookkeeping devices to brighten their results'. [Allis-Chalmers was at the time faced with a takeover; and it had a new president who wished to write off the effects of past mistakes.] 'Allis-Chalmers resolved this conflict with some intricate accounting ... the company reported a loss of $55 million. That was, however a whole lot better than the $122 million that the company *actually* lost last year.' [It was pointed out that the greater part of the difference was due to taking immediate credit for the tax (at about 50 cents in the dollar) on the losses carried forward, as losses would diminish the amount of future taxable income. The auditors disclaimed responsibility for the management's judgment in the matter. Neither the SEC nor the New York Stock Exchange objected to the company's mode of reporting.]

☐ 'AMK Corporation, a diversified conglomerate, was able to boost its fiscal 1968 net profit 74 cents a share over the previous year ... simply by three accounting switches. Without these its profit would have declined by 25 cents a share, Two of these changes were possible because AMK had just acquired a new subsidiary, John Morrell & Co., a meat packer. AMK shifted Morrell from more conservative to more liberal methods of depreciation and valuing inventories ...; AMK itself had been using the more liberal methods.' / 'Conglomerate Earnings: Credibility Gap', *Wall Street Journal*, 24 July 1969 /

☐ In the issue of *Wall Street Journal* just cited, it was reported that Copperweld Steel Co. had announced a gain for the second quarter of 1969, 'but it said the increase was assisted by accounting change'. In fact, the depreciation charge was $2·8 million in 1969 compared with $5·0 million in 1968. The effect of changing the company's depreciation method from an accelerated to a straightline method was to increase 1969 earnings by $918,852 or $0.38 per share. / Annual Report, 1969 /

It will be noticed that, in the majority of cases we have cited, changes in methods of accounting had the effect of reducing the burden of charges on the current and later years' revenues, and thus of increasing the amounts reported as profits. Whether the change was made deliberately to boost reported income cannot be said, for we have no way of knowing the intentions behind the changes. We can, however, observe the effects. But for the change in method, many companies would have shown lower profits than in the preceding year. As the change in accounting methods was at the discretion of managers or directors, it is difficult to avoid the conclusion that changes were made with the objective of boosting reported income.

That the number and effects of these changes are substantial was indicated by Lee Berton in *Wall Street Journal* of 24 July 1969.

☐ 'According to a Value Line investment service study, if accounting practices hadn't been changed between 1966 and 1968, earnings of companies comprising the Dow-Jones Industrial Average, the cream of solid blue-chip firms, would have fallen 0·5% in this period rather than risen 2·6% as actually reported.'

Berton quoted two opinions which associate the general tendency to vary methods of accounting with the pressure exerted by the attractive *apparent* growth rates of conglomerates. Professor

Abraham J Briloff of the City University of New York said: 'old-line companies that once achieved solid financial successes are being forced to employ balance-sheet razzle-dazzle to please stockholders'. Thornton O'glove, a security analyst at Blair & Co. said: 'It doesn't take long for a stick-in-the-mud company to see how quickly its stock is being dumped by mutual funds or institutions in favor of a go-go outfit whose stock is skyrocketing in price'. Berton also reports the 'chief executive of one fast-growing conglomerate' as saying: 'Accounting tricks are taking over. There's no rule on how to keep the books. You can make up your own mind'.

Of course the United States is not the only country in which changes have been made in methods of accounting for the depreciation of property, plant and equipment. We give just a few examples from other jurisdictions:

☐ In 1964 Ready Mixed Concrete made a capital profit of £5 million from the sale of its UK business. It proposed to use this profit 'to eliminate the intangible assets and to reduce the book values of land held primarily as deposits of raw materials for future extraction and thus reduce the burden of future depreciation charges in the accounts'. The 1963 Report included only £319,700 for depreciation and amortization against all the group's freehold and leasehold land and buildings, valued at £7·5 million. Editorial comment: 'The net effect [of the £4 million write-down] would be to reduce shareholders' funds today in order to make trading profits look better in the future. The record of the capital profit will in effect have been rubbed out of the books in as real a piece of 1984 accounting in 1964 as one could wish to unthink'. / *Australian Financial Review*, 6 February 1964 /

☐ Associated Engineering in 1965 decided to reduce by one-fifth the rate at which depreciation was charged on plant, and by one-quarter the rate charged for depreciation of freehold buildings. The 1965 charge was consequently £340,000 less than if it had continued to use the former bases. / Digested from Annual Report, 1965 /

Of course the net profit was 'boosted' by the change in the method.

☐ In 1968 Lake & Elliot changed the period over which certain assets were written off from six years to eight or ten years. The change 'benefited this year's profit figure (1968, £333,881; 1967, £264,432) by approximately £60,000.' / Directors' Report, 1968 /

Without the change there would have been only a slight rise in profits from 1967 to 1968.

☐ In 1969 Bath and Portland Group revised the expected lives of its plant and equipment. 'If the depreciation for the year to 31 October 1969 had been calculated on the basis applied in the previous year the provision necessary would have been £92,448 greater than the amount provided in arriving at the group trading profit.' / Annual Report, 1969 /

The trading profit for 1968 was £1,463,113; for 1969, £1,507,137. Without the change in depreciation charges, the 1969 trading profit would apparently have been lower than the 1968 profit.

☐ The 1969 Annual Report of Fisons referred to difficulties in one division and a fall in profit in another. The directors reported a change in the method of accounting for depreciation of plant. '... as from 1 July 1968, the lives of all existing plant and equipment will be reviewed annually on [the basis of obsolescence of process]. The effect of this year's revision has been brought into the accounts to 30 June 1969, resulting in a reduction in the provision for depreciation for this year of £548,000 compared with the amount which would have been charged on the previous basis.'

And resulting also in a shot in the arm for profits.

INVENTORY VALUATION

The valuation of inventories affects both the reported income and the reported assets of a company. But, as we have shown earlier in this chapter, the number of permissible ways of valuing inventories is very great. In particular, the use of the term 'cost', as a description of the basis used in any balance sheet, may mean many quite different things. Surveys of accounting methods used by companies may fail to provide evidence of changes in accounting method simply because the term 'cost' is used of any one of these methods.

A rule commonly followed is 'the lower of cost and market price'. This rule clearly makes it possible for companies to switch from one cost method to another, and to switch from cost to market price and back again to cost, without any indication of the switches on the face of the balance sheet. Whether companies avail themselves of the opportunity to smooth reported incomes by making such undisclosed switches cannot be known. But if switches are made which must be disclosed (such as changes in depreciation accounting) it seems quite likely that switches may be made even more readily if their occurrence can be concealed by the use of such vague terms as 'cost'.

Other rules have been invented, much like the accelerated depreciation rule for plant, to overcome some 'undesirable' consequence of using the original cost rule. Suppose a good is bought for $5, that it is sold for $10, but that between the dates of purchase and sale the buying price rises to $7. Under the original cost rule the profit would be $5. But if the whole of this were paid out as a dividend, the firm would only have $5 to replace the good, whereas the price of replacing it (to stay in business) would be $7. For these reasons the original cost rule is held to overstate the amount of profit. In the United States, the LIFO (last-in-first-out) rule was developed, from an earlier base-stock rule used in the United Kingdom, to alleviate the 'distortion' due to use of the original cost rule. It came into favour during the thirties when rising prices imposed strains on the financial capacities of companies—another instance of practical exigency showing up the defects of the entrenched cost rule.

The effect of the LIFO rule may be illustrated more fully by comparison with the FIFO (first-in-first-out) rule which charges the sales revenues of a period with the purchase prices of the goods earliest purchased.

	FIFO	LIFO
	$	$
Suppose 10 units of inventory were bought at $5 each	50	50
and *later*, 10 units were bought at $7 each	70	70
Total outlays	120	120

Suppose 10 units were sold at $10 each	100	100
This is to be charged with the cost of goods sold		
under FIFO, at earliest cost	50	
under LIFO, at latest cost		70
Net income	50	30
Value of inventory on hand at end of transactions		
under FIFO, at latest cost	70	
under LIFO, at earliest cost		50

The LIFO rule gives a 'more realistic' net income, if more realistic is understood as relating current levels of selling prices to current levels of cost prices. But it gives a 'less realistic' balance of inventory in the balance sheet, because the inventory is reported at out-of-date prices (the earliest prices paid). In short, LIFO gives a 'better' income statement, but a 'worse' balance sheet. One undesirable result of the original cost rule (assuming regular turnover of inventory) is eliminated but another distortion arises in its place!

Now, because both FIFO and LIFO as well as other rules, are professionally endorsed, companies may change from one to the other, boosting or depressing reported income as a consequence. When prices are rising, whether from general inflationary causes or from special efficiency or advantages of a company, a switch from FIFO to LIFO will moderate reported profits. When prices are falling, from general causes or particular inefficiency, a switch from LIFO to FIFO will boost reported profits. The effects do not come under observation in any quantity. But here are three examples:

□ R J Reynolds Tobacco Company changed its method of valuing inventory in 1957 from the average cost method previously used to the LIFO method. The effect of this 'and related adjustments' was to reduce net income before taxes by $27 million and net earnings by $12 million. The difference, $15 million, was described as income tax saving for the year. Inventories were shown at $28 million less than they would have been shown under the previous method. / Digested from Annual Report, 1957 /

□ In 1969 Gulf & Western Industries reported that one of its subsidiaries had changed the basis of accounting for its inventory of feature films. 'These accounting changes ... had the effect of increasing fiscal 1969 cost of goods sold and reducing year-end inventory by approximately $22 million. Also effective in the 1969 fiscal year, those subsidiaries of the company which formerly determined the costs of their inventory using the last-in-first-out method changed to the first-in-first-out method which had the effect of decreasing cost of goods sold and increasing year-end inventories by approximately $7 million. The net effect of the above changes resulted in a reduction of net earnings of approximately $7 million ($.34 a share on a primary basis) for the year ended July 31, 1969.' / Note to Consolidated Statements /

☐ In 1966 Wheeling Steel Corporation changed the basis of accounting for inventories from LIFO to standard cost. Its Annual Report noted that the change 'decreased the net loss in 1966 by approximately $9 million'.

Changes in inventory valuation rules occur elsewhere than in the US:

☐ 'For the third successive year the shareholders' funds of [Henry Jones Cooperative] have been boosted by book entries. Directors revalued the assets of the New Zealand subsidiaries prior to sale to J Wattie Canneries by $972,000 and credited this to asset revaluation reserve. In the 1964 balance sheet, the funds were boosted by $2·6 million as a result of a change in the method of valuing stock, while in 1963 they rose by $2 million when the company decided to accept the standard basis of conversion for its investments in overseas countries.' / *Australian Financial Review*, 16 February 1966 /

☐ In 1959 Rolls Royce changed the basis of valuing partly and wholly manufactured goods in stock. 'The increase in value amounting to £4,878,794 ... represents the amount by which profits would have been increased in previous years if this basis had then been used and it has therefore been included in these accounts under the heading "Profits retained in the business".' / Annual Report, 1959 /

☐ 'The basis on which overhead expense has been included [in stock valuations] has changed from that used in previous years. Application of the new basis to stocks at 1 January 1967 gave rise to a surplus of £346,018 which has been credited to reserve. In addition the profit for the year is estimated to include approximately £162,000 relating to the change in basis.' / Hoover, Annual Report, 1967 /

☐ In 1968 Newall Machine Tool Company changed the method of valuing stock and work in progress of one of its UK subsidiaries; 'this has produced an exceptional profit of £174,454 ...' / Directors' Report, 1968 /

☐ 'The effect of changes in [the basis of stock valuation] compared with previous years adds approximately £110,000 to the value of stock at 3 October 1969.' / Jute Industries (Holdings), Annual Report, 1969 /

Group profit for the year was £358,706.

☐ '... the existing valuation [of inventories] founded on prime cost was unsatisfactory. Consequently a new basis of valuation has been agreed with the company's auditors, the effect of which is to include a limited proportion of expense associated directly with production and warehousing. The adoption of this new basis has resulted in an increase in the value of stock at 1 July 1968 of £235,285 of which £233,019 attributable to Norvic shareholders has been credited to the balance of retained profits brought forward from last year.' / Norvic Shoe Company, Directors' Report, 1969 /

To what extent and in what direction the profits of the year of report were affected by the changes made by Rolls Royce, Jute Industries and Norvic Shoe Company is not disclosed. A reader cannot know whether the amounts previously reported as net profits, by any of the five UK companies referred to, represented the trend of those companies' profits.

☐ We have noted above (p. 99) that Fisons changed its method of depreciation accounting in 1969. A footnote to the accounts of that year also mentioned a change in inventory valuation. 'At 30 June 1969, £561,000 additional overheads are included. If stocks at 30 June 1968 had been valued on the same basis they would have been increased by approximately £456,000.' The effect of the two changes in accounting was to reduce the charges against the year's results by about £653,000. The 'trading' profits actually reported in 1968 were £7,011,000 and in 1969, £7,096,000. But for the change in accounting method there would have been a fall of 8 per cent in reported profit instead of the rise of 1·2 per cent actually reported.

☐ A report on the preliminary 1971 figures of Davy-Ashmore was accompanied by an explanation in terms of a change in the method of valuing work in progress. Reported trading profit was £1·7 million compared with £1·0 million in the previous year. The effect of the change was to bring into the 1970–71 accounts £0·9 million of profit on work done during the year, which on the previously used basis would have been brought into the results of subsequent years. / *Accountant*, 19 August 1971 /

CONCLUSION

We have alluded to only some of the devices that may be used to bolster or depress the amount of reported profits. The variety of alternative methods of accounting for different assets, equities, costs and revenues, indicated early in the chapter, suggests that the possibilities of tinkering with the reported profits by changing accounting methods are enormous.

Indeed, there is some support for the notion that preoccupation with the possibilities of manipulation is continuous. In respect of the 'short-term' reports of some companies, a 'leading certified public accountant' in the US, presumably knowledgeable in the matter, is reported to have said:

> '... in the unaudited reports filed quarterly some companies tended to estimate earnings conservatively so that the last quarter result—the one leading to the audited figure—would provide a pleasant surprise for shareholders. On the other hand, if such companies felt earnings were going to fade in the next year the emphasis would shift into looking as good as possible in terms of the similar quarter of the previous year.' / *Australian Financial Review*, 26 March 1969 /

We are not raising the question at this point whether manipulation is culpable. What is striking is that the rules of accounting are so flexible that, at unexpected and unpredictable times, companies may switch the rules they use subject only to the proviso that they state what they have done. This adds an element of contingency and risk to the investments of shareholders, and in some cases to the advances of creditors, from the very quarter to which they look for reliable information and guidance.

The statistical frequency of switches is immaterial; the average magnitude of the effects of switches is immaterial. If switches from one acceptable method of accounting to another can influence reported profits and asset values to the tune of millions or tens of millions, there can be little satisfaction with 'acceptable' standards of practice. The laxity of the rules permits, if it does not encourage, companies to put on a better face in the short run. For, clearly, if they can change once to produce an immediate effect on what is reported, they can change again with similar or opposite effects to produce 'favourable' short-run effects whenever they wish. That this shuffling seriously affects the determination of trends in performance and comparison of the performances of companies seems to be considered of no consequence. It is no defence to say that explanations of the changes in any year of change are given in footnotes or in other ways. When companies give tabulated summaries over series of years in their reports (and many do this) the footnotes disappear. And when stock exchange information services give tabulated summaries of the same kind (a common practice) the footnotes do not appear in them either.

The looseness and diversity of accounting rules have been under attack for many years. Two observations, one from an official governmental inquiry and one from the financial press, show that the problems to which this laxity gives rise are still considered to be serious:

□ 'If accounting is a tool designed to facilitate a rational assessment of business success or failure, its techniques should give a timely and accurate representation of an enterprise's current operations, permit comparison with results in previous years, and allow comparison with other comparable enterprises.

'As currently practiced, accounting does not always meet these expectations. On a number of key issues, generally accepted accounting principles permit a range of reporting choices that can materially alter reported company operating results. There need be no consistency in the treatment of depreciation charges, inventory evaluation, the expensing of research and development, and other factors. The specific method of reporting selected by management may be changed from one period to another. It may be said categorically that accounting statements often are neither consistent over time nor comparable between firms.' / *Economic Report on Corporate Mergers*, Washington 1969, p. 120 /

☐ '[The announcement from Klinger Manufacturing] showing a £400,000 write-down in the value of the company's stocks [inventories] and a £675,000 half-year trading loss only three months after the company was hoping for a £2 million profit, is the latest in a series of events that make published accounts look pretty arbitrary documents for investors. [The article went on to describe how differences between the accounting methods of companies, in respect of inventory valuation, depreciation and 'development' costs could lead to marked differences in the profits and assets reported.] The result of all this is that the profits you see described as "true and fair" in an auditor's report could in many cases be doubled, halved or pitched anywhere in between and still be "true and fair" using a different but equally respectable set of accounting principles . . . Unless the Stock Exchange and big investors insist on measures to make company accounts more comparable, we shall miss a golden opportunity to make the capital market a more efficient place and ordinary shareholders less likely to be duped by the few insiders adept at reading between the lines.' / 'Time to Clean up the Accounts Chaos', *Sunday Times*, London, 7 September 1969 /

9
FROM THE OUTSIDE LOOKING IN

'The rule is, jam tomorrow and jam yesterday—but never
jam today', [the Queen said].
'It *must* come sometimes to "jam today",' Alice objected.
'No, it can't,' said the Queen. 'It's jam every *other* day;
today isn't any *other* day, you know.'
/ *Through the Looking Glass* /

Some might suppose that the products of widespread accounting
practices cannot be as misleading or as uninformative as our argument and illustrations suggest. It may be alleged that the argument
and the evidence are biased. In this chapter, therefore, we draw on
the practices and observations of a number of 'outsiders'—persons
other than accountants. Some of these—regulatory officials, analysts, financiers, managers—have had occasion to use, or to
disregard, or to observe the use of, financial information derived
by accounting processes. Others—economists—in the course of
analysis of the modes of rational economic calculation, have
expounded the meaning of 'wealth' and 'income' which, of
course, are what balance sheets and income accounts respectively purport to represent. We shall find that outsiders are critical
of the information that traditional accounting yields; and we shall
find further evidence of the propriety of financial statements that
report financial position and results in up-to-date terms.

We have shown that many of the figures that appear in financial
statements are, or are based on, out-of-date costs. On the other
hand, all calculations of depreciation and other distributions of
'cost' over the current and future years entail guesses about the
future—the future 'life' of the asset, and its future scrap value (see
p. 124)—guesses which may be far from what is subsequently experienced. There has, in fact, been a considerable increase in the
amount of guessing about the future which finds its way into company financial statements. Potential liabilities for future payments
of taxes, lease rentals, pensions and other things—none of them
actual liabilities at the date of the balance sheet—are increasingly
being shown in balance sheets. Costs of assets, yesterday; guesses

about amounts of liabilities, tomorrow; but little about the values of assets, today. 'The rule is, jam tomorrow and jam yesterday—but never jam today.'

AN EYE TO THE FUTURE

It has become common among accountants to consider that the most important function of published financial statements is to aid in forecasting the future performances of companies. Whether this view is traceable to the expressed opinions of investment analysts is not certain; but it certainly is supported by the following:

> 'The investment analyst is concerned *only* with an evaluation of the future return opportunities and risks within a given enterprise. Therefore, accounting data are useful *only* to the extent they provide clues to these opportunities and risks. As a consequence, it would be desirable for the income statements to reflect *only* that flow of revenues, costs and related income that seems pertinent to future operations. Similarly, the balance sheet would be stated in a form to reflect clearly the financial obligations of the firm, the nature of the assets, and the equity of the shareholders. Then ... from a series of such statements it is anticipated that an insight into the potential trends and fluctuations of these items can be obtained.
>
> 'As a consequence of these objectives of investment analysis, it would follow that (1) transactions involving gains and losses to the firm that are unusual or non-recurring in nature should be excluded from reported income and (2) all financial commitments related to future operations would be clearly presented in the balance sheet.' / Douglas A Hayes, 'Accounting Principles and Investment Analysis', in *Law and Contemporary Problems*, vol XXX no. 4, 1965, p. 755 /
>
> [Italics have been added. Hayes is also author of *Investments: Analysis and Management*, 1961.]

We have already noticed the adverse features of income-smoothing. It is no doubt useful to draw attention, through the directors' report, to abnormal items of revenue or cost in any year. It seems to be going too far though to urge that 'unusual and non-recurring' items should be excluded when calculating the income to be reported. The amount of reported income serves other purposes than forecasting. It is the amount out of which dividends are paid and reserves are created, the whole amount of income, inclusive of the effects of unusual and non-recurring items; is indicative of the prospect of regular dividends and the need for reserves (if income does, in fact, fluctuate) to secure the regularity of dividends.

The view that unusual items should be excluded, in effect, confuses the reportorial function of accounting with the predictive function of analysis. This was pointed out long ago by the US Securities and Exchange Commission, in an opinion that seems to have been unnoticed or disregarded. For the latter reason we quote from it at length:

□ 'In our opinion financial accounting is essentially historical in nature—it consists of an accounting for costs that have actually been incurred by the business and for the revenues that have been actually derived from the business ... financial accounting is in our opinion concerned with what did happen, not with what might have happened had conditions been different. And it does not attempt to forecast the future even though it supplies much of the material used in making such a forecast. There is, on the other hand, another field of financial statistics in which statements are used which in form and language are closely similar to the financial statements used in presenting actual balance sheets and income statements. This is the field of financial analysis and forecasting. In essence, the analyst begins with reports of actual operations and conditions and adjusts them to give effect to expected future changes and events in order to arrive at his estimate of future earnings. In one form of analysis and forecasting the analyst is content to comment upon the actual past results, to point out what parts of the past results are due to factors which are not expected to continue and how the existence of new factors and conditions is expected to alter past results. At times, however, the analyst goes further and attempts to prepare an 'adjusted' statement which purports to show how past operations would have worked out had certain specified subsequent events taken place earlier. Finally, the analyst may seek to forecast as accurately as may be what he expects will be the results of future operations ... ... In contrast to such forecasts, a statement of past operations, even though it is based in important part on opinion and judgment is primarily an historical record of actual events, not of prophesied future events.

The two types of financial statements are obviously in wholly different categories and have different uses in examining the investment merits of a security.

Particularly because of the similarity in form, great care must be taken to ensure that the reader will be aware of the nature of the particular statement. Nothing, in our opinion, would be more misleading than to present, in the guise of an actual earnings statement, data which, in fact, was an estimate either of expected future earnings or of the effects of subsequent conditions and transactions on prior operations ...

... disclosure should be made as to significant, known factors that might render past earnings statements, or particular items therein, not indicative of probable future operations. With such information at hand the reader of the statement is informed of what the past operations were, and of the conditions or transaction, which in the draftsman's judgment, are apt to be unusual and not apt to recur. In our opinion, this is the boundary line of financial accounting. It is the place at which the financial accountant in his capacity as such should stop. He is, we feel, essentially a historian, not a prophet.

This desire to prepare statements in a form more readily usable in estimating the future has led some to attempt to present what can be called a 'normal' income statement, the inference being that the statement shows about what can be expected to happen year after year. The broad justification alleged for the practice is that if the actual results of the year's operations are unusual a reader may be misled into thinking the abnormalities will recur and that the last, if not the only way, to avoid such misconceptions is to 'normalize' the statement—that is to exclude therefrom the effects of some or all of the conditions which in the opinion of the draftsman are deemed to be unusual.

The dangers inherent in such a practice are numerous. In the first place, the draftsman's judgment as to what is abnormal can scarcely be considered infallible. In the second place, there is certainly as much danger that the reader will fail to understand what has been done by the draftsman as that he will fail to recognize that the unadjusted statements are abnormal. Finally, the method is extremely susceptible of misuse through conscious or unconscious bias in making decisions as to what is unusual or abnormal about the current year ...

We conclude then that the proper function of an income statement presenting the results of operations is to present an accurate historical record ... the amounts shown should be in accordance with the historical facts and should not be altered to reflect amounts that the draftsman considers to be more 'normal' or likely to recur in future years ... We think that such [financial] statements should be historical records of the results of whatever financial events actually took place. It is not the role of the financial accountant to adjust them so as to eliminate the effect of unusual circumstances which actually occurred.' / *Accounting Series Release* no. 53, 16 November 1945 /

Need anything more be said? Let the analyst guess about the future and predict if he must. He will do poorly unless the financial statements fully report the effects of *past* events and transactions, right up to the date of the report.

BALANCE SHEET INFORMATION — THE INVESTMENT SERVICES

A practical test of the adequacy of the information published is the use made of it and the comments made on it by those who analyse financial statements for the benefit of financiers, clients and the public generally.

From time to time, in response to suggestions for reform, accountants have been found to question the use made of information contained in published balance sheets. Many have alleged that shareholders and analysts are primarily interested in net income, not in the particulars in balance sheets. This view overlooks the fact that the figures of the balance sheet and the income (or profit and loss) account are technically interlocked—the income account is one of the accounts whose balance appears in the balance sheet. This interlocking entails that any mis-statement of asset values has a corresponding effect on the income account or on the balance of some reserve account. Likewise if any additional information on asset values, obtained from parenthetical or foot-note statements, is used to adjust asset values shown in the main balance sheet columns, the adjustment should be accompanied by some corresponding adjustment to the income account.

Perhaps the view that users of financial statements make little or no use of balance-sheet information stems from the knowledge (of accountants) that this information is practically useless under the traditional mode of accounting. But there is abundant evidence to the point that balance-sheet information is needed.

☐ In the USA Robert Morris Associates publishes *Annual Statement Studies* periodically. The 1968 edition gives the median value and upper and lower quartiles for fourteen financial ratios of companies in 223 industries. Every one of the fourteen ratios has, as one of its elements, a single balance-sheet item, or a sub-total or grand total of balance-sheet items. (Incidentally, the three basic ratios to which we have frequently alluded—the current ratio, the debt-to-equity ratio and the rate of return on shareholders' equity—appear in this set.)

☐ In the USA Dun and Bradstreet have published similar tabulations. The successive editions of *Practical Financial Statement Analysis* by R A Foulke, who was for thirty years associated with Dun and Bradstreet, contain samples. (The three ratios on which we have concentrated also appear in this series.)

☐ In the USA *Standard NYSE Stock Reports* give up to ten years statistics for particular companies whose securities are traded on the New York Stock Exchange. The information given includes security prices, company income, certain balance-sheet items, and such derived figures as the current ratio and the book value (asset backing) of common stock.

Similar information services are associated with other large securities markets. The fact that these services are sustained, at substantial costs to subscribers, is evidence of the belief that balance sheets are, or should be, more serviceable than merely as indicators of how the original capital and loan subscriptions were deployed. The argument of Chapter 4 is corroborated. The publication year by year of ratios for individual companies and ranges of ratio values for industry groups is evidence of the particular uses to which the raw data may be put. But as long as the raw data are mixtures of figures, some up-to-date, others long out-of-date and others incomprehensible, those who use the investment services mentioned are still at risks of which they are unaware.

☐ One such investment service has attempted to reduce the risk, at least in one respect. The Investment Service of the Sydney Stock Exchange Research and Statistical Bureau, like most such services, gives tabulated summaries of assets, equities and other matters for listed companies. For some years, where the assets of a company included listed securities, the Investment Service has given the market value of those securities as a footnote to its tabulations, and has given the net tangible assets per share both on the basis of balance-sheet values and market values of a company's security holdings.

This may seem a small matter but it is indicative of the significance that the Service attaches to the knowledge required by investors and others of the effects of changes in the market prices of assets.

FINANCIAL AND SECURITY ANALYSTS

If the information given in company balance sheets is less than ideal for the purposes of security analysis, we might expect the standard textbooks on investment and investment analysis to comment on its deficiencies. Many writers have referred generally to the 'limitations' of the products of conventional accounting processes. But we consider more pertinent the remarks of those who point directly to the need for up-to-date valuations of assets.

☐ Montgomery Ward's 1963 financial statement 'therefore shows net fixed-asset values based on the prices which existed at the time the assets were acquired. There are three reasons why these net figures may be far removed from present market values. First, changes in general price levels may have made the basic cost figures obsolete. Second, the estimates of total accumulated depreciation may be too large or too small, resulting in inaccurate net values. Third, the economic usefulness of a fixed asset is not necessarily measured by its cost; some are well chosen and profitable, others may be white elephants.' / John C Clendenin, *Introduction to Investments*, 4th ed., New York, 1964 /

☐ 'At the end of 1960 Bishop Oil Company owned 88,000 shares of Flintkote Corporation ... carried at cost of $164,000 but worth $2,550,000 at market. For analytical purposes these shares should be considered as current assets at their market value less capital-gain tax on the indicated profit.' / Graham, Dodd and Cottle, *Security Analysis*, 4th ed., New York, 1962, p. 206 /

☐ 'In December 1960 Kaiser Industries showed Investments in Affiliated Companies of $182 million with a footnote indicating that their market value was $388 million. This market appreciation

of $206 million is relevant to an analysis of Kaiser Industries shares.'
/ Graham, Dodd and Cottle, *Security Analysis*, p. 207 /

Dealing with plant and property, Graham, Dodd and Cottle say
that 'shareholders and security analysts should be supplied with
more information regarding the present value of the property
account than is contained in the ledger figures, which reveal
only original cost or a substitute value selected many years ago'
(p. 207). They say that some companies give estimated replacement value less depreciation, 'generally for the purpose of justify-
ing a higher depreciation rate than is allowed for tax purposes.'
It seems not unlikely that the use of the higher replacement
value basis is connected with tactical income-smoothing in years in
which gross revenues are higher than usual; Chapter 8 of this book
gave some examples of tactical income-smoothing in the opposite
circumstance, when gross revenues or the result before charging
depreciation is lower than usual. The present point however is that
analysts require more up-to-date information than the traditional
accounts give.

□ Graham, Dodd and Cottle also note that some companies give
figures on the insurance values and assessed values of their buildings and equipment. In 1949 Equitable Office Building stated that
its building and contents were insured against fire for $18 million,
whereas the book value was $5·4 million. The land and building
were assessed (for local tax purposes) for $27·8 million, whereas the
combined book value was $19·9 million. The difference between
current values and book values can scarcely be considered immaterial. In 1949 Diamond T Motor reported the insured value of
its buildings and machinery to be $4,878,000, against a book value
of $939,000. 'If figures such as these were required to be supplied
by all companies as a footnote to the balance sheet, a much more
informative picture of the plant account would be available to those
who really own the assets,' say Graham, Dodd and Cottle (p. 208).

□ 'The Cessna Company used a certificate from the federal government which gave the company authority to write off the cost of
$4,648,000 of its gross plant and equipment costs over a 60-month
period. The basis for this certification was that this plant and equipment was constructed in the interests of national defence. This
plant and equipment probably has a much longer economic life.
The net effect of this rapid write-off is to understate the value of

the plant and equipment account on the balance sheet and also to understate the reported net incomes.' / Plum, Humphrey and Bowyer, *Investment Analysis and Management*, Homewood, Ill. 1961, pp. 212–3 /

In the light of such comments as these by writers in the United States it is not easy to understand why the profession and the Securities and Exchange Commission hold so strongly to the belief that financial statements should be based on the costs of assets.

APB Hearing: In 1971, under the aegis of the Accounting Principles Board of the American Institute of CPAs, there was conducted a public hearing on accounting for investments in certain equity securities—stocks and shares. The Board was considering the desirability of accounting for these investments on the basis of current market value. The 'general practice' at the time (except for certain types of organization, mostly subject to governmental regulation) was to show such investments at cost (or at market value if less than cost); to bring in, as income of each year, dividends received or receivable; and to bring into account the effect of changes in the market values of such securities in the year in which they are sold.

A number of submissions supported retention of the present method. In particular, the SEC believed that 'a market or fair value basis for general practice is not desirable or feasible', though market or fair value should be disclosed parenthetically or otherwise.

The Financial Analysts Federation submitted that equity securities (and marketable debt instruments) should be shown in balance sheets at market value, net of the tax effect on the sale of such securities. Both realized and unrealized appreciation or depreciation should be accounted for in the same way, to avoid the possibility, available under present practice, of 'managing' reported income by 'selective realization of gains and losses'. Gains and losses, through changes in market values, should be reported separately in the income statement. The Federation held that exclusion of changes in market value would result in an 'incomplete picture of the income for the period'. It set aside the objection that fluctuations in market value would produce 'distortions', since management when making the investment is aware of the possibility of variation in market prices and 'indeed intends to profit from it'. It set aside the argument that gains or losses through changes in market value may never be realized, on the ground that 'the decision to hold or sell a security does have economic consequences'; these would be accounted for under the proposals it submitted.

As we are concerned in this chapter with the beliefs and opinions of a variety of different persons, it is pertinent to notice that the submissions to the Hearings by the American Insurance Associ-ation, the American Life Convention/Life Insurance Association of America, and the Panel on Corporate Law and Accounting of the American Bar Association agreed substantially with the sub-mission of the Financial Analysts Federation. (The full transcript of hearings and the written submissions are published in *Cases in Public Accounting Practice*, vol. 8, Arthur Andersen & Co.)

It may be noted that investments in securities may be bought to hold for income, and may be sold for the gain on sale if the market price is sufficiently attractive. Substantially the same applies to all kinds of assets of a commercial or industrial firm; we have already cited some examples of this (p. 65). It would perhaps be improper to suppose that the professional groups mentioned above would support the same principles for all assets. But the specific points mentioned by the Financial Analysts Federation are equally relevant to the accounting for all assets of commercial and industrial companies.

CURRENT ANALYSIS

Perhaps more cogent, in one sense, than the views of the writers of textbooks, may be the actual observations, comments and speculations of reporters, analysts and financial editors on the accounts of companies, as they have been published or as they have come before investors.

Consider, first, some UK examples:

☐ 'But with £3,172,525 within the properties figure [in the balance sheet of J Hepworth & Son Ltd] applicable to properties still at the 1955 valuation and £2,611,387 bought since 1955 and unvalued, there is a majority of "unvalued" as against "revalued" properties in the figures. A more up to date idea of the property value would not come amiss.' / *Accountant*, London, 14 December 1968 /

☐ 'Properties in the books [of Thomas Robinson and Son] at £278,000 were professionally revalued last in December 1963, and were then on a going-concern basis estimated to be worth £581,000. Taking no account whatsoever of the rise in property values since 1963, the shares have an asset backing of 90s. each of which 40s. is liquid. [The quoted price in January 1969 was 72s 6d.] The shares should move higher.' / *Investors Chronicle*, 31 January 1969 /

☐ 'As the bulk of the assets [of Hay's Wharf] has not been revalued for twenty years, they almost certainly are considerably understated at book values. The directors do their best to play down this possibility. They concede that certain London office buildings would probably be worth £2·3m more than their £1·1m book value, but say that other properties, figuring at £10·5m in the accounts would probably not be worth very much more if valued on a going-concern basis. On the other hand, if requisite development permission could be obtained, there is no doubt that the true worth of land bordering the Upper Pool of London would be substantially higher than book values ... At what could be a substantial discount on the underlying asset potential, the shares should be retained.' / Analysis, *Investors Chronicle*, 14 March 1969 /

☐ 'There is little to get one's teeth into in the full accounts from George Wimpey despite a wealth of information about the progress of particular contracts ... It is known that Oldham [Estate company in which Wimpey has a 40 per cent stake] itself is worth quite a bit more than the £72m disclosed in connection with the abortive merger talks with City of London Real Property. At £90m, Wimpey's stake would be worth 22s. 8d. per share.' / Analysis, *Investors Chronicle*, 11 April 1969 /

The investment in Oldham was only part of the business of Wimpey; yet the net assets per share of Wimpey were shown to be only 19s. 11d.

And now some Australian examples:

☐ '... the value of the premises and equipment [of Brisbane Permanent Building and Banking Co.] ... in 1931 was £33,500. Their value with certain other furniture and sites as shown in the

1960 balance sheet is £45,556. It may thus be reasonably assumed that there is a very substantial element of undervaluation in the book figures of these assets.' / *Australian Financial Review*, 4 May 1961 /

□ '... the hotel itself is listed in the [Australia Hotel Company's] books at £1·6 million—extremely conservative when compared with an estimated market value of £2·7 million.' / *Australian Financial Review*, 9 August 1962 /

□ 'Fixed assets, including the large modern brewery and the hotels, are in the books [of Castlemaine Perkins] at £5,333,735 and their value is several times that amount.' / *Australian Financial Review*, 27 September 1962 /

□ 'During the year the New South Wales Valuer-General placed a value of £702,500 on the Rosebery freehold and factory [of James Stedman]. Many people ... believe it is worth even more.' / *Australian Financial Review*, 8 November 1962 /

□ 'The current difference between the book value and market price of Cuming Smith's listed holdings is enough to add an additional 46s. or so on to the stated asset backing of 37s. 3d. a 20s. share, even at a most conservative reckoning.' / *Australian Financial Review*, 2 July 1963 /

□ 'There has apparently been no revaluation of any of the [Commonwealth Industrial Gases] group's fixed assets during its existence and their book value of £10·7 million is only 56 per cent of their cost of nearly £19 million after accumulated depreciation allowances of £8·3 million.' / *Australian Financial Review*, 26 March 1964 /

□ 'However, these assets are conservatively valued. Many of them have never been updated—at least since the last bonus issue in 1927.' / Comment on Henry Jones Co-operative, *Australian Financial Review*, 13 May 1964 /

□ 'One property alone, the State Shopping Block and theatre in Sydney's Market Street, must have a realisable value running close to the £3,902,129 at which the company [Greater Union Theatres] assessed the whole of its freeholds at December 31 last.' / *Australian Financial Review*, 14 September 1961 / 'In the 1965 balance sheet the value the company put on its Australia-wide chain of theatres was $10 million—and many of these theatres were built, or their sites bought, in the depression years.' / *Australian Financial Review*, 23 June 1967 /

INTER-COMPANY COMPARISONS

The examples just given relate mainly to the reports of single companies considered by themselves. It is very common to consider each company as a unique company, having and entitled to have its own special kind of accounting—its own set of rules. The idea is fostered by the laws, which make directors responsible for the contents of financial statements but leave them extraordinarily wide latitude in their choice of rules. More and more information is being required to be given—but without any concern for its comparability between companies.

Investors and their advisers need to be able to compare the financial features of companies if they are to make informed choices of investments and, subsequently, to protect their interests. But comparisons of information derived by different rules are likely to be misleading. Only by the uniform use of well-chosen rules is proper comparison made possible.

If the same rules are not used uniformly, there may always arise the question whether the assets, profits and financial position of one company are comparable with those of others. Here are two comments made—one in the setting of a takeover bid, the other in relation to two companies that subsequently merged:

☐ Comment on a bid by Tecalemit for Dennis Brothers, equivalent to 22s. 9d. per share: '... whereas the net asset value per share in the accounts is 22s. 7d., if allowance is made for the property revaluation in 1965 it shoots up to 34s. And one shareholder who claimed to know something about property values in the Guildford area, where Dennis has its works, claimed at the recent annual meeting that an up-to-date valuation would bump up the figure to 40s.... it is rather unfortunate that the agreement of terms between the parties makes no reference whatsoever to Dennis' asset value—which is really the vital point.' / *Investors Chronicle*, 14 March 1969 /

☐ 'Adelaide Chemical looks a poor performer when the return on ordinary capital is compared with other industries—one wonders how well Wallaroo-Mount Lyell Fertilisers would look if, like Adelaide Chemical, it revalued its assets and adjusted shareholders' funds to what they could be. Return on the assets employed by Wallaroo, adjusted for present day values, would look rather low in comparison with most other industries.' / *Australian Financial Review*, 5 September 1963 /

And here is a stockholder's plea for comparability—and the response it attracted:

☐ At the 1967 meeting of Twentieth Century-Fox the following observations were made:

Mr Lewis Gilbert [a stockholder]: 'At the MGM meeting ... the question was raised by me as to whether or not they were using the predominant method used in the industry, and the answer was that they were not because in the opinion of [the auditor] and in the opinion of [the chairman] it would overstate the earnings. My question is, may we have some comment as to this as far as Twentieth Century is concerned? Are we overstating these earnings?'

Representative of the Auditor: 'Twentieth Century-Fox uses the policy predominant in the motion picture industry, and we do not believe the earnings are overstated ... We believe the policies used by Twentieth Century-Fox are correct and correctly report the earnings and we don't try to compare it with any other company.'

Gilbert: 'It is all very well to boast about the earnings but we are entitled to know if the other method were used, rightly or wrongly, how much difference there would have been in our earnings ... This is a matter of information. It doesn't say who is right or who is wrong.'

Comptroller of Twentieth Century-Fox: 'When you say "difference", you are now comparing us to the MGM policy?'

Gilbert: 'That is correct. He [chairman of MGM] said, "If we followed the method of others, our earnings would be much higher". And from your reticence, it gives the impression it must be really a substantial amount.'

Comptroller: 'We have not taken the necessary steps to try to compare what our earnings would be with that of other companies had we followed their policies.... I don't think we should be asked to compare what our figures would be in comparison to what other policies are.' / Lewis D and John J Gilbert, *Twenty-Eighth Annual Report of Stockholder Activities at Corporation Meetings during 1967* /

In this case the officer of the company (the comptroller) seems to have been unconcerned with the stockholder's wish to make comparisons.

But there are circumstances in which the uneasiness is on the other side.

☐ The chairman of Cunard Steam-Ship Company explained a £2 million trading loss in 1970 in the following terms: The company had in 1970 adopted a new rule, recently recommended by the Institute of Chartered Accountants, for dealing with the profits and losses of associated companies. Other companies had not followed the rule in 1970. In answer to questions from members, he said: 'I can only speak for our own business. It is a fact that if Cunard's accounts had been prepared on the same basis as those that seem to have been used by others, we should have reported a loss of £200,000 for 1970 instead of £2 million ... Methods of accounting that produce such widely different figures as that cannot both be right—and the unwitting stockholder is left to guess which gives the true and fair view.' / *Accountancy*, June 1971 / The chairman was himself a chartered accountant.

For the same reason, concern that one company should appear in no worse light than its competitors, United States Steel changed its method of accounting in 1968 to conform with the practices of other companies in the industry (see pp. 94–5, above). To fall into line may facilitate comparison. But if a whole industry follows a rule that is not 'well-chosen', doubt about the value of comparisons will remain.

It is worth noting that at various times during the sixties individual commissioners of the SEC have affirmed that comparability of information on different firms, and hence greater uniformity of practice, is desirable in the interest of investors. But, consistent with its established stance, the Commission has taken no direct steps to reduce the basic causes of diversity in reporting.

COMPARATIVE ANALYSIS — WITH GUESSWORK

We have seen that analysts and critics are often reduced to guess-work. And we know that investors may well wish to compare the financial characteristics of companies in different industries. It is an interesting exercise to see what differences in important indicators may arise if an attempt is made to reduce the different kinds of information on two companies to comparable and up-to-date magnitudes. We have said that it is impossible to do this properly without detailed knowledge of a company's accounting methods—knowledge that is not available to shareholders or analysts. A careful investor or his analyst may be reduced to guessing, in the interest of comparison, when he has no reliable and comparable information.

The figures in the table below are based on information contained in the 1970 annual reports of two UK companies. A is a company in the foodstuffs industry, B a company in the consumers semi-durables industry. Both have been in business for over fifty years. A has made numerous revaluations of assets; B has made no such revaluations. We do not give the names as we do not wish the conclusions to be taken as anything else than the product of plausible guesswork. We made the following adjustments:

Comparison of financial features of two UK companies (money figures in £ million)

Reports of December 1970	As published		As adjusted (see text)	
	A	B	A	B
Turnover	278	541	278	541
Net profit, less tax and minority interests	8·8	9·1	8·8	9·1
Ordinary shareholders net equity	133·4	122·6	133·4	135·4 (a)
Land and buildings				
at cost	16·8	61·8	22·4	82·4
at revaluation	56·3	—	56·3	—
less depreciation	(7·0)	(26·0)	(9·3)	(34·6)
Net value	66·1	35·8	69·4	47·8
Add to net equity			3·3	12·0 (b)
Plant and equipment				
at cost	85·0	260·5	102·0	312·6
at revaluation	9·7		9·7	
less depreciation	(51·3)	(140·9)	(61·6)	(169·1)
Net value	43·4	119·6	50·1	143·5
Add to net equity			6·7	23·9 (c)

Comparison of financial features of two UK companies (money figures in
£ million)

Reports of December 1970	As published		As adjusted (see text)	
	A	B	A	B
Investments				
at book value	2·8	11·9	2·1	16·7
Add to net equity			(·7)	4·8 (d)
Adjusted net equity			142·7	176·1
(a + b + c + d)				
Rate of return on net	6·6%	7·4%	6·2%	5·2%
equity				
Tangible assets per share	£2.56	£2.55	£2.74	£3.66
(of nominal £1)				

Ordinary shareholders' net equity: For *B* we added in £12·8 million,
described as 'provision' and shown as liabilities in the balance
sheet, but which appear to be reserves.

Land and buildings: A revalued many of its assets during the past
15 years. We take them at their face value though this is likely to
be below current value. We have no idea when the other assets of
A or all the assets of *B* were bought. As a guess, we suppose their
present prices are one-third higher than the book values; and that
the cumulative depreciation charges in respect of them should be
one-third higher. The figure 'Add to net equity' is the difference
between the 'adjusted' figure and the published figure for each of
the companies.

Plant and equipment: The same remarks apply to land and buildings.
But because plant and equipment wear out faster, we suppose the
items shown at cost to have current values one-fifth higher than
book values, and that the cumulative depreciation charges in
respect of them should be one-fifth higher.

Investments: For the book values of investments we substitute the
market valuations or directors' valuations given in the reports.

We make adjustments for these three items to the figure for ordinary shareholders' net equity, since any increment in asset values runs to the equity of ordinary shareholders. We make no adjustments to the reported net profit—either for the higher depreciation or the gain or loss in value of investments; there is no information that enables such adjustments to be made to the net profit of a single year.

The result of the exercise is in the last two lines. On the reported figures A has a lower rate of return than B; on the adjusted figures the opposite is the case. On the reported figures A has slightly higher assets per share than B; on the adjusted figures B has substantially higher assets per share than A. What effects these reversals in ranking might have on an investor thinking of investing in either A or B we do not know. As long as the law and practice of financial reporting remain so loose, investing must be a very chancy pursuit.

POTPOURRI

Diverse kinds of people, practically concerned in one way or another with accounting, finance and financial dealing, have expressed dismay or puzzlement over the practices of accounting, or have been moved to make good in other ways the defects of those practices.

There have been many and varied admonitory or caustic remarks on the loose and ambiguous nature of the accounting process and its products.

☐ 'To the layman, and in this I include myself, it appears that the accounts of companies can now be presented to show either a profit or a loss from the same set of figures. Nothing has done more injury to your reputations than the somewhat squalid sight, which we have recently seen, of firms of accountants with international reputations giving totally different views of the worth and results of the same company.' / Chairman P G Balfour of Newcastle and United Breweries, at annual dinner of the Association of English Chartered Accountants in Scotland, reported in *Accountancy*, January 1971 /

☐ In the Duple Motor Bodies case (an English taxation case of 1960), it was shown that the profit in a 'slack' year could be greater than the profit of the preceding year of higher sales volume, if overheads were included in the valuation of work in progress. In effect 'a loss could be made into a profit according to whether overheads were excluded or included in the valuation of stock and work in progress. Told that either course was in accordance with accepted accounting principles, the (then) Master of the Rolls is reported to have said: "That absolutely defeats me" '. / Vice President D S Morpeth of the Institute of Chartered Accountants in England and Wales, reported in *Accountant*, 24 September 1970 /

☐ '... over the last 30 years the SEC might profitably have invested the energies of some of its best analysts and some of its funds to the development of a better set of indices offering some hope of prognosis for economic behavior. It is clear that what we call accounting and our standard methods of accounting are of remarkably limited usefulness for purposes of figuring out what is going on in the real world of economic activity.' / Bayless A Manning, Dean, Stanford School of Law, in *Economic Policy and the Regulation of Corporate Securities*, 1969, pp. 84–5 /

There is some evidence that even the directors of companies have themselves been in ignorance of the values of their companies and their assets through reliance on traditional accounting information.

☐ A partner of Barings, advisers to Courtaulds on the occasion of the ICI takeover bid in 1961–62 is reported to have said: 'We had become convinced that Courtauld's assets were much higher than they themselves had realized'. And, speaking generally, 'many boards do not know the real value of their own properties. They don't realize, for instance, that a building outlet may be more valuable than a trading outlet.' And, of another client: 'Among our clients is one of the biggest brewing companies in this country. Their directors are primarily interested in making and selling a lot of beer; that's what they get paid for. They sit inside and have no time to look out. We at Barings are outside looking in; we can see the whole operation in financial terms though we know nothing about the making of beer. We looked at their balance sheets and discovered that some of their assets were still listed at the prices they had been bought for, thirty years ago. The directors didn't realize

that their assets are now worth many millions more.' / Joseph
Wechsberg, *The Merchant Bankers*, 1966, ch. 3 /

There are regulatory and assistance-granting agencies which
administer particular trades or classes of trade or terms of trade.
For them it is important, in the interest of equity, to be able
to compare firms in terms of their results and other financial
characteristics. So:

☐ The US Small Business Administration found it was unable
to make satisfactory comparisons and judgments from information
derived by the style of accounting in common use, based on original
costs. Its agents were Small Business Investment Companies which
helped to finance small business ventures. In 1969 its regulations
were revised so that each Investment Company was required to
report the 'unrealized appreciation of assets' of each venture it
assisted. The amount was to be the difference between 'total assets
as recorded in the small business concern's books' and 'total assets
based on their estimated market value or fair value as at the close of
the fiscal year'. / 'SBA Revises Reporting Requirements for SBICs',
Journal of Accountancy, June 1969 /

SOME ECONOMISTS

The theoretical work of economists seldom makes allusion to
the problems of ascertaining the states of affairs of persons or
companies, or the calculation of income earned by companies. For
some purposes economists make use of the products of accounting;
but they tend to take the figures for granted, on the assumption
that accountants have done what they could do.

Further, economists are commonly concerned with what happens in general, or what follows from certain assumed conditions
and actions. They are not concerned with anomalies beyond their
own domain. A comment to the point was made by a writer in *New
York Times* on an institutional investor study sponsored by the SEC:
'As economists, the authors ... were mainly interested in
discovering the overall, the "usual" impact of the institutional
investing—in the general case, rather than in the aberrational
one. It is the aberrational one, at least in markets that are func-
tioning reasonably well, that points toward the need for additional

regulation to safeguard not only the smooth working but the very fairness of the securities market.' / Eileen Shanahan, as reproduced in *Australian Financial Review*, 25 March 1971 /

There have been economists however who have taken positions on the meaning of wealth (net assets) and income that are consistent with the position taken throughout this book.

It will be recalled that we have referred to the total assets of a company, and to the amount of the net assets. We could as easily have used the terms 'wealth' and 'net wealth', for that is substantially what gives security to creditors and the prospect of gain to investors. The terms may be applied equally well to individuals. What then is 'wealth'?

□ 'To be wealthy is have a large stock of useful articles, or the means of purchasing them. Everything forms therefore a part of wealth which has a power of purchasing ... To an individual anything is wealth, which, though useless in itself, enables him to claim from others a part of their stock of things useful or pleasant.' / John Stuart Mill, *Principles of Political Economy*, 1848 /

□ 'Wealth [is used by the author] to signify material objects owned.' The value of a given quantity of wealth is found by multiplying the quantity of it by the price, in exchange, for a unit quantity. It is not necessary that an exchange shall take place, or shall have taken place, in order that this calculation may be made. Recourse may be had to an estimate of 'what price the article would or should fetch'. Value is thus 'not a subjective magnitude in the mind of man, but purely objective'. / Abstracted from Irving Fisher, *The Nature of Capital and Income*, 1906, pp. 3–14 /

□ 'The firm's fortune at any moment comprises the market value at that moment of all the material objects and legal rights which it then possesses, plus the money it has, plus the debts owed to it less those it owes to others.' / G L S Shackle, *Expectation, Enterprise and Profit*, 1970, p. 28 /

And what is income?

□ 'Personal income may be defined as the algebraic sum of (1) the market value of rights exercised in consumption and (2) the change in the value of the store of property rights between the beginning and the end of the period in question ... without regard for anything which happened before the beginning of that interval or for what may happen in subsequent periods ... The essential connotation of income, to repeat, is *gain*—gain *to* someone during a specified period and measured according to objective market standards.' / H C Simons, *Personal Income Taxation*, 1938, p. 50 /

□ '[The definition of income of a past week, which] for most purposes ... is the most important [is that it] equals the value of the individual's consumption *plus* the increment to the money value of his prospect which has accrued during the week; it equals consumption *plus* capital accumulation ... [it is] an objective magnitude ... [involving] a comparison between present values [i.e., market prices] and values which belong wholly to the past.' / J R Hicks, *Value and Capital*, 1946, pp. 178–9 /

□ With the object of distinguishing the products of conventional accounting from the information necessary in deliberate economic analysis, Lipsey and Steiner set up the accounts of an imaginary firm on two bases. They deprecate information produced by the conventional process. By contrast, the 'economist's balance sheet' is shown clearly to be based on market prices of assets at the balancing date, depreciation is shown as the difference between opening and closing market prices of assets, and the income of the preceding period is the difference between the opening and closing amounts of the net equity calculated in the same way. / Richard G Lipsey and Peter O Steiner, *Economics*, 1966, p. 207 /

These economists wrote quite independently of debates about accounting rules, but with the object of clarifying the meaning of wealth and income and their relation to action, choice and policy. Clearly they contemplate the discovery of wealth by reference to market prices (selling prices to the present holder) and the discovery of income by reference to wealth so measured at two points of time.

Finally, we note an observation (typical of observations by others) relating to the connection between the costs of goods and the decisions made by their holders. The writer makes it plain that the *present* cost of a good—the alternative forgone—is the cost that is presently relevant to decisions.

□ 'What are the costs of production of a stock of goods already in the seller's possession? It is tempting to reply that the costs are the sums of money which were previously paid for the stock of goods, but is this really a sensible answer? Is the money spent in the past an alternative to holding the stock of goods? It is apparent from this question that past outlays cannot directly influence present alternatives, and hence present costs. If I "bought" Brooklyn Bridge for $500, that is not its present cost—or foregone alternative—to me, and similarly, if I bought wheat at $1.00 a bushel, that is not its present cost to me. To insist on recovering historical costs is irrational, and people who obstinately insist on doing so must be phenomenally lucky to avoid the bankruptcy courts.' / George J Stigler, *The Theory of Price*, 1946, p. 149 /

The alternative forgone by holding any asset is, of course, its present market price. In all settings, therefore, from trading decisions to financial analysis and decisions, market prices are pertinent to choice and action.

CONCLUSION

Experts in every field develop their specialties in ways understandable to themselves. But the products of every specialty are expected to serve others than their producers. It is reasonable therefore to judge the product by reference to its uses, the opinions of its users and the views of independent observers of the conditions under which it is used.

Accountants have justified some of the conventional rules in terms of pure stewardship or custodial reporting, with an eye entirely on the past; and other rules in terms of the formation of expectations, with an eye largely on the future. From the circumstances and opinions considered in this chapter it seems clear that users need to have information from time to time, substantially about the present—'jam today', in the words of Alice.

The tasks of security analysts, administrators and tribunals, it seems, have been hindered rather than aided by established, conventional accounting practices. Financial analysts, journalists, jurists, merchant bankers, economists—all find the products of company accounting far from satisfactory. Some have deplored the looseness in practice which makes abortive all attempts to compare the financial features of companies. There is quite clear evidence, in what they have said, to the effect that statements of the financial positions and results of companies are significant only if they are based on the current market prices of assets.

10

'WILL YOU WALK INTO MY PARLOUR?'

'Shareholders must be put in possession of all the facts necessary for the formation of an informed judgment as to the merits or demerits of [a takeover] offer. Such facts must be accurately and fairly presented and be available to the shareholder early enough to enable him to make a decision in good time.'
/ Rule 14, *The City Code on Takeovers and Mergers*, London, 1968 /

'He never wants anything but what's right and fair; only when you come to settle what's right and fair, it's everything that he wants and nothing that you want.'
/ *Tom Brown's Schooldays* /

Builders of conglomerates 'were helped by a number of American accountancy practices which bordered on the whimsical'.
/ Wall Street Correspondent, *Investors Chronicle*, 12 November 1971 /

'Takeover bid' is a relatively new term in the language of corporate business, but the operation it signifies is much older. The merger movements of the 1950s and 1960s are not so very different from the amalgamations and combinations engineered by Rockefeller, Carnegie, Mellon and the Du Ponts about the turn of the century; or the horizontal combinations in a wide range of trades and industries in Britain about the same time. These earlier movements gave rise to debates about the economics of rationalization, the merits of competition, the regulation of monopolies, and the relative efficiencies of large and small scale business. Of course these issues are still of consequence but we shall be concerned with smaller issues.

Many of the earlier mergers, acquisitions or takeovers could serve, and perhaps did serve, as models for more recent exercises. Concealed or distorted information, common enough in the earlier stages of the growth of corporate business, did not, however, attract the kind of attention it has attracted more recently. Even now, more attention is paid to the immediate mechanics of bids, and the fairness of the mechanics to shareholders of offeree companies, than to the fairness of the information available to shareholders in both offeror and offeree companies.

TAKEOVER BIDS AND COUNTERACTIONS

No doubt many mergers and amalgamations are arranged amicably. The parties agree both on the advantages and on the terms of the merger or sale. But a significant number of mergers or proposed mergers come to public notice because there is a substantial public shareholding in either or both companies, and because the alleged advantages or the terms of the merger are contested.

The object of the offeror or bidder is to acquire all, or a sufficient part, of the shares of the offeree company to control the operations and assets of the company. The offeror may seek to use the assets of the offeree in ways more profitable than the management of the offeree: to sell off and lease back properties, thus increasing the working funds available to the offeree company when it has been acquired; to sell off security holdings, or inventories whose values are far greater than those reported in the financial statements of the offeree; or to use the liquid assets and proceeds of sale of other assets of the offeree, either to defray in part the costs of acquiring the offeree, or to boost the funds available to the offeror, saving it recourse to other kinds of financing.

Whatever the aim of the offeror, the directors of the offeree company have a direct and personal interest in the outcome. The offeror must therefore propose terms that are satisfactory in all respects to the board of the offeree, or be prepared to deal directly with shareholders in the face of possible countermeasures by the offeree board or counter-bids by others.

We have already seen that in jurisdictions where assets may be revalued upwards, directors may make revaluations, so that shareholders will be *better* informed about the values of company assets if a takeover bid is made (pp. 59–60). In other jurisdictions, other changes in accounting methods seem to have been prompted by the threat of takeover bids. In March 1969 a member of a panel of leading US certified public accountants expressed the view that the changes in depreciation accounting made in 1968 by a number of steel companies (see, for examples p. 97 above) were intended 'to make the steel companies less subject to takeover bids'.

B F Goodrich, at the time it changed its methods of accounting (see p. 97), was also engaged in staving off a bid for its
ordinary shares (*Australian Financial Review*, 26 March 1969).

So much for threats of takeover bids. The pressure to release
information not previously disclosed to shareholders is even
greater when a bid has been made. The following comment
on an Australian bid both illustrates the release of additional
information and states the case for disclosing that information in
the ordinary course of events:

☐ 'It has taken this bid [by Marra Developments for Squatting Invest-
ments] to prompt directors of Squatting Investments to admit to
shareholders that their shares are backed by at least twice as much
in assets as the last balance sheet shows. The Marra bid, for £1
million in cash, had put a value on each 10s. share that was 6s.
higher than the 35s. 8d. value Squatting directors placed on the
shares in the latest balance sheet. Now Squatting directors say that
this is not enough; that in reality their shares are worth "in excess of
60s." If it is good enough for directors to tell shareholders the real
value of their shares when the potential buyer is trying to take the
company over, it seems curious that shareholders intending to sell
their shares at other times are not entitled to the same information.
But they are not given it. Instead the company's properties are
shown in the books at cost—and it has been operating since 1882!'
/ 'Investor's Notebook', *Australian Financial Review*, 8 October
1963 /

The market price of Squatting Investments shares one month
previous to this date had been 27s. 6d.; the bid raised the market
price to 40s. by early October.

The course of some UK takeover bids in the early 'fifties, before
attempts were made to regulate takeovers, illustrates both the
motivation of some bids (control of assets worth far more than
their reported values) and the extent to which shareholders were
previously misinformed. For the details, our principal source is
Bull and Vice, *Bid for Power* (London, 1961).

☐ J Sears and Company controlled a chain of shoe stores and
other property, 900 shops in all, having a reported 'book' value of
£2·59 million. Its $22\frac{1}{2}$ per cent dividend was covered five times by

available earnings. Late in 1952 the prices of the Sears 5s. ordinary shares began to move upwards; in a few months they rose from 13s. 3d. to 21s. 3d. The Sears directors seem to have suspected a bid for control for, in December, they announced an interim dividend of 15 per cent, and proposed a scrip (or bonus) issue which suggested a liberalization of dividend payments. Early in 1953, Investment Registry (of which Charles Clore was a director) made an offer of 40s. cash for the Sears ordinary shares (or an alternative approximately equivalent). The Sears board raised the dividend to an annual rate of $62\frac{1}{2}$ per cent, proposed a scrip issue of two for one and gave some idea of the current value of Sears' assets. The directors said that £6 million could be raised if necessary on the properties, even disregarding the 350 shops occupied by tenants. The dividend, the proposal and the information were not sufficient to raise the market price to 40s. Investment Registry's offer succeeded. Under Clore's control, property worth £4·5 million was sold; long leases were acquired for the shoe chain; £1·76 million of Sears' debentures were redeemed; and the company still had £4 million worth of property at the end of the year. Sears has since had a very successful history as a holding company.

Consider the defects in the information available to shareholders before the bid by Investment Registry. The company's borrowing power could have been assessed only by reference to the reported value of its properties. Shareholders could have had no idea that the company's earnings could be 'geared up', by borrowing to the extent of £6 million; properties reported to be worth £2·59 million could not support such borrowing. In fact, if the company could have borrowed £6 million on the security of part of its assets, it was likely that Sears' properties were worth in excess of £10 million. Lacking this knowledge, shareholders were unable to calculate a rate of return on the current value of the assets. The incumbent directors would thus have been credited with results superior to the effective current results and would have been shielded from criticism by the scale of the reported results. Further, the disclosure of Sears' borrowing power was quite a roundabout way of indicating the worth of the company's assets. How much more than £6 million the assets were worth, shareholders were left to guess. At the least this seems a strange way of acting in the interest of the company or of its shareholders, a function usually ascribed to company directors.

Other bids have been substantially similar in pattern:

☐ When House of Fraser acquired Scottish Drapery Corporation in 1952, it acquired net assets worth about £4·6 million for approximately £3 million. For shares which were quoted at 30s., Fraser had offered £3. When Fraser bid for Binns of Sunderland in 1953, it offered over £18 for the Binns ordinaries which just previously had been quoted at £6 5s. The Binns properties were shown in the accounts at a value of £1·6 million. The directors of Binns countered with the information that a revaluation put the net tangible assets at £4·8 million; and with a proposal to raise the dividend rate from 25 per cent to $187\frac{1}{2}$ per cent. Fraser raised the amount of the bid to just over £19, at which price the bid succeeded against the opposition of the Binns board.

☐ In 1954 Great Universal Stores (GUS), under the management of Isaac Wolfson, became interested in acquiring Jones and Higgins, a drapery and furnishing store. Wolfson would offer one GUS 5s. 'A' ordinary share (market price about 75s.) for every Jones and Higgins £1 ordinary share (market price about 42s.) The offer was rejected. (Note that these events occurred before it became obligatory to make the existence of bids known to shareholders.) Some months later the directors of Jones and Higgins proposed to pay £2 to shareholders for every share held, but to cut the dividend rate from $13\frac{1}{2}$ per cent to 10 per cent. The cash required was to be obtained by the sale of certain freeholds. This intimation seemed to suggest that Jones and Higgins' assets were much greater in value than the market price of 42s. per share. The market rose to 72s. GUS then made an offer of 90s. cash. The Jones and Higgins board countered: GUS would be gaining for 90s. assets worth £6; Jones and Higgins was prepared to sell its remaining freeholds and distribute the gains to shareholders. But this proposal would not reach the value offered by GUS. Jones and Higgins next obtained a bid of £5 cash from Macowards, another store group. GUS reverted to the offer of one 'A' ordinary share, by this time worth about 115s. An offer from another quarter worth about £6 was never confirmed by the bidder. Jones and Higgins capitulated.

THE MISINFORMED SHAREHOLDER

From cases such as these we may depict the general circumstances of those offeree companies that are especially attractive to bidders.

They are commonly companies that have been in business for many years, over which the values (market prices) of their land, buildings and other assets will have risen. The use of original costs or other out-of-date asset values will seriously understate the value of the risk capital (or the net assets) employed, and it will tend automatically, and artificially, to boost the rate of return. Suppose a company earns 15 per cent per annum on the *cost* of its assets over a series of years in which the market prices of those or similar assets have risen by 20 per cent. The maintenance of a 15 per cent return indicates that the company has not sought (or has not found) ways of raising its revenues while other prices have been rising. Its financial efficiency will have declined relatively to other companies, for the rise in the market prices of its assets entails that other companies can earn satisfactory profits on investments made at those higher prices.

The incumbent management may be ignorant of the decline in financial efficiency, and complacent with its performance, if it pays attention only to the rate of return on the *cost* of the company's assets. It may forgo the opportunity of borrowing, on the higher current values of its assets, to increase its earnings, in the belief that shareholders will be satisfied with the maintenance of the company's rate of return. The management of a static or declining company may even be secretly grateful for a professionally endorsed style of accounting which represents that the rate of return has not declined, and which therefore shields it from criticism by shareholders.

But no company is an island. Ignorant and complacent managers and directors leave their companies and shareholders at the mercy of diligent and inquisitive outsiders or competitors. Property values are a matter of record (for rating and taxing purposes); the value of the association of Clore and other property developers with experts in real estate is made clear by Oliver Marriott in *The Property Boom* (London, 1967). Several studies have pointed out the frequency with which offeror and offeree companies have been in the same trade or industry; it is not difficult to imagine that useful estimates may be made of the relative strengths and asset values of companies in one's own industry. On both grounds an offeror may be far better informed of financial facts that are relevant to shareholders of offeree companies than those shareholders themselves. It is unimaginable that such large premiums on the pre-bid prices of shares would be offered by bidders without substantial grounds for their bids.

The success of the offeror thus turns largely on his superior knowledge of the values of the assets of the offeree company. He also has the tactical advantage of having explored the prospect of redeploying those assets. Shareholders of the offeree company, and in some cases the directors, suffer the disadvantage of surprise. If shareholders are given new information on asset values, or new dividend promises, they are unable to relate these to the 'old' information and dividend rates to which they have become accustomed. Little wonder that offerors may make handsome gains when they are successful. Indeed, if they have bought into the offeree company to lay a foundation for a bid for control, they may make handsome gains even if the offer fails—for it will have pushed up share prices, sometimes substantially, at which higher prices they may sell off their holdings. The main point, however, is that the element of surprise stems from the degree to which conventional accounting has concealed past results and the present worth of the offeree's assets.

'FAIR EXCHANGE?'

A bid made in terms of an exchange of shares may seem to be straightforward, for the market value of the shares of the two companies may be said to be comparable; they are amounts of cash, prices established in the market. But the market value of the shares offered often exceeds by material amounts the market value of the shares sought in exchange. This indicates that there is more at stake than the disclosed position and results of the offeree company; for if the real position and results coincided with the reported position and results, the market prices of the shares would be considered to have been fairly established, and an exchange on the basis of market prices of the two shares would be a fair exchange. What is unfair about some takeovers by exchange of shares is that the share prices are not prices established in a fairly informed market.

Suppose Company A has net assets worth $4 per share, and a rate of return of 15 per cent on the amount of its net assets. Suppose B Company has net assets worth $5 per share, and a rate of return of 15 per cent on its net assets. Suppose also that the figures given for the two companies are derived from accounts kept uniformly in terms of up-to-date asset values, or prices. All other things being equal, the price of B shares would be higher than the price of A shares. An offer by A to acquire the shares of B would have to compensate for the greater value of assets per share of B.

Now suppose that the methods of accounting of A and B (for exactly the same assets, equities and transactions as before) are different—as in fact is the case for almost any two actual companies. Suppose that A reports in terms of up-to-date asset prices as before; but B reports, conservatively or in terms of out-of-date prices, net assets worth $4 per share and a rate of return of, say, 13 per cent on net assets. In this case, all other things being equal, the price of B shares would be lower than the price of A shares. The market will have undervalued the B shares, due solely to the conservative (or unrealistic) mode of accounting that B followed. An offer by A to acquire the shares of B by a one-for-one exchange of shares would seem to be attractive to B shareholders. If the offer succeeded, B shareholders will have sacrificed a higher equity in the assets of B for a lower equity in the assets of (A + B); and A shareholders will have gained. This would occur through no fault of B shareholders and no special wisdom or skill on the part of A shareholders. The cause of the involuntary redistribution of rights and interests will have been the differences between the accounting methods of the two companies and the effects on share prices of what the accounts of the companies disclosed.

In practice, there may be no way of telling whether an offeror company or an offeree company is the more wealthy or the more profitable of the two. But the analysis suggests that companies valuing assets at up-to-date prices and calculating profits on that footing will be able to bid successfully and inexpensively for the shares of companies that in fact have superior assets per share and rates of return. A securities market in which such inequities can occur cannot reasonably be described as a fair market. Nor can a system which produces financial information having such inequitable consequences be considered an adequate auxiliary to a fair market.

TAKEOVER BIDS AND SHARE PRICES

There are, of course, some who hold that investors make some allowance for the possible undervaluation of assets and understatement of past gains. How those allowances may be made and how they affect market prices of securities has not been explained.

The history of many takeovers makes it clear that, if any such allowance is made (by way of higher share prices than the reported results and position warrant), it is very modest by comparison with the premiums that bidders are prepared to offer. The price obtained by shareholders in Sears was about three times the market price of the shares before Investment Registry entered the market. Scottish Drapery shareholders obtained double the pre-bid price; Binns shareholders, three times the pre-bid price; Jones and Higgins shareholders, just under three times the pre-bid price.

An aggregative study of movements in the share prices of 'victim' firms in the United Kingdom in 1967–68 lends support to the view that the 'pre-bid' market is inadequately informed.

☐ 'The final bid prices in [161] uncontested mergers were on average 33·4% higher than the prices four weeks before the first bid; the mean increases for the [62] contested bids were much higher, 77% in the case of those [27] contested by directors and 73·9% where [in 35 cases] third parties were involved,' / Gerald D Newbould, *Management and Merger Activity*, Liverpool, 1970, p. 56 /

Or consider some Australian examples. The following rises in the market prices of shares of offeree companies occurred, following the making of takeover bids at substantial premiums, up to the announced closing date for acceptance of the offer:

Offeror	Offeree	Year	Percentage rise in market prices of ordinaries of offeree company
David Jones	Charles Birks	1954	112
G J Coles	Manton & Sons	1955	256
David Jones	Finney Isles	1955	153
G J Coles	John Connell	1958	121
Colonial Sugar	Masonite	1959	120
H C Sleigh	Adelaide Steamship	1959	148
Ralph Symonds	Beale	1960	168
Howard Smith	Melbourne Steamship	1961	177

Rises in the market prices of offeree shares to two or three times the pre-bid price may not be typical. However the offeree companies were all long-established listed companies, grounds enough for considering them as companies whose share prices depended in part on the financial information they published.

As none of the English or Australian offeree companies mentioned were speculative in character, the only causes of such marked changes in share prices can have been the occurrence of the bids and the clues that they gave to concealed assets or profits.

It may be foolish to entertain sympathy for shareholders, whose investments necessarily entail risks. But there is no good reason why the risks should be compounded by the concealment of asset values and by the unpredictable emergence of well-informed bidders. A holder of £1,000 worth of Sears shares in late 1952 would have found himself with £3,000 a few months later; an investor who sold £1,000 worth of Sears in late 1952 could scarcely feel satisfied with a system which dropped a £2,000 gain into the lap of his successor in a few months, from what would seem an entirely fortuitous event—the takeover bid.

One final example:

☐ The Australia Hotel Company owned and operated a hotel in the centre of Sydney. It reported a loss in 1967; its ordinaries sold from $1.20 to $0.40 during the year. Two bids were made for its shares in late 1967, at 80c and 90c cash per share, no doubt to acquire the real estate for redevelopment. In early 1968 it was disclosed that MLC Assurance Company and Lend Lease Corporation had acquired in the market substantial holdings of the shares; by August, they held over 80 per cent between them. As share prices in 1968 varied between $1.05 and $0.90, it may be supposed that MLC and Lend Lease acquired their holdings at about $1.00 or less. The reported value of the company's assets in June 1968 was $4.75 million, equivalent to 66c per share. In February 1970 the hotel was sold at auction to MLC on a 'walk-in, walk-out' basis for $9.6 million or almost $2 per share after allowing for prior charges. In July 1970 M.L.C. announced the closing of the business and forecast a return to shareholders of $2.02 per share.

Whether so many shareholders would have sold at $1 or less per share in 1967–68 if they had known that the assets were worth $2 and not 66c per share, no one can say. Certainly they lacked the information that MLC and Lend Lease—as financiers and developers—could have had. It is hard to avoid the conclusion that the absence of current valuations from the accounts was contributory, at least to some extent, to the profit of the order of $4 million which in two years accrued to the two companies mentioned.

A TRUE AND FAIR VIEW

No one can say after the event what the pre-bid prices of the shares of offeree companies would have been if the financial statements of those companies had been based on up-to-date asset prices. But it seems to be entirely reasonable to hold that the published financial statements did not give a true and fair view of the financial positions and results of those companies.

To judge fairly the merits of a bid, shareholders of offeree companies would need to know the current market values of the assets of their companies. The value of the net assets is the lower limit to the price they should accept from a bidder, for this amount could be obtained from piece-meal sale of the assets. Undervaluation of assets lowers this 'floor'. Shareholders would need to know the full rate of periodical growth in net assets. Conventionally the only periodically reported source of growth is net profit from trading operations; the periodical growth (or decline) in asset values is disregarded. Yet this may be just as important an element of the growth of a company as its trading gains, and just as important an indication of strength and prospects as conventional net profits. Shareholders would need to know the present real relationship between debt and equity. For if the debt-to-equity ratio of an offeree company is high, merger may enhance the prospects of growth of its class of business; and if the debt-to-equity ratio is low, merger may be a device of the offeror company for improving its own debt-to-equity ratio. Shareholders would need to know the effective current rate of return (inclusive of all gains). But understatement of asset values and of the periodical rate of growth in asset values yields a rate of return that may be distorted upwards or downwards to an unknown extent. As merger or takeover proposals may occur at any time, clearly shareholders of all companies should have information on all these matters, free of understatements and distortions.

But what do we find? In the case of Sears, property values were reported at about one-quarter of their current market values in 1952. In the case of Binns, property values were shown at about one-third of their current values in 1953. House of Fraser offered double the market price for the shares of Scottish Drapery and still acquired, for £3 million, net assets worth about £4·6 million.

Property development may seem to be a highly speculative exercise; and property development in London after long post-war years of constraint and regulation may seem to be in a class by itself. However the rate at which urban redevelopment is occurring all round the world suggests that out-dated property valuations will continue to provide developers with opportunities for gain at the expense of uninformed shareholders. Marriott (*The Property Boom*) gives a number of instances of the extent to which financial statements prepared on traditional principles were grossly misleading.

☐ 'The accounts of Stock Conversion [a property development company] were prepared on some ultra-conservative principles. By 1960 a writer in the *Investors Chronicle* had laboriously dug around behind the published figures and came up with what then seemed the rather wild estimate that the net asset value backing each ordinary share was not 3s. 6d. as the figures showed, but closer to 120s. Robert Clark [Chairman] was asked about this by a shareholder soon afterwards at the company's annual meeting. All he would reply austerely, in his clipped Scottish accent, was that the estimate was "very enterprising".

By 1960 insiders and students of obscure companies had woken up to the possibility that Stock Conversion might be a vast ice-berg. One clue had been a dramatic and regular increase in the company's borrowing powers. In 1954 these had been raised to £1 million. In 1957 ... to £2 million, in 1958 to £4 million and in 1960 ... to £8 million. 1959 was the year in which the share price began its long climb, having drifted for two years between a bottom of 6s. 4d. and a top of 20s. In 1959 ... [the price] leapt from a low of £1 to just over £3. The next year ... to £12. In 1961 it hit £25 10s. In the space of three years [shareholders] had seen their shares multiply in value by a cool twenty-five times.'

Dealing with the growth of Nigel Broakes' Trafalgar House company, Marriott recounts Broakes' 'discovery' of three companies he might wish to acquire.

☐ '[Broakes] decided to investigate them property by property. They were all publicly quoted companies run by the same highly respectable but sleepy management. The assets sat in the balance sheet at well under true values, no attempt had been made to develop old properties and the capital structures were archaic.' (p. 207).

Broakes acquired one of the companies and assisted others to acquire the other two.

If the differences between reported asset values and current market values of assets are small, they may not have a material effect on the values of rates of return, of assets per share, and of debt-to-equity ratios. But where book values are as low as one-third or one-quarter of market values, it cannot reasonably be said that a true and fair view of a company's state of affairs or its results is given. It may be argued, of course, that the cases we have mentioned are unusual, that in only relatively few cases are there such discrepancies as those we have noticed. But the practices that lead to gross understatement are generally acceptable practices, and many takeover bids are accepted without contests that lead to the disclosure of up-to-date asset values. It follows that shareholders of offeree companies may be misled on a greater scale than is suggested by the mere number of contested bids or the mere number of cases of (subsequently) revealed understatement.

SHAREHOLDERS' PROTESTS

If things are as bad as they seem, it might be expected that there would be aggrieved and bitter protests from shareholders who parted with shares at prices far below the prices offered shortly afterwards by takeover bidders. There are plausible reasons for the lack of protests. Those who claim expertise in investment and security analysis would naturally be unwilling to expose their earlier mistakes in evaluating shares and their prospects. Those who are not expert may well believe that the shift in share values was due to matters of which they could not have had prior knowledge. The curiosities of accounting doctrine and practice are beyond them. They cannot help but believe that financial statements, duly audited and said to give a true and fair view, could not be so wide of the mark as to grossly mislead them. Notwithstanding this, there have been some protests:

☐ A shareholder in Borax Consolidated complained in 1955 to 'Candidus' (a financial columnist) about his dealings in the shares. When the market price was about 80s., a broker advised him that the break up (or asset) value of the shares was about 40s. He sold. An American bid was subsequently made of 100s. per share. The directors thereupon pointed out that the assets were worth more than the amount of the bid. The market value of certain shares held by Borax was £3·6 million; the balance sheet value was £339,464. The company's buildings, plant and machinery (excluding land) in the US had recently been valued at £7·1 million; the group balance sheet showed £5·9 million for all physical fixed assets, including the assets in the US and factories and mines in at least six other countries. Under pressure from the bid, the directors pointed out that if shareholders sold at 100s. or even more they 'will not only be deprived of the steadily improving rewards that your Board foresees, but will be parting with assets far below their true value'. / *Investors Chronicle*, 29 January 1955 /

Unfortunate indeed for the shareholder who on advice sold at 80s.

☐ Mark Foy's ('the home of good value'), Sydney retailer, experienced a series of difficult trading years in the sixties. Its 50c shares had sold at as little as 25 cents in 1967 following a reported loss for the year ended in January 1967. In February 1968 there were 'informal talks' with an undisclosed bidder for the shares at $1.10. By then the shares had risen to $1.25. In March, McDowells, also a retailer, offered $2.05 per share, or $4·3 million in all. Mark Foy's directors recommended acceptance of the bid, but dissident share-holders, representing about 20 per cent of the shares, counselled shareholders against 'selling their equity too cheaply'. In April the company reported a 1968 profit of $183,000, in contrast with a loss of $140,000 in 1967; and the directors forecast that the profit for the current year, 'should be more than double that for the year just closed'. It was also disclosed that in the previous year the company had sold two of its properties for $750,000, for a 'capital profit' of $463,000.

Dissident shareholders pressed for up-to-date valuations of the company's properties. But it was not until the annual general meeting on 15 May that directors advised that an expert valuation of the freeholds in December 1967 put them at $6·95 million—3 times the figure reported in the 1968 accounts. Needless to say, the long silence of the Mark Foy's board on the current value of the properties provoked injured expostulation from shareholders at the meeting. The current valuation would have given ordinary shareholders' equity of $8·29 million (or $3.84 per share) instead of the reported $3·32 million (or $1.44 per share). But the information was 'too late'. By June, McDowells had acquired nearly 95 per cent of the shares.

P.S. In April 1969, McDowells announced that three of the Mark Foy's properties had been sold for a profit of $1·76 million. This prompted a former managing director of Mark Foy's to write with some irony of the takeover: 'In the event, McDowells were pressed to accept $7 million in real estate for a price of $4 million and, if further inducement were needed, they were asked to accept $2 million worth of stock and assets and the goodwill of a large competitor for nothing ... To the death, Mark Foy's remained "the home of good value".' / *Australian Financial Review*, 1 May 1969 /

One form of protest is to challenge the basis of compulsory acquisition of shares when the majority of shareholders have accepted an offer.

☐ The *Press Caps* case was an English case in which a shareholder objected to the acquisition by Metal Box Company of his shares at a rate based on the market prices of Press Caps and Metal Box shares. His argument was that the Press Caps balance sheet understated the then current value of the company's freehold by some £60,000, and that the market price of Press Caps shares was based on inadequate information about the company. Finding for the applicant, the judge said: 'If you find admitted so large a discrepancy as an undervaluation of the most important asset in the balance sheet of this company, an admitted undervaluation of no less than £60,000, I should have thought that threw a great deal of doubt on the appropriateness of the balance sheet as an estimate of value, and through that, therefore, it also threw doubt on the market price of the shares'.

Metal Box appealed the decision and the Court of Appeals found in its favour. The judgments of the Court turned to some extent on the 'fairness' of the rate at which the shares of the two companies were to be exchanged. The effects of undervaluation of assets in the Press Caps balance sheet on the price of Press Caps shares were not explored. In any such case, if the shareholders of an offeree company were to know the market prices of the assets severally, they would be able to judge whether it were better to sell the assets piecemeal than to dispose of the assets and undertaking, lock, stock and barrel, by an exchange of shares. The possibility of doing this is foreclosed against shareholders when they have no knowledge of the current values of assets. The appeal judges seem to have depended, in part at least, on the notions (a) that balance-sheet figures are not valuations (which gives rise to the question, what then is the use of such figures?), and (b) that balance-sheet figures do no more than accurately represent the state of accounts in the books of the company (which seems to be quite at odds with the legal dicta cited in an earlier chapter; see p. 26). These two lines of argument are of a piece with the conventional practices of accounting. But they are obscurantist in effect and interfere with the right of shareholders to be reliably informed of the properties in which they have equities.

WHAT IS 'NOT MISLEADING'?

Rule 10b-5 under the US Securities Exchange Act of 1934 makes it

> 'unlawful for any person, directly or indirectly, ... to make any untrue statement of a material fact or to omit to state a material fact necessary in order to make the statements made, in the light of the circumstances under which they were made, not misleading ... in connection with the purchase or sale of any security.'

The rule is very wide in scope. We consider its application to the case where a company has a majority shareholding in one company and seeks to acquire the shares of the minority shareholders. The rule operates against the use of inside information by principal shareholders to their advantage and to the detriment of other uninformed shareholders. The cases we shall notice are not typical takeovers of the kind dealt with so far in this chapter but they illustrate the significance to shareholders, in the view of the tribunals, of knowledge of the up-to-date market prices of company assets.

☐ / *Speed* v. *Transamerica Corporation* (1951) / Transamerica Corporation was a majority stockholder of Axton-Fisher Tobacco Company. Axton-Fisher's financial statements showed the value of its large tobacco inventory at average cost. Transamerica, by virtue of its position, knew that the market value of the tobacco was greatly in excess of the reported values; the minority shareholders did not know this. Transamerica bought most of the minority-held stock at a price in excess of the current market value of Axton-Fisher shares, but far below the value of the Axton-Fisher assets. It then caused Axton-Fisher to sell some of its tobacco, distribute the rest to its stockholders by means of warehouse receipts and dissolve. One, Speed, and others brought an action based on Rule 10b-5.

The Court found for the plaintiffs. The difference between the book value and the market value of the tobacco inventory was held to be a material fact affecting the value of Axton-Fisher stock, and the judgment of the sellers of that stock. Said the Judge: 'The duty of disclosure stems from the necessity of preventing a corporate insider from utilizing his position to take unfair advantage of the uninformed minority stockholders. It is an attempt to provide some degree of equalization of bargaining position in order that the minority may exercise an informed judgment in any such transaction'.

The above account is digested from *Securities Regulation* by Professor L Loss, a standard work on its subject (see 2nd ed., 1961, vol. III, pp. 1458–62). Loss notes that the Judge emphasized that his conclusion was based on his finding that Transamerica had intended to merge, dissolve or liquidate Axton-Fisher. This intention certainly gives point to the significance of the market price. But, as Loss observes, the intention to liquidate

□ 'is not an indispensable element of an insider's violating Rule 10b-5 by non-disclosure. Suppose an insider has advance knowledge that his company has struck oil or is about to obtain an extremely profitable contract. Clearly his buying stock without disclosing that fact violates the rule whether or not he plans to liquidate, or could if he wanted to; for the market is going to go up when the news gets out. What is the difference when the hidden information is the fact that the company has an inventory worth twice the amount at which it is carried on the books?

'It is no answer that accounting practice normally favors the carrying of assets at cost or market, whichever is *lower*, so as to present a conservative rather than a roseate view of the company's affairs. The cost-or-market-whichever-is-lower formula operates in quite the reverse manner, of course, when the company is *buying* rather than *selling* its securities. Nor is it an answer that the [Securities and Exchange] Commission's accounting rules do not specifically require inventory to be priced at market value. For Regulation S-X does provide that the specified information shall be furnished "as a minimum requirement to which shall be added such further material information as is necessary to make the required statements ... not misleading".'

Such cases as this seem to be treated as if the circumstances were special; Rule 10b-5, it will be recalled, refers to 'the statements made, in the light of the circumstances under which they were made'. But the rule is of perfectly general application. No buyer or seller of shares in a company can know when it will become the subject of another's intention to merge, acquire or liquidate the company. So much for the merger or takeover situation. Equally, no buyer or seller of shares can know when the issuing company will itself choose to liquidate one or more of its assets at a price materially different from a book value based on traditional accounting rules, for such decisions may not even confront company officers until some substantial offer is made by previously unknown outsiders.

□ / *Gerstle et al* v. *Gamble-Skogmo Inc.* (1968) / The plaintiffs were minority holders of stock in a company, General Outdoor Advertising Company ('General' hereafter), in which the defendant ('Gamble' hereafter) was a majority holder. At various dates in 1962 and 1963, General had obtained appraisals of its assets which indicated that they had a sales value of two-and-one-half to four times the book value. In 1962 General received advice from one investment banker that the fair market value of its assets was $13 per share greater than the book value of the assets. General and Gamble proposed to merge. General's balance sheet, mailed to shareholders with statements soliciting proxies in favour of the merger, showed its property, plant and equipment at cost, $20 million. The proxy statement stated also that, based on appraisals and prices obtained on previous sales, the remaining parcels of real estate had a value, under certain conditions, of approximately $3,700,000 or $839,000 in excess of the book value of $2,861,000. In the nine months following the merger General sold the remainder of its properties and its Mexican business for $25 million, realizing a profit before taxes of $14 million (i.e. a surplus over book values). The action was brought on the ground that the information disclosed had been insufficient to make the proxy material not misleading. The Court found a violation of Rule 14a-9.

In the course of the proceedings, the SEC submitted a memorandum, as *amicus curiae*. It affirmed the general rule of the Commission that fixed assets should generally be carried at historical cost less depreciation. It then proceeded to discuss the Commission's Rule 14a-9, under Section 14(a) of the 1934 Act, which prohibits the use of a proxy statement that 'omits to state any material fact necessary to make the statements therein not false or misleading'. A number of cases bearing on the matter were cited and the following opinion was quoted:

☐ 'It is the duty of one selling securities ... not only to state truthfully what he actually tells, but also not to suppress any facts within his knowledge which will materially change or alter the effect of the facts actually stated. To tell less than the whole truth may constitute a false and fraudulent misrepresentation. A partial and fragmentary disclosure of certain facts ..., accompanied by the wilful concealment of material facts which change the effect of the facts actually stated, is as much a fraud as an actual positive misrepresentation.'

Continuing, the Memorandum pointed out that the Commission's accounting rules and generally accepted accounting principles often prescribe a single set of accounting standards regardless of the use to be made of the financial statements.

But 'in many instances the disclosure needs of a particular situation may not coincide with the assumed purposes on which the accounting standards are based'. Where this is the case the proxy material must contain 'the additional material information that may not be put in the financial statements themselves but is necessary under the circumstances to make the proxy statement not misleading'.

Such additional information, said the Commission, may be necessary if the balance sheet gives asset values substantially below resale prices, (a) where there is a definite intention to liquidate one company after a merger, (b) where there is a fairly ready market for the assets of a corporation, even in the absence of a definite intention to liquidate, and (c) where a ready market exists for only a substantial portion of the assets and partial liquidation of the assets is possible.

The concluding section of the Memorandum included the opinion that existing appraisals of the liquidating value of assets (their resale prices) must be disclosed in proxy material, if they have been made by a qualified expert, if they have a sufficient basis in fact and if their omission would render the proxy statement materially misleading. Attention was drawn to the Commission's brief, *amicus curiae*, in *Speed* v. *Transamerica Corporation* where it took the position that the amount of the appreciation was required to be disclosed even in the absence of intention to liquidate the appreciated assets. Other cases are mentioned in which it was held that the fair market values should be disclosed where failure to do so would make the proxy statement materially misleading.

The SEC's argument draws a distinction where there seems to be little difference. It was empowered to prescribe the kind of financial information to be given in periodical financial statements, which it deemed 'necessary or appropriate for the proper protection of investors and to insure fair dealing' in company securities. Whatever 'assumed purposes' underlay the accounting standards it proposed or endorsed, they must relate to the protection of investors (against ignorance) when buying or selling securities. Now, if there is a 'fairly ready market' for some of the assets of a company, there is no less reason for the disclosure of the 'liquidating values' of those assets in periodical financial statements, than there is for their disclosure in proxy material in the 'particular situations' of *Speed* and *Gerstle*. The SEC did not carry its argument to that point, however; the circumstances did not require it to do so.

But the element of contradiction remains. The SEC rules on periodical financial statements oblige investors to deal in ignorance of the up-to-date values of assets in all circumstances other than those similar to Speed and Gerstle. And the position of the SEC on proxy material arbitrarily discriminates between investors who buy or sell up to the issue date of proxy material and those who buy and sell after that date. For before that date they have access only to the information in the latest published financial statements; after that date they may have information, as well, on the current market prices of at least some assets. Further, in taking two different positions on asset valuation, the SEC takes no account of their differential effects on debt-to-equity and rate of return calculations; its rules oblige analysts and others to use figures in these calculations which are irrelevant to the proper assessment of the financial characteristics of securities.

Professor Homer Kripke, formerly an officer of the SEC and now Professor of Law, New York University, has recently summed up the situation of the SEC thus:

□ 'First, the Commission seems to say that [current market] values need only to be disclosed if they seem likely to be realized by a sale of the properties. This reverts to the old argument that values of most fixed assets are irrelevant because they are not going to be sold, and that cost is the relevant basis for the depreciation charge. To this there are now two answers: (1) The view increasingly prevalent among economists and academic accountants is that the true economic measure of the cost of using fixed assets is depreciation based on values, not depreciation based on historical cost, because it is the opportunity to realize values by sale that is being forgone by continuing operations. (2) Neither the SEC nor anyone else can properly determine whether the assets are going to be sold until the facts are disclosed to stockholders and they decide whether they want to install a management which will sell the properties to realize the values. Disclosure of values thus seems relevant in any proxy statement in which stockholders elect management, and surely in any proxy statement covering a merger or similar situation in which the stockholder must decide the future of his investment ... and in any information on which existing stockholders and prospective stockholders may determine whether to buy, sell or hold ...

'My second major concern is with the concept in the SEC brief [in the *Gerstle* case] that accounting is to remain purely on a cost basis, while the really necessary disclosure of financial facts is to be made outside the accounting system. This would reduce accounting to a decorative role ...

'In summary, the SEC has both substantively and administratively created a dangerous dilemma between its insistence on the cost basis of accounting and its own full disclosure and anti-fraud concepts. It will find its position increasingly impossible unless it re-examines its whole insistence on historical cost accounting.' / 'The SEC, The Accountants, Some Myths and Some Realities', *New York University Law Review*, December 1970 /

'POOLING' ACCOUNTING

One outgrowth of the general acceptance in the United States of the historical cost principle of accounting was the 'pooling of interests' method of accounting for business combinations.

Suppose that the net assets of Company *B* were $600,000, based on historical cost valuations, and its net income was $60,000. Suppose that Company *A* acquired Company *B* by an exchange of shares, issuing Company *A* shares worth, say, $1 million on the market at the date *B* was acquired. Suppose also that the fair market value of the assets of *B* was $800,000 at that date, so that in effect $200,000 was being paid for 'goodwill'. The long-standing way of bringing the assets of *B* into the accounts of *A* is to value them at fair market value, that is, the cost to *A*.

Now, whereas the income of *B* was at the rate of 10 per cent on the reported value of the net assets of *B*, the same income would only be 6 per cent of the consideration given by *A* for *B*. *A* would have to make the assets and business acquired from *B* 'work much harder' to keep up the rate of return after paying $1 million for *B*. To avoid this, and to obtain certain other tactical advantages, the 'pooling of interests' idea was developed. *A* would record the assets acquired at their book values to *B* before the combination; and the consideration given by *A* would be recorded at the book value of the shares issued to shareholders of *B*.

Whatever the justification for this kind of accounting, it will be clear that it ranks book values as superior information to market prices and results in the misrepresentation of the real financial terms under which the combination was negotiated. And insofar as it understates the values of assets that depreciate (plant, buildings), it enables the income of future years to be relieved of depreciation charges which would be based on the higher market values under accepted principles of accounting.

☐ In 1956, Union Carbide and Carbon Corporation acquired the business and assets of Visking Corporation. The book value of the assets of Visking was $25 million. The market value of the shares issued by Union Carbide was approximately $97 million. By using the book values of Visking in its accounts after the combination was effected, Union Carbide understated the 'cost' to it of Visking by $72 million, and reduced 'by $72 million the charges to future income accounts, charges which would otherwise have been made if the $72 million was apportionable to tangible assets or to goodwill subject to amortization'. / Arthur R Wyatt, *A Critical Study of Accounting for Business Combinations*, 1963 /

☐ When Litton Industries acquired American Book Company and Jefferson Electric Company and accounted for the assets on a pooling basis in 1967, it 'suppressed' $80 million in values. 'As a result the corporation's earnings will be exaggerated over the [subsequent] years by the amount thus suppressed.' / Abraham J Briloff, 'Distortions Arising from Pooling of Interests Accounting', *Financial Analysis Journal*, March-April 1968 /

There are many other examples in the periodical literature. When so much turns on the proper valuation of assets—solvency, borrowing power and rate of return—it is impossible to see how investors can knowledgeably watch their interests in these circumstances. It is not to the point to say that, if asset values are concealed, the solvency and borrowing power of a company may therefore be the higher. Concealment means that no one can tell whether solvency and borrowing power are better, or worse, than what is disclosed.

Pooling has other tactical consequences. If the market prices of 'pooled' assets exceed their book values, the company can sell off assets selectively, boosting its reported income by the realized difference between book value and selling price. This difference is quite properly a gain, but a gain previously concealed. The criticism relates to the fact that it can be 'made to appear' when its inclusion in the results of any year is 'desirable' to the management, and that is principally to maintain or boost reported earnings per share.

Pooling has come under sharp criticism by the accounting profession in recent years. But astute managers have found that they can obtain similar effects by a version of 'purchase' accounting which does account for the full purchase consideration. The tangible assets are brought into the acquiring company's accounts at their old book values; the difference between these book values and the consideration given is described as goodwill or by some other euphemism; and the company has stated its intention to defer (perhaps indefinitely) the amortization of goodwill. There the difference sits in the balance sheet; an asset that is not an asset.

◻ For a consideration of $49 million, National General Corporation acquired the shares of Grosset & Dunlap in 1968. It brought into its accounts $16 million in tangible assets and put the remaining $33 million in an 'excess of cost' account. 'There it will stay until management decides otherwise.' / Abraham J Briloff, 'Much Abused Goodwill', *Barron's*, 28 April 1969 /

It does not seem to matter which way the wind blows; the variety of acceptable accounting practices makes it possible for companies to arrange the representation of their financial affairs as they please.

OFFICIAL COMMENT ON US MERGERS IN THE SIXTIES

A Staff Report of the US Federal Trade Commission in 1969 considered many aspects of the unusually high merger and takeover activity of the sixties. One of the incentives to merge was said to be the possibility of acquiring assets and going concerns at bargain prices. A contributory to this has been prevalent financial reporting practices.

◻ 'In recent years, it has been increasingly recognized that accounting practices are wanting in their presentation of adequate investor information ... Many instances can be found where the reporting system understated earnings and earnings potential. Assets have been carried at historic rather than at greatly enhanced true market value ... depreciation has been overstated ... Operating revenues have been systematically understated, liabilities and accruals overstated.

'In other words, a balance sheet or an operating statement may conceal as much as it reveals of a company's true economic condition. To the extent that this is true, it increases the probability that the market valuation of a firm's security will not accurately reflect its earnings potential ...

'The techniques adopted for both tax and public reporting purposes have not been uniform. Some companies have taken conservative approaches. Others have been liberal. Conservative firms have generally tended to understate their profits and asset values. Some merger bargains represent exploitation of this understatement. Price level changes, too, can undermine the accuracy of accounting balance sheet statements, which have a historic orientation and thus need have no direct relation to current economic value ... this creates bargain opportunities for expert investors.' / US Federal Trade Commission, *Economic Report on Corporate Mergers*, 1969, pp. 76–80 /

The report gives other examples of the flexibility of accounting practices and of practices that have similar (and also opposite) effects. In the light of all this, a discriminating shareholder seems to have little of substance on which he can exercise his wits.

THE REGULATION OF TAKEOVERS
AND MERGERS

The size, the side effects and the manoeuvring which accompanied takeover bids at various times in the last twenty years have given legislative, regulatory and other bodies occasion to believe that some greater restraint and supervision were necessary. We consider the attempts made in the United Kingdom to rationalize aggressively acquisitive operations.

Restrictive legislation is not favoured in the City of London. Some in the United Kingdom (and in Australia) have thought the remedy might lie in regulation along the lines of the SEC in the United States. But it was more generally believed that informal devices, guidelines and persuasion were sufficient to curb the rambunctious elements of some of the earlier bids and defences.

We have seen that, in some of the cases of the fifties, defences against bids included disclosure of the current values of assets and increased dividend proposals. There were other cases. The bid by Sears Holdings for Watney Mann in 1959 led to the disclosure of asset undervaluation by £6·8 million. Courtaulds, defending against a bid in 1961 by Imperial Chemical Industries, revealed that assets shown in the books at £70 million were worth £120 million at current prices.

Some other defences were more objectionable. When, in 1953, a bid was made for Savoy Hotels, the directors created a property-holding company which effectively prevented shareholders from controlling the disposition of the company's properties. An official investigator appointed by the Board of Trade found the action of the Savoy board to be an invalid use of its powers. A somewhat similar device was used by Scottish Motor Traction in defence against bids by Sears Holdings and House of Fraser (1956). In 1958 the board of British Aluminium sought to 'defend' the company against a bid, by Reynolds Metals in association with Tube Investments, by a proposal to sell 4·5 million unissued shares to Alcoa—in effect, to dilute the voting power of existing shareholders by one-third without consulting them about the approach of Tube Investments. The sequel was an acrimonious tussle which seems to have been the proximate stimulus to the setting up of the City Working Party which prepared the first 'Notes on Amalgamation of British Businesses' (1959).

In the sixties some offerees defended themselves by 'side deals' with other companies. Watney Mann thus assisted International Distillers and Vintners to defeat a bid by Showerings (1967); Thorn Electrical Industries assisted Metal Industries to defeat a bid by Aberdare Holdings (1967). Other bids and defences were made in terms of profit forecasts, many of which turned out to be quite wide of the mark. The 'Notes on Amalgamation' were revised in the light of these tactics. They became 'The City Code on Takeovers and Mergers' in 1968.

The principles and rules enunciated in the Code are clearly directed to the fairness of dealings between offeror and offeree companies, their directors and their shareholders. Thus, for example, the boards of both companies 'have a primary duty to act in the best interests of their respective shareholders': all parties must 'use every endeavour to prevent the creation of a false market in the shares of an offeror or offeree company'; 'all shareholders of the same class of an offeree company shall be treated similarly by an offeror company'; and so on.

Of particular interest in the present context, however, is the principle:

> 'Shareholders shall have in their possession sufficient evidence, facts and opinions upon which an adequate judgment and decision can be reached, and shall have sufficient time to make an assessment and decision. No relevant information shall be withheld from them.'

The financial experts of the City must have been well aware of the extent of the differences between reported asset values and current market values of assets which we have illustrated in this and previous chapters. They must have been equally aware that the legislature had, in 1967, required directors to comment in their annual reports on these differences in respect of property assets. They should have been equally aware that balance sheet figures and net profit calculations may be based on quite different rules for any two companies. It seems odd, therefore, that no attempt was made in the Code to specify what kind of financial information is 'relevant' to the judgments of shareholders, to insist on the giving of up-to-date asset values, or to require information to be given that would enable shareholders to compare directly the financial features of the two companies and the features of the combination of the two. The closest the Code comes to any of this is the rule that, *when* revaluations of assets are given in connection with an offer, they should be supported by independent expert opinion.

There is, of course, one condition under which stipulations of the kind we have suggested would be unnecessary in the Code and that is: if the law or rules of practice relating to the regular financial statements of companies were explicitly to require accounting figures to be or to be based on up-to-date prices or values. The history of recent takeovers has shown repeatedly that shareholders have long been misinformed or inadequately informed. Yet the evidence—pointed as it is—has not been taken as a cue for the rectification of the accounting rules and practices which give rise to inadequate judgments and inequities.

CONCLUSION

The occurrence of takeover bids is just one set of circumstances in which shareholders are confronted with the choice of holding or disposing of their shares. Because bids may be contested, they also provide tests of the adequacy of the financial information provided periodically to shareholders in the ordinary course of events. If investors were well-informed as a matter of course, there would be no occasion for panic or surprise on the part of directors or shareholders when bids are made. There would be no occasion for the vacillation of official or regulatory bodies as they seek to justify a current valuation of assets 'in some circumstances' while tolerating out-of-date valuations in general practice. And there would be less opportunity for industrious and inquisitive bidders to 'make a killing' at the expense of shareholders whose interests are supposed to be protected by adequate financial publicity.

To bids and bidders generally there can be no great objection. They perform a prophylactic function in corporate finance and management, weeding out inept managers and inefficient companies and freeing assets for more economical use. If they can do this at great profit, so much the better for them. But if they are aided and abetted by the inadequate and misleading information provided by others, some more substantial corrective than those yet tried seems to be necessary.

11

WATCHDOGS, BLOODHOUNDS, ET AL.

'An auditor is not bound to be a detective, or … to approach his
work with suspicion, or with a foregone conclusion that there is
something wrong. He is a watchdog, but not a bloodhound.'
/ Lopes L J, *Re London & General Bank*, 1896 /

'They have mouths and speak not; eyes have they, and
see not. They have ears, and hear not; noses have they,
and smell not. They have hands, and handle not; feet
have they, and walk not: neither speak they through
their throat.'
/ Psalm CXV.5. Cited by Gordon Samuels, 'Protecting your
Practice Against Liability', *Chartered Accountant in Australia*,
August 1971 /

To err is human. Hence the practice of one man checking the
work of another, particularly where the consequence of error may
be serious or costly. In the command of aircraft and seacraft,
in medical diagnosis and surgery, in building construction and
industrial processes, in scientific inquiry, testing or checking is
commonplace. Its object is to ensure that the conclusions reached,
or the results of the tasks performed, are reliable bases for the
next step in a chain of actions. What is tested is the *result* of some
previous action, not that action itself. If the result is found to be
suitable or serviceable for the known and intended use of it, the
tester is unconcerned with the steps that led up to it. The tests
that are applied have to do with the way in which the thing tested
will 'fit in with' other things, or will do what it is expected to do.
In effect all testing is a form of quality control.

A quality control inspector in a chemical or engineering plant
tests the product as it comes to him. He tests it by reference to
the specification which is set up to ensure that the product, when
put together with other things (other parts, or power supply, or
liquid or air pressure, for example), will work smoothly and not
break down unexpectedly. He checks the product independently
of the previous processes or processors. He does not go back to
the processor, check what he did, and affirm that he did it. If he

were to do this he would be relying on the report of the processor; no such report, and no check that depends on such a report, can give assurance that the product meets the specification of what is required for the next step in processing or use.

The audit of accounts is a kind of quality control, control of the quality of the information on which managers, investors and creditors will make judgments about the performance and prospects of companies. The tests that auditors should apply, therefore, are tests of the fitness of the financial figures for use in further calculations and in making judgments about the past or decisions about the future on financial grounds.

WHY AUDIT?

Directors must both act upon knowledge of the financial affairs of companies and report upon those affairs. But the handling of money and goods and the keeping of records of them is done by a variety of officers and servants. Any one of these officers may make errors, mislay goods or misappropriate goods or money. Checks made of the actual balances of money and money's worth from time to time enable the account balances to be rectified if necessary, so that neither directors themselves nor the recipients of their reports will be misled indefinitely as to the financial state of a company.

However, directors and managers may themselves influence the quality of the information reported. They may in any year 'succeed too well'. They may wish to conceal the fact from competitors to avoid counteraction, or from shareholders to prevent excess of optimism, or to carry over the fruits of success to some later year when results may be less satisfactory. Or they may have erred, so that a year's results are less rosy than they and others may have expected. They may wish to conceal the fact to avoid adverse reaction of shareholders, creditors and others, and to give themselves time to straighten things out. In both cases they could justify concealment as being in the 'long-run interest' of the company and its shareholders. The variety of acceptable asset valuation methods and other accounting rules provides the means of concealment. They may select and change rules to meet *their* circumstances; the evidence in Chapter 8 strongly suggests that the directors of many companies have done so. Ideally, an independent check of the balances of assets and equities would eliminate the possibility of concealment or manipulation, even if innocent or with the best of intentions; for the object of audited accounts is to inform, not to conceal.

INDEPENDENT VERIFICATION

Whoever is to act upon financial information is entitled to suppose that what is reported is actually the case. The auditor's report is commonly considered to be the outcome of an independent verification of what is stated in the balance sheet and income account. But there are three reasons why in practice this belief is not justified.

We saw in Chapter 3 that many have held that accounts should tell the truth, irrespective of audit, and we saw that the courts have held that the accounts should correspond with the facts, not merely with the books of record. But the standard type of audit report makes reference to the proper keeping of books of account or to the keeping of those books in accordance with generally accepted accounting principles. What the financial statements say, therefore, tends to correspond with the books of record rather than with the facts.

Secondly, 'independent' in 'independent verification' has come to be linked more strongly with the status of the auditor than with the verification of what is reported. The laws and regulations relating to auditors state or imply that the auditor of a company shall be financially independent of the company and free of other business relationships with its officers. However, independence in these senses may have nothing to do with independent verification of financial statements. Curiously, the laws and rules contain no amplification of what constitutes independent verification.

Thirdly, the notion of verification seems to have eroded or to have been whittled away. It is understandable that, while the choice of accounting rules is vested in directors, auditors may be reluctant to say they have 'verified' the balances that result. It is less onerous to assert that the financial statements are in accordance with the books of account or with generally accepted principles. Neither directors nor outsiders should be satisfied to use statements that were not true of the company, its assets and equities. So that what is less onerous for auditors is of doubtful value to others—unless or until the general principles of accounting are so designed that they lead to true statements.

What, then, happens when there are alternative permissible accounting rules and the choice of rules is at the discretion of directors?

HOW AUDIT?

The contemporary practice of auditing is an uneven mixture of independent authentication or verification and entirely dependent non-verification. Consider the auditing of asset balances.

It is common practice to check independently the amount of cash on hand. This balance is the result of all operations involving cash holdings and movements. It is not considered sufficient to accept the assertions of any party having control over cash balances that the amount of cash shown in the books to be on hand is actually on hand. The amount of cash ascertained, independently of the books of account, to be on hand is the amount that an auditor will insist on having reported in the accounts. To check the balance in this way conforms with the usual quality control rule mentioned above.

Since the *McKesson and Robbins* case in 1940, independent checks on the balances of accounts receivable and on the physical quantities of inventory have become more common. But there are still important phases of checking that cannot be independent. There have been notorious cases in which the balances of debtors' accounts in respect of terms sales have been overstated, due to the discretion of management in determining whether debts are good, doubtful or bad; examples are given in this and later chapters. More pervasive is the dependence of the auditor on management for the money value assigned to inventories. When inventories are valued at cost, and where cost is determined by such of the usual formulae as are chosen by management, the auditor is obliged to accept the chosen formulae; his checking consists only in testing the application of the formulae. The resulting monetary amount of the inventory balance is thus not independently authenticated. The process does not qualify as a form of quality control. It is as if a quality control inspector were to pass a batch of screws with no threads, on the ground that the machinist knew what he was doing, and he 'must' be right.

The same applies to machinery and other durable assets. Suppose a company buys a machine for $10,000. To account for it over its life in the customary way, there must be a *decision* on its expected service life (say the decision was five years); there must be a *decision* on its expected scrap value at the end of that life (say, $1,000); there must be a *decision* on the spreading of the difference between cost and scrap value over the service life (say, straight-line distribution). Given these decisions, the depreciation charge each year would be $1,800; and the book value of the machine at the end of, say, the second year would be $6,400. To audit the accounts for the machine and the depreciation, the usual steps are to see what *decisions* were made and that the calculations are consistent with the decisions. Of course, the calculations may be correct and yet the balance of the asset account and the amount of the depreciation charge may have nothing to do with the financial or commercial value of the machine at the end of any year. These amounts are not authenticated independently of the company and its accounts; they are dependent entirely on the say-so of the management.

It should now be clear why such anomalous differences can occur, as were illustrated in Chapter 8, consequent upon changes in accounting methods, without any comment or objection on the part of auditors. By habit or convention, they do not seek external independent evidence of the propriety of the book values. They see that the bookkeeping process is correct, given the decisions of management; not whether the resulting figure is one that a company or its shareholders and creditors can reliably act upon.

The account given of the steps taken in the course of auditing is sketchy, though in principle correct. But it may be said by some to be incomplete. The Committee on Auditing Procedure of the American Institute of CPAs has stipulated, among its 'generally accepted auditing standards', that 'In all matters relating to the assignment an independence in mental attitude is to be maintained by the auditor or auditors'. It is a nice prescription, and one that auditors would claim to follow. But it is not linked to the quality of the information contained in audited financial statements. Nor indeed can it be so linked as long as auditors accept, without corroboration by reference to independent evidence, the allocations, apportionments, charges and valuations determined by the managers or other officers of companies.

☐ Sydney Guarantee Corporation was originally a company engaged in financing hire purchase and similar transactions. In 1957 it extended its operations to other fields—land development and other commercial undertakings. It borrowed extensively from the public in the years 1956 to 1959, its debt rising in three years from £135,000 to £1·6 million. In February 1961 it was reported that a depositor of £100 could not obtain payment of that amount when payment fell due. This was the beginning of consternation. One month later a receiver was appointed for one of the creditors. Liquidation and official investigation followed. The investigators estimated that only some £170,000 would be realized out of £4·4 million supplied by shareholders, depositors and creditors. The credit of the company had been sustained, though 'it was rotten to the core', by the directors' failure to take account of bad debts arising from its financing business. And the auditors had failed to check, independently of the directors of SGC, the reliability of the figures for accounts receivable. In the words of the investigators, the auditors failed 'to appreciate that their duty required them to exercise an independent and critical approach to the representations of the directors and, in the final analysis, to form their own opinion and report it'. / *Report of the Inspectors* ..., 1964 /

☐ Pacific Acceptance Corporation was also a finance company. It successfully brought an action for damages against its auditors on grounds which included failure to check, independently of the managers of a subsidiary, the security for loans to customers. Said the Court ' ... the auditor does not satisfy himself merely by being content that management is responsible and is satisfied about the matter ... In principle an auditor is really in no different position from any skilled inquirer. To the inquirer in any field to know by direct examination is surer proof than to believe on the hearsay of others or by inference.' / *Pacific Acceptance Corporation Limited* v. *Forsyth and ors*, 1970 /

It seems that, in these and other cases, auditors have concerned themselves principally with the formal task of checking, without consideration of the protective function of an audit or of the wider consequences of what was reported. Many finance companies have a high debt-to-equity ratio; they are highly geared. For this reason alone the equity of shareholders may be at greater than ordinary risk. However, the financing of terms sales is subject also to shifts in the availability of credit, as monetary and governmental authorities seek to boost employment on one hand or temper inflationary tendencies on the other—another source of risk. The risk is increased manyfold if the company borrows short-term money for long-term use, as in speculative land and commercial development. Further, the risk spills over to lenders and depositors if asset values are overstated by failure to write off bad debts and other reductions in market value. The deed securing the rights of certain depositors in Sydney Guarantee, for example, allowed the company to borrow up to six times the shareholders' equity. Therefore each £1 by which asset values, profits and shareholders' equity were overstated enabled the company to borrow an additional £6—on non-existent security! The potential damage to investors and creditors from this magnification of the consequence of overstatement should be well known to auditors, sufficiently well-known to make careful independent verification of asset values a matter of binding principle. Yet pervasive reliance on conventional accounting rules and managerial judgments persists.

INDEPENDENT EVIDENCE

A company is better off at one date than at another, and it stands in a certain financial relation to the rest of the world at any date, because of the transactions in which it has engaged and the events it has experienced. No decision by managers or directors about how those transactions and events will be recorded or reported can influence what has happened in a period. No decision about the valuation of inventories or plant 'for reporting purposes' can affect the gains or losses that a company has in fact made. Whether gains or losses are made depends on operations in the market place, not on operations in the counting-house.

There is only one way in which the particular statements in a dated balance sheet may be checked *independently* of the accounting process and *independently* of the influence of managers and directors. That is by reference to the market prices of assets and the contractual amounts of liabilities. The only effects of decisions to use values other than market values is to distort in some way the report of what has occurred.

The conclusion just stated agrees with the conclusion reached already in earlier chapters, namely that financial statements should be based on asset valuations at current prices, but it has been reached on quite different grounds. Earlier we held that such information is the kind which is useful and informative to managers, investors and others. Here we hold that such information is the only kind which can be independently verified. The convergence of the two lines of argument on the same conclusion strengthens the belief that this kind of accounting is the kind which the law contemplates for the protection of creditors and the investing public. We will presently show that it also tends towards the protection of auditors.

We anticipate some objections.

Some will argue that there may be many different market prices for any asset at a given time. Maybe so, but the objection could only be sustained if it can be shown that the range of market prices is greater than the range of values obtainable by the application of different established and accepted accounting rules. We have already shown (Chapter 8) how varied may be the consequences of applying possible combinations of accounting rules; and we shall give some other examples later in this chapter.

Others will argue that as the financial statements are the responsibility of the directors, the valuations assigned by directors are the best possible valuations. In fact, considerable reliance is placed by auditors on directors' valuations. But as, under this argument, directors are not necessarily bound by any accounting rule or convention, it is quite possible that directors *could* value assets at market selling prices, without objection on the part of auditors.

MATERIAL INCLUSIONS, EXCLUSIONS
AND DIFFERENCES

However, suppose that there were a range of market prices for any particular asset at a given time and that it were not possible to obtain an exact and unequivocal figure for the value of any asset, or the amount of any charge or credit in the income account that depended on that value. What degree of approximation would be sufficient to enable an auditor to give a 'clean' report?

This question does not attract a great deal of attention but it has been answered indirectly on occasions. For example, in evidence before the Royal Commission on the Atlantic Acceptance Corporation, it was said by a chartered accountant that the limit would be about 10 per cent either way in an assessment of losses from bad debts. In *Escott* v. *BarChris Construction Corporation* (US, 1968), the Court held that a 16 per cent overstatement of the current ratio was a material overstatement. In the Westec case, *Carpenter* v. *Hall* (US, 1968), the complaint alleged that a difference of 23 per cent in a reported figure was a material difference. / Henry B Reiling and Russell A Taussig, 'Recent Liability Cases—Implications for Accountants', *Journal of Accountancy*, September 1970 / And in 1971, the Securities and Exchange Commission was reported to have held that amounts of $4·5 million and $8·9 million, by comparison with incomes approximating $175 million reported by Occidental Petroleum, were material amounts. Thus, as small a proportion as 3 per cent of a reported figure may be judged to be material.

Now consider some of the examples given in earlier chapters. A glance at the figures on pp. 81\endash 82 will show that in no case was the amount of the real property revaluation as low as 10 per cent of the pre-revaluation figure; and that in fifteen out of twenty cases of revaluation the increase was greater than 50 per cent. It seems most improbable that a bona fide attempt to obtain independently a current value for these assets before the revaluations would have produced figures as divergent as 50 per cent from a reasonable commercial valuation. On the basis of the '10 per cent test', the financial statements of all these companies should have been 'qualified', if independent authentication were the rule. But we have found no examples of qualification on this score.

Consider also the examples of marketable security valuations given on pp. 98\endash 99. There is no difficulty in obtaining up-to-date valuations, but where the differences between book values and market values so greatly exceed 10 per cent it seems odd that the balance sheet may be said to give a true and fair view, without qualification, when the market values appear only in footnotes.

Numerous other examples are given in other places. We have in many of the illustrations given other figures with which the amounts under notice may be compared in order to show that the differences are material.

No further comment seems necessary on these cases of omission to draw attention to the very substantial differences between figures reported in the financial statements proper and figures given as footnotes or obtainable, by inquiry, from evidence independent of the company or its records. The case against the use of market prices in the body of audited financial statements seems weak indeed, particularly when such prices are required to be given as footnotes or otherwise in respect of certain kinds of assets.

GENERALLY ACCEPTED PRINCIPLES

There can be no doubt that the laws which provide for the audit of company accounts intended that the users of those accounts would be assured of their reliability. It is, of course, impossible for auditors to check in detail all the transactions and operations of a client. The courts have laid no greater duty on auditors than a duty to exercise reasonable care and diligence, and what is reasonable care and diligence has turned on the general standards of the profession. 'Accountants should not be held to a standard higher than that recognized in their profession', said the Court in *Escott* v. *BarChris Construction Corp.* The dictum is well established.

But auditors are actionable for negligence; and the US Securities Act of 1933 makes auditors (and other experts) actionable, at the suit of innocent buyers of securities, for untrue statements made or omissions to state material facts. Consistently with the dicta of the courts, defendant auditors in litigated cases have relied, at least in part, on the testimony of other practitioners on the prevailing standards of practice. Plaintiffs have not been notably successful, for two reasons as it seems.

Firstly, the duty of auditors (and others giving information or advice) has been deemed to run only to limited persons or classes of person, notwithstanding the fact that many persons and classes of person may rely upon and act upon audited financial statements. The court in the US case, *Ultramares Corporation* v. *Touche* (1931), declined to make auditors liable at the suit of any person who might act upon a company's ordinary financial statements even though they contained misstatements. Auditors could not be exposed to 'a liability in an indeterminate amount for an indeterminate time to an indeterminate class'. In a more recent English case (*Hedley Byrne*), the law lords on appeal indicated that a 'special relationship' must exist between the giver and receiver of statements or advice if an action for negligence against the giver were to have a chance of success. It seems therefore that the case law is ineffective as protection of shareholders and creditors generally against unreliable accounts or against the general 'debasement' of audited accounts.

Secondly, the law is loose and vague on what is meant by a true and fair view, or fair representation in accounts. It is therefore possible—and as our examples have illustrated, it has been the case—that accounting practices have been developed that fail to secure to investors reliable and pertinent information. When such practices fall, as they do, under the rubric 'generally accepted accounting principles', and when what is 'untrue' or 'material' turns on what are generally accepted principles, legal actions alleging negligence may be defeated by reference to the general standards of the profession. The possibility that judgments of the courts may stem the spread of practices that operate against the protection of investors is consequently minimal.

We are not concerned in this book with the specific precedents established in litigated cases. We are concerned with indications of the drift of decisions and dicta insofar as they bear on the *general* protection of investors. There are some signs that generally accepted accounting practices and auditing standards which give inadequate information are not tolerable and may not be tolerated. We have already noticed some earlier observations of the British judiciary on the auditor's duty to ascertain the facts and the potential deficiency of technical rules of accounting (p. 35).

Breakdown in United States: A recent US case suggests that the courts will not invariably consider as satisfactory defence the plea that accounts are in accordance with generally accepted principles and that the auditor acted in accordance with generally accepted auditing standards.

☐ / *United States* v. *Simon et al.* (Continental Vending Machine Corp. case, 1969) / Roth was founder and president and holder of 25 per cent of the stock of Continental Vending. He was also an officer, director and major stockholder of Valley Commercial Corporation. From 1958 to 1962 Roth caused Continental to lend large sums of money to Valley which he, in turn, borrowed to finance personal stock market operations. At 30 September 1962, Valley owed Continental $3·5 million, which it could not repay since Roth could not repay Valley. Roth agreed to give collateral security for his debt, but 80 per cent of the collateral consisted of securities of Continental. At the insistence of the auditors of Continental, a note to the 1962 financial statements stated that the amount receivable from Valley was 'secured by the assignment to the company of Valley's equity in certain marketable securities ... the amount of such equity at current market quotations exceeded the net amount receivable'. The auditors also insisted on writing off certain research and development costs which resulted in a net loss for the year and wiped out the balance of retained earnings. When the report was released in February 1963, the price of Continental shares slumped, the collateral which supported the loan to Valley became inadequate, and the auditors could not certify the annual return to be filed with the SEC. The SEC took action to appoint a receiver. Debenture-holders of Continental brought a civil action against the auditors for $41 million dollars, claiming negligence; the action was settled for $2 million. But the principal case was a criminal action against two partners and a manager of the auditing firm, charging that they had knowingly drawn up and certified a false and misleading financial statement of Continental Vending for the year ended 30 September 1963. The defendants were convicted and fined; the verdict was upheld on appeal.

We deal here only with the adequacy of the footnote disclosure of the security supporting the Valley account receivable. The auditors, in defence, held that they had followed generally accepted accounting principles. On their behalf, other expert accountants testified that neither generally accepted accounting principles nor generally accepted auditing standards required disclosure of the composition of the collateral for Continental loans to Valley. Said the Court of Appeal,

☐ 'As men experienced in financial matters, they must have known that the one kind of property ideally unsuitable to collateralize a receivable whose collectibility was essential to avoiding an excess of current liabilities over current assets and a two-thirds reduction in

capital already reduced would be securities of the very corporation whose solvency was at issue—particularly when the 1962 report revealed a serious operating loss ... Since disclosure that 80% of the securities were Continental stock or debentures would have led to inquiry who could furnish so much, the jury could properly draw the inference that the failure to reveal that the bulk of the pledged securities was of the one sort most inappropriate to 'secure' the Valley receivable, rather than being a following of generally accepted accounting principles, was part of a deliberate effort to conceal that defendants knew of the diversion [through Valley to Roth] of corporate funds that Roth had perpetrated.'

It seems then that a statement may be false and misleading if the terms used to describe an account balance are insufficiently explicit, and the amount of the balance is insufficiently indicative, to enable investors to draw proper conclusions about the real current financial state of a company; and that it is not a reliable defence to claim that any such practice conforms with or is not in violation of generally accepted accounting principles. Commenting on the case, Kripke observes that

□ '... accounting information cannot be a closed system based on rules that are meaningless and misleading to others. The accountants' position with respect to civil and criminal liability cannot rest on the assumption that all readers understand that generally accepted accounting principles permit assets to be shown at cost (thus concealing or overstating the value of assets) ...' / 'The SEC, The Accountants, Some Myths and Some Realities', *New York University Law Review*, December 1970 /

The complaint is not new, nor is it confined to the defects of using original costs, nor does it stem from the courts and legal scholars alone. Here are some earlier observations of a banker:

□ '... we should expect accounting procedures to be consistent from year to year within companies and consistent among companies; secondly, that they be reliable; and thirdly, that a certification of the use of "generally accepted accounting principles" gives us a clear navigational fix by which we can judge the suitability of footnoted departures from those principles ...

'[But] generally accepted accounting principles have permitted some of the largest firms in the country to change their accounting procedures primarily because someone else is following a particular practice. And all of this happens without departing from the "principles". Under these circumstances, you may wonder just who is doing what and to whom.

'The fact is . . . that the accounting profession cannot say precisely— or perhaps even approximately—what those "generally accepted accounting principles" are.... Some auditors seem to see themselves as non-questioning reporters working within the confines of "generally accepted principles".' / J Howard Laeri, Vice Chairman, First National City Bank, 'The Audit Gap', *Journal of Accountancy*, March 1966 /

Breakdown in Australia: Similar things had happened before, and on a large scale.

☐ *Reid Murray Holdings.* Formed in 1957 by the merger of two well established companies, Reid Murray Holdings grew rapidly by the takeover of other companies. In 1962 the group consisted of 222 companies. Originally engaged in retailing and the financing of sales of consumer goods, it later ventured into property and commercial development. In 1958 a subsidiary, Reid Murray Acceptance, was formed to facilitate hire-purchase financing. R M Acceptance borrowed regularly and extensively from the public. The proceeds were used, increasingly from mid 1959, to finance R M Holdings and its subsidiaries instead of for the direct financing of hire-purchase sales. In late 1961 the trustee for the debenture-holders of R M Acceptance became concerned with the absence of security over the assets of R M Holdings and its subsidiaries, a concern that was heightened by delay in meeting interest on debentures in mid 1962. The group appears to have made no plans, or quite inadequate plans, for the payment of interest and the repayment of maturing debt. It seemed to rely on belief in its capacity to go on raising new money. But the supply of new money dwindled. R M Acceptance defaulted on interest payments in late 1962. Various makeshifts were canvassed to preserve the group, but none was acceptable to the principal creditors. Receivers were appointed in January 1963; in April an official investigation of the group was ordered by the Victorian government, and in May an order was made for the winding up of the group.

We pass over many matters of administration which the inspectors found deserving of critical comment and confine attention
to features of the reported results and financial position of the
group.

☐ The consolidated net profits (after tax) of the group had been
reported to be: 1958, £536,000; 1959, £859,000; 1960, £1,543,000;
1961, £856,000. For 1962 a net loss of £5,386,000 was reported but
the report did not become available until July 1963 when the group
was in the hands of the liquidators. The 1962 balance sheet showed
that paid up capital was £9·3 million, shareholders' equity was
£7·6 million, and total liabilities amounted to £56 million. In 1963
the liquidators estimated that shareholders would lose the whole
of their equity, that debenture holders might lose approximately
£12 million and unsecured creditors some £15 million—about £35
million in all. Up to October 1971 some $47 million (note the
change in the Australian currency unit) had been paid out to
secured creditors, and the total losses were estimated to be likely to
exceed $100 million. / *Australian Financial Review*, 27 October 1971
/

It is not possible to say how far the reported profits of all years
were boosted by the use of 'favourable' accounting principles. The
investigators found that almost £1 million of the £1·27 million
profit (before tax) of Reid Murray Holdings in 1961 was due
to changes in accounting methods or the use of methods that
were objectionable. For more elaborate comment on the group's
accounting methods we turn to the reports of the investigators.

☐ '... we have been greatly disturbed to find that thousands of
people invested in the group in reliance, not upon their own
judgment, but upon the advice of men who held themselves out
in the community as skilled to give such advice. It seems to us,
therefore, that either the published reports and accounts of the
group must have been deceptive or inaccurate or that these advisers
were either incompetent or negligent. We do not think the latter
is the case ... We believe that ... the accounts of the group
must have fallen short of their supposed objective—namely that of
presenting a true and fair view of the state of the affairs of the group
and of the results of its operations ... neither of us is skilled in
accountancy and we are aware that much of what we have said [on
the accounts of the group] will not be accepted by the profession

generally. On the other hand we believe that we are accustomed to the use of common sense, and common sense has compelled us to reject a number of the accounting practices used in the group and, apparently, regarded as acceptable by accountants.' / *Interim Report of an Investigation ... into ... Reid Murray Holdings ...*, 1963 /

The investigators found that the Payne's Properties companies (part of the Reid Murray group) had adopted accounting practices that led to grossly misleading financial statements.

☐ 'The methods to which we refer are the taking to account of total book profit upon terms sales as at the date of sale without any provision being made for bad debts, and the capitalization of holding costs [of properties] without adequate steps to ensure that book values were not increased beyond realizable values. We think these policies ... were deliberately adopted ... in order to produce accounts which would show at the earliest possible date the largest possible profit by the use of recognized accounting principles ...

'We would stress, however, that the object was throughout to use accounting methods which were recognized by accountants, and accordingly, we do not think that the methods adopted were deliberately designed to deceive. We think that it was thought that since the methods were recognized the results must be proper. However, in our view, the result of combining in one set of accounts a series of extreme techniques all of which maximized [reported] profits ... was to produce grossly misleading figures.' / *Final Report of an Investigation ... into the affairs of Payne's Properties ...*, 1964-65 /

Finally, on the accounts of Reid Murray Holdings:

☐ 'The 1961 accounts ... combined what was plain dishonesty with misleading exploitations of recognized accounting practices ... in the circumstances in which the 1961 accounts were prepared many of the devices which I have called misleading exploitations of recognized accounting practices received the imprimatur of the various accountants who were auditing the accounts involved. Now it is true that some of the auditors of the companies whose affairs I investigated were supine and gullible but most were not and I do not think that any were dishonest—and yet the accounts were approved.... In my opinion the investigation has shown that ... the whole question of how company accounts ought to be prepared and presented requires urgent and critical examination.' / *Final Report of an Investigation ... into the affairs of Reid Murray Holdings ...*, 1966 /

QUALIFIED AUDIT REPORTS

The cases we have dealt with at some length are admittedly unusual; but the elements of them are more pervasive—sufficiently pervasive to cause auditors to take more seriously the right to 'qualify', or to express reservations about, the financial statements on which they report. There has been an increase, at least in Australia, in the number of qualified audit reports; one newspaper on this account described 1971 as 'the year of the auditors'. Many of the matters mentioned in qualified reports however are relatively trivial beside the understatements and overstatements of asset values which pass without comment. Some of the matters mentioned are disputable and are the subject of differences of opinion among practicing auditors. Some have been disputed by directors on what seem perfectly proper grounds.

In many cases the qualifications seem to be beside the point. The position has long been taken that annual financial statements report on the past up to the date specified in the balance sheet. On this ground, nothing that 'might happen' in the future is properly a matter for qualification. Yet:

☐ The 1969 audit report of R J Reynolds Tobacco Company read, in part: 'In our opinion, subject to adjustments, if any, that may result from the divestiture of Penick & Ford Limited described in [a footnote to the financial statements], the accompanying balance sheet and statements of earnings and earnings retained present fairly the financial position ... and results ...'

☐ Great Boulder Mines reported a loss of $1·2 million in 1971. It showed shares in Western Mining Corporation acquired during the year at cost, $47·3 million. The market value of these shares at balancing date was $39·5 million; by the date of the audit report the market value had fallen to $21 million. The auditors reported that they were 'unable to form an opinion to what extent, if any, the fall in value of shares in Western Mining Corporation is permanent'. For that reason they were unable to 'express an opinion whether the accounts were properly drawn up ... so as to give a true and fair view of the state of the company's affairs ... and results ...'

The mention of a future event (Reynolds) and the reference to the permanence of the amount of an asset (Great Boulder) seem to be quite gratuitous remarks, unrelated to the positions of the companies at the latest balancing dates.

☐ The 1964 report on the accounts of Chevron Sydney was qualified thus: 'The realizable value of the hotel and equipment, standing in the balance sheet at a figure of £5,105,566 cannot be assessed, but it is a matter of public knowledge that during the year an option was granted for its sale of £2,500,000 ... No provision for a possible loss on realization has been made in the accounts ... Subject to this important reservation ...'

☐ The 1968, 1969 and 1970 audit reports of Mr Whippy Holdings were qualified in respect of the reported values of certain assets. The book value, it was said, 'whilst appropriate to the business as a going concern, is unlikely to be realised on a sale'. The company had made losses since its incorporation in 1965.

Perhaps the reservations in these two cases were prompted by the 'threat' of liquidation. But the allusions to *future* realization are inconsistent with the traditional line that accounts are historical in character, and that the audit report is a report on such accounts. The style of these qualifications suggests that auditors tread an uneasy path between 'the long past' and 'the speculative future'—that is the closest they come to affirming something about the present (or near-past) state of affairs.

☐ The 1970 audit report of Hothlyn Corporation was qualified: 'Depreciation has not been charged in respect of freehold buildings held ... as income producing assets which at balance date had book values totalling $1,807,008. Subject to this reservation ...'

The reports on a number of other companies, large and small, have been qualified for the same reason. The Institute of Chartered Accountants in Australia has recommended that, as a matter of principle, depreciation should be provided on buildings. Notwithstanding this, a survey in 1971 of 80 Australian companies indicated that 30 companies had not made such provisions and that the audit report of none of them was qualified (*Australian Financial Review*, 5, 6 October 1971). The professional recommendation related to buildings alone. However it is often impossible to distinguish that part of an amount paid for land and buildings which may be described as the value of the buildings. And although buildings may depreciate, urban and industrial land tend to appreciate. Of the appreciation the professional recommendation says nothing. To insist on showing depreciation and to disregard appreciation seems to be on odd way of securing that accounts give a true and fair view of position and results. It is not surprising, therefore, that some companies have declined to comply with the recommendation on the ground that appreciation in land values more than compensates for any decline in the value of buildings.

☐ In 1971 the auditors of Aberfoyle disagreed with the auditors of Storeys Creek Tin Mining (a subsidiary of Aberfoyle) on the necessity of providing for 'deferred taxation'—taxes that *may* become payable in future years because under the tax laws a smaller amount of income tax was paid in a given year than the 'normal' tax.

The audit reports on other companies have been qualified for failure to provide for deferred taxation; for example, Australian and Kandos Cement Holdings (1971), Broken Hill Proprietary Company (1971), Western Mining Corporation (1968, 1969, 1970). The auditors of other companies in similar circumstances have been less demanding.

☐ The 1970 audit report of Jardine Matheson (Aust.) was qualified. The company had charged a provision for loss in respect of shares in unlisted companies against past accumulated profits. The auditors held that the provision should have been charged against profits of the year.

As in the case of depreciation for buildings and deferred taxation, practice differs in the treatment of gains or losses in asset values, and gains or losses on the sale of assets—and auditors differ among themselves in their attitudes towards the same practice. Let it be granted that the market values of the assets such as those mentioned in the cases of Great Boulder Mines and Chevron Sydney deserve notice, if those values do not appear as the principal values in the balance sheets. But all the other examples given do not seem to be instances that deserve qualified reports, since they relate to hypothetical futures or to accounting practices disputed among accountants. It is difficult to avoid the conclusion that many of the reservations of auditors either are not pertinent to what the financial statements cover, or are not contributory to a better understanding of the state of affairs of the companies under report.

THE PROTECTION OF AUDITORS

The sixties was a poor decade for auditors. In the United States, suits against auditors alleging the certification of misleading reports grew 'from a trickle to a flood'. We have already noted that a debenture-holders' action against the auditors of Continental Vending was settled out of court for $2 million. The auditors of Mill Factors, an insolvent finance company, settled with shareholders and creditors for $5 million. Several years ago it was reported that some 80 actions were pending for amounts aggregating upwards of $100 million; the position is said to have become worse. In Australia a judgment for $1,500,000 was given in 1970 against the auditors of Pacific Acceptance Corporation in an action for negligence.

Professional indemnity insurance no doubt provided some cover against claims such as these. But insurers have become increasingly reluctant, in the face of such large settlements, to underwrite the risks. Premiums are reported to have risen substantially.

In the face of all this there has been an upsurge in discussion of the possibility of limiting the liability of auditors. However desirable this might be from the viewpoint of auditors, it would seriously restrict what might be considered the legitimate claims of misinformed shareholders and creditors. It would not remove the nuisance. It would merely shift to other, innocent shoulders the financial consequences of misleading information. The possibility of inequities can only be removed by some more rigorous basis for the forming of auditors' opinions.

Company directors, of course, value a 'clean' audit report and generally auditors would prefer to give a clean report. They may and do discuss with directors matters which should in their opinion be more fully described; and they put forward their views on the reported values of assets and equities where they do not readily accept those of the directors. However when disagreements are not resolved, reports are usually qualified.

Any serious qualification puts readers on notice of disagreement. It may issue in demands for explanations at annual meetings, or inquiries by official or regulatory agencies, or notice and comment in the financial press. As qualification may in these ways be damaging to the confidence of others in the directors, to the confidence in the company of investors and creditors, and to the value of outstanding securities, the caution of auditors and their reluctance to give qualified reports is understandable. Fears have been expressed that auditors may be actionable for defamation at the suit of directors. And there have been cases where auditors have not been reappointed following disputes over the contents of company reports. These add to the caution and reluctance that auditors may feel on other grounds.

The potentially uneasy situation of auditors is due substantially to the fact that so much of what appears in traditional financial statements is a matter of opinion—and opinions may differ, materially. Where matters to be reported are in dispute between directors and auditors, shareholders and others may *not* become the better informed, for compromise on one side or the other may enable both to save face. It would be far better if there were fewer matters of opinion, and fewer occasions for dispute.

The argument and evidence we have adduced points the way to the removal of grounds for disagreement. If it were required that financial statements should be based on current market values of assets, the possibility of dispute would be narrowed substantially. Directors (or company officers) would be obliged to demonstrate that the values used in balance sheets were or were based on some current or recent market price and that serious attempts had been made to obtain such prices. Auditors would be obliged to see that there was adequate evidence of attempts to obtain current market prices and they could, as we have already said, independently test the figures of the client company by reference themselves to market prices.

Auditors would be aided in this task by access to the market prices used by other clients. This is no breach of professional secrecy, since market prices are by definition public knowledge. Auditors would thus bring to the benefit of companies, managers, directors and investors the wider knowledge of market prices which professional contact with other clients gives—in much the same way as medical, legal and other experts draw on their experiences of many clients for the benefit of each client. There may still, of course, be some latitude for opinion, for market prices may be obtained from different sources and they may be divergent. Nevertheless some such prices, however different, are surer grounds for opinion than figures arising from idiosyncratic calculations based on cost.

A number of present difficulties would be eliminated.

No auditor need fear removal by directors on the ground that another auditor would more readily comply with the wishes of directors, for all auditors would follow the same practices, relying on independent evidence of the prices of assets, and no great advantage could be gained by switching auditors.

If, in the ordinary course of events, one auditor were to succeed another, the successor could more readily and more reliably test the quality of the work of the previous auditor. The necessary information on market prices would be of recent date and within his own recent experience; checking of long sequences of past book entries would not be necessary to be assured of the propriety of the opening figures under the new audit.

There would be less necessity for all companies in a group of companies to have the same auditor. Transactions between the member companies of a group of companies are commonly effected at 'prices' that are not ordinary market prices. The 'profits' or 'losses' on these internal transactions are usually eliminated when preparing consolidated financial statements of groups, and difficulties have been experienced in checking the eliminations and other adjustments where member companies have different auditors. No such difficulty would arise if all financial statements were based on market prices and all auditors tested the financial statements by reference to evidence of market prices. The auditors of parent companies or holding companies could rely more safely on the independently audited accounts of subsidiaries.

Finally, public accounting and auditing firms have increasingly engaged in work of a consultancy nature, described generally as 'management services'. There have been misgivings in some quarters about the possible conflict between serving as advisers in some sense to management and serving as independent auditors.

The conflict may be serious where accounting rules and their products are matters of opinion: for if professional accountants have influenced managerial opinion on methods of accounting, their judgment on the truth or fairness of financial statements cannot be said to be independent. However if the final financial statements of any period must be authenticated by reference to external evidence, and if the auditors' task is specified in these terms, the possibility of conflict between the roles of adviser and auditor is greatly reduced.

REMEDY

It can no longer be supposed that auditors may carry on their assignments with the limited objectives of seeing that the book-keeping is correct. Auditors have for some years devoted considerable attention to the 'internal controls' of companies. This may serve to limit the possibilities of internal error and perhaps minor defalcation. But it has little to do with the usefulness of financial statements to other parties, as long as the traditional asset valuation rules are followed. In connection with the *Yale Express* case (1957) the court held that the responsibility of an auditor of financial statements filed with the SEC (and available for public information) runs 'not only to the client who pays his fee, but also to investors, creditors and others who may rely on the financial statements which he certifies ... The public accountant must report fairly on the facts as he finds them whether favorable or unfavorable to his client. His duty is to safeguard the public interest, not that of his client.'

Notwithstanding the heavy financial burdens that have fallen on some auditors, there has been no change in the general style of accounting and auditing in the direction of protecting both investors and auditors simultaneously. Accounting rules that conflict with common sense are unfair to investors. And to make auditors liable in negligence to all and sundry shareholders and creditors would be unfair to auditors. Amelioration of the lot of both does not seem possible through the processes of the courts while the law remains vague on the style of information that is protective of investors and while reliance is placed on the prevailing standards of the profession.

The only remedy seems to be in the hands of the legislature. That remedy, we hold, is not in the direction of heavier penalties or burdens on auditors at the suit of large classes of investors but in the direction of clearer specification of what constitutes fair and proper representations in financial statements.

12

HOT SEAT IN THE BOARDROOM

'Honest Abe Lincoln could lose a shareholder suit today. It's more than a question of honesty. You have to be candid, careful, lucky, and have an attorney watch your every move. Even then you can't be sure you might not lose a shareholder suit.'
/ Anonymous lawyer, *Forbes*, September 1968 /

'. . . the ballot as an instrument of control is fictional. The right to vote in corporate affairs is not identical with the right to vote in politics . . . the market place, the price of stock, often is a polling place. If a stock persistently declines while other stocks in the same industry rise, then it is reasonable to conclude that the smart investors—the insiders—are getting out, unloading . . . . the market place vote has power. It is a positive warning, a financial warning, to an incumbent management, that dissatisfaction has got beyond the discussion stage.'
/ J A Livingston, *The American Stockholder*, 1963 /

The directors of a company are its agents. They determine, initiate and authorize the actions that the officers of the company will take on its behalf. Their powers are extensive. They are not limited, as are trustees, to specified courses of action. They are allowed wide discretion in dealing with the resources under their control but they do occupy a fiduciary position in relation to the company. They are expected to exercise their powers with care and skill for the benefit of the company. They are not entitled to make use of information they obtain as directors for their own benefit to the detriment of the company.

We shall be concerned with several of the terms used in these last sentences.

CARE AND SKILL OF DIRECTORS

Directors as a class are not required by law to possess any specific technical qualifications though they are expected to bring to bear on the company's affairs such knowledge as they have.

'A director's duty has been laid down as requiring him to act with such care as is reasonably expected from him, having regard to his knowledge and experience. He is, I think, not bound to bring any special qualifications to his office. He may undertake the management of a rubber company in complete ignorance of everything connected with rubber, without incurring responsibility for the mistakes which may result from such ignorance; while if he is acquainted with the rubber business he must give the company the advantage of his knowledge when transacting the company's business.' / Neville J, *Re Brazilian Rubber Plantations & Estates Ltd*, 1911, 1 Ch. 425 /

'A director of a life insurance company, for instance, does not guarantee that he has the skill of an actuary or of a physician.' / Romer J, *Re City Equitable Fire Insurance Co. Ltd*, 1925, Ch. 407 /

It may be good sense to have on a board of directors some persons who have technical knowledge of the technical business of a company—whether the company is a rubber planter, a pharmaceutical manufacturer, an engineer or a banker. It may be reasonable also to have on a board some persons skilled in financial and some in legal matters. But in the absence of any legal prescription—which, in any case, it would be almost impossible to devise—a board of directors may consist of persons having none of these competences.

The standard of care and skill required by the above dictum is thus a modest standard. The directors of a company are entitled to engage whatever specialists may be required for the purposes of the company, and generally to rely on them.

'The larger the business carried on by the company the more numerous, and the more important, the matters that must of necessity be left [delegated] to the managers, the accountants and the rest of the staff ... In respect of all duties that, having regard to the exigencies of business, and the articles of association, may properly be left to some other official, a director is, in the absence of grounds for suspicion, justified in trusting that official to perform such duties honestly.' / Romer J, *Re City Equitable Fire Insurance Co. Ltd* /

Thus, no action can lie against directors for mistakes or errors of judgment arising in the course of business. Managers, their aides and subordinates may be relied upon for knowledge of technical processes and of the statistical, legal and other processes necessary, for example, for market analysis, quality control and protection of the company against litigation. The consequences of failure in any of these directions fall on the company, not on the directors.

Now, just as the contracts and transactions of a company affect its legal and commercial relations with others, so do the contents of balance sheets and income accounts affect the financial relationships between a company and its members and others. Are directors, then, permitted to rely on the technical knowledge of accountants to produce these accounts? May they escape the consequences of failure to keep proper accounts and failure adequately to report on the financial positions and results of companies?

Legislation on the UK pattern provides that every company shall keep or shall cause to be kept proper books of account; that, annually, directors shall lay before the company in general meeting a profit and loss account and balance sheet; and that any director who fails to take all reasonable steps to secure compliance with these provisions shall be liable to imprisonment or fine. It is also provided that the accounts shall be approved by the board of directors and signed on their behalf, usually by two of them. Further, the frequent reference, through the 'accounts sections' of the statutes, to specific matters of which the directors are aware, or on which they must or do form opinions, or on which they must report, seem to make clear their responsibility for the particular and aggregate statements made in the accounts.

But the law hedges. The penalties for false statements (in financial statements or elsewhere) fall only on any person who wilfully makes a statement false in a material particular, knowing it to be false. As accountants are one of the classes of officers on whom directors may rely (see the dictum in the *City Equitable* case above), directors will ordinarily escape liability, under the 'false statement' rules, for the contents of financial statements. They would seldom, if ever, have the means of knowing whether or not a statement in the accounts is false, unless they themselves were directly responsible for it.

☐ Over 12 years of trading, Federated Industries reported a profit in every year. Aggregate reported profit for the period was $3·6 million. In 1969 it was forced to revalue its inventory; $2·5 million was written off the book value. The directors explained that profits anticipated from the manufacture of highly sophisticated electrical systems had been eroded by the costs of research and engineering of the products, and the costs of financing the long term contracts involved. The outlays had not been authorized by the board and had been carried in the accounts as work in progress. To what extent in each year, and for how many years, profits and assets had been overstated by the overvaluation of inventories was not disclosed. But, presumably in the light of the reported profits and asset figures, creditors had increased the amounts advanced to the company from $6·6 million in 1963 to $14·7 million in 1969. Heavy losses would be faced by shareholders and creditors.

To charge development costs into asset accounts, however misleading the result may be, is not an uncommon practice. It would not necessarily involve, and in this case apparently did not involve, a decision of the directors. It would therefore be difficult to sustain a complaint against the directors (and even against other officers of the company) that the statements of inventory values and net profits over years were false statements, wilfully and knowingly made. The same difficulty would be faced in every case where, by the use of what has come to be accepted as an accounting rule, reported figures are materially different from the financially significant values of any assets at a given time. Inadequate accounting practices that result in misleading information are thus not likely to be eradicated by decisions in litigated cases under the false statement provisions.

In US law, the general requirements of directors are not greatly different. Directors are expected to use 'such care and diligence ... as ordinarily careful and prudent men could reasonably be expected to exercise on behalf of' a similar company under similar circumstances (*Ballantine on Corporations*, 1946, p. 158). As elsewhere, there is no other stipulation as to requisite skills. For the same reasons as we have already given, it would seem to be difficult, in the absence of fraudulent or other unusual circumstances, to contest successfully the figures yielded by accounting rules in common, or even not so common, use.

In the light of all this, the statute seems to confer on directors power without determinable responsibility—the power to decide what shall appear in financial statements but, in the absence of fraud, no responsibility for what appears therein.

THE BENEFIT OF THE COMPANY

Granting that directors have discretion in the choice of accounting rules, what choice may be considered to be in the interest of or for the benefit of the company?

It is possible to set up plausible grounds for almost every form of idiosyncratic accounting that we have noticed in previous chapters. Consider some broad classes of effects produced by the choice of rules.

Secret reserves: Secret reserves arise through the undervaluation of assets, whether deliberate or inadvertent or in consequence of some so-called accounting principle. They may be said to be for the benefit of the company insofar as they constitute 'inner' strength, unknown to competitors and others. But the advantage of inner strength arises only when that strength comes to be disclosed to others. The company *may* then benefit from the 'surprise value' of the operations it can support when confronted by testing circumstances. The element of surprise is of equivocal value, however; even greater surprises may be produced by antagonists, as the failure of countermeasures against many takeover bids has shown (see the cases of J Sears, Binns of Sunderland and Jones and Higgins pp. 166–67 above).

A more direct justification of secret reserves is the opportunity they create for normalizing reported profits. If profits are understated in good years, the undisclosed increment in asset value may be drawn upon in poorer years. The company is thus given the appearance of having a steadier and more reliable income than is the case. To create this impression may be said to be in the interest of the company, especially if it has frequent need for credit or new share capital subscriptions. No great harm may arise if the variations in profit from year to year are really 'temporary fluctuations'. However deviations from the past level of income may turn out to have been the beginning of a sustained rise or fall in income, which directors may not be in a position to foresee when deviation first occurs. If the deviation is the first step in a downward turn in income, shareholders and creditors who supplied additional funds on the strength of the normalized income may seriously embarrass the company by off-loading their shares, refusing further credit or pressing for settlement of existing obligations of the company.

What seemed to have been in the company's interest may thus become quite contrary to that interest.

Conservative income reporting over long periods (and consequential understatement of assets) may be said to be in the company's interest. It reduces the amount reported to be available for distribution, reduces the pressure for higher dividend payments, and enables a company to finance correspondingly greater growth out of the undisclosed income retained. But this too has drawbacks. If directors are not accountable in terms of the total quantum of assets under their control, they may devote increasing amounts to developmental or speculative ventures. This is fine, if those ventures pay off; but they may eat into the very heart of the company's operations and prospects if they fail.

Changes in accounting method: These may be similarly justified—and on equally hazardous grounds.

A change that keeps up the level of reported profits may be said to be in the interest of the company, since it tends to keep up the market price of the company's shares and its credit rating. But if the level of reported profit is artificially sustained—by bookkeeping entries, rather than by actual achievement—the market's judgment of the company may be the more seriously influenced when the advantage of the change in accounting method is exhausted. A change that influences the reported income of one year may give directors the breathing space necessary to improve the substantive operations of a company. But it may just as readily remove the feeling of uneasiness and the pressure for improvement which arise from a publicly reported reversal of income—and that is not in the interest of the company.

A change that reduces in one or more years the level of taxable profits may be said to be in the interest of the company. In the first place, it reduces the amount of tax payable (the cash outflow) in respect of that year or those years, in the second place, it may improve the reported income net of tax. However these are short-run advantages only. Generally the expenses allowable in the calculation of taxable income are limited in amount; the total amount allowable for depreciation of an asset, for example, is limited to the difference between the cost of the asset and its finally ascertained scrap or resale value. Any advantage gained in one year therefore entails some higher impost in a later year—and the later year may be a year in which it is much less convenient for the company to pay it.

☐ In 1970 Chrysler Corporation changed its inventory valuation method from LIFO to FIFO. Since it defers the time-incidence of taxes, LIFO could be said to be in the interest of the company, but it was an advantage Chrysler could not 'afford' when profits fell. The switch to FIFO enabled Chrysler to charge lower costs against revenues. By virtue of the change, the company was able to declare a profit of $7·6 million in the fourth quarter of 1970; without the change it would have had to declare a loss of $3·6 million. For the full year it reported a loss of $7·6 million; but for the change in accounting it would have reported a loss of nearly $24 million for 1970. Consequent upon the change in accounting, the company would have to pay additional taxes dating back to 1957; it would pay to the federal government $53 million over the next twenty years. / *New York Times*, 10 February 1971 /

The latter arrangement constitutes an interest free loan to Chrysler. This would favourably affect its earnings over the next two decades, in a manner that may not be discernible from its reports. What the reported earnings (after tax) would have been, over the previous 13 years, if the FIFO method had been used consistently, is not known. And whether it will be more convenient in the future than it was in the past for the company to pay out the $53 million tax owing is entirely speculative. What may seem to be in the interest of a company obviously may bounce.

☐ Rocla Industries since 1969 followed a policy of estimating the gross values of fixed assets at current price levels. Against land improvements, buildings and plant, it had charged depreciation 'on the basis of replacement values which recognize the effects of inflation'. The amounts provided were considerably higher than the amounts allowed by the taxation authorities. The company's policy in this respect may be considered as progressive and in the company's interest, insofar as it takes account of some of the effects of rises in asset prices. In 1972, subsequent to a takeover bid, the company announced that it would change its method of profit calculation. Its general manager said, in explanation, that the company expected 'when introducing its current value accounting policy and related higher depreciation rates several years ago, that professional analysts would recognize the understating effect on net profit'. However experience did not support the original view of directors. 'The analysts often used tabulated data that did not distinguish between the sorts of profits Rocla had been arriving at and the sorts of profits other companies had been arriving at.' No credit was given for the company's foresight and more realistic reporting. It would therefore revert to the method of calculating profit 'used by normal manufacturing industry'.

/ Annual Reports and *Australian Financial Review*, 9 May 1972 /

Even 'progressive' changes in accounting when made by isolated companies may turn out to be an embarrassment to them.

Review: The immediate advantage to the company from any of these practices is probably comprehensible to all directors. Profits and taxes are understandable notions, even if directors know little of their components. But the direct justifications of secret reserves and changes in accounting are one-sided, biased. They may turn out to be to the advantage of a company, and they may not. Further, although directors may grasp the immediate advantage, they may not know or may ignore the fact that artificial change contains the seeds of its own defeat. Under- or overstatement of profits, or the change in net assets, in one year must be compensated by changes in the opposite direction in other years, since the closing balances of one year are the opening balances of the next.

DO DIRECTORS INFLUENCE FINANCIAL STATEMENTS?

As many directors do not ostensibly have special financial and accounting skills, are we making too much of the provisions of the statute? Do directors in fact wilfully adopt and change accounting rules? It is impossible to answer these questions in general terms. It seems certain that directors of many companies have chosen forms of accounting which have 'desired' effects in certain circumstances, for the forms chosen have been inconsistent with previous accounting.

☐ All revaluations of assets (see Chapter 6) may be supposed to have been incorporated in the accounts with the knowledge of, if not on the initiative of, the directors. Whether the object has been to reduce the apparent dividend rate, or the apparent rate of return, or to counter takeover bids, it can scarcely be supposed that the internal accountants of the companies concerned would have acted on their own initiative.

☐ All changes in accounting which have had the effect of improving the earnings per share or reducing immediate tax burdens may reasonably be supposed to have been made with the approval of, if not at the instigation of, the directors. The adoption of LIFO valuation for inventories and accelerated depreciation for plant assets, and the reversal to FIFO and straight-line depreciation are cases in point (see Chapter 8).

☐ In 1967 International Telephone and Telegraph Corporation received compensation for war damage in the amount of $17·4 million and charged an equivalent amount to a provision for contingencies arising from foreign operations. In 1969 Litton Industries made a profit of $23·2 million from the sale of security investments, and made a provision in an equivalent amount for start-up costs over the next three years while shipyards would be under construction. A similar set-off by Ready Mixed Concrete in 1964 was noticed at p. 131 above. In all these cases the sizes of the amounts involved, and the identity of the amounts of the set-offs, make it clear that the accounting was at the directors' discretion.

We cannot imagine a board of directors instructing a competent engineer to adopt different rules or principles having inconsistent consequences from time to time, nor instructing a competent statistician to adopt different methods of calculation to make statistical measures 'look better' than previously, nor instructing a competent legal officer to disregard a material legal principle in any specific circumstance under advice. The rules and processes by which factual statements of financial position and income are derived are in principle no different from, and no more at the whim or discretion of directors, than the rules and processes of science, technology, statistics or law. It seems just as inconceivable as in the latter cases that directors should decide, or should be considered to have discretion to decide, the rules used in accounting.

GROUNDS FOR SUSPICION

We have been concerned principally with the ordinary conduct of business, not with the special circumstances of deliberate fraud or deceit. But it is very difficult to distinguish between the two classes of circumstance when directors or some of them may determine the contents of a company's financial statements. The dictum of the court in the *City Equitable* case made reference to the absence of grounds for suspicion.

A set of financial statements, drawn up according to firm and consistent principles, may be one of the sources of doubt or suspicion. If the figures there represented are materially different from what was expected, or different from the position of the previous year or the trend of previous years, or different from the results of other companies in significant respects, there are grounds for inquiry by the directors, and there may be grounds for suspicion. However if any dominant officer, chief executive or managing director, is able by the choice of accounting rules to interfere with the evidence of performance or its comparability, doubt or suspicion may not arise in the minds of other directors. We cite a few of the many cases in which dominant officers or directors have concealed the drift of company affairs from directors and outsiders.

☐ The failure of the London and Globe Company under Whitaker Wright was marked by the dominance of one director over the others, speculative investments, inadequate cash for ordinary business purposes, a downward drift in the stock market, inter-company sales of shares at fictitious profits, window-dressing of balance sheets including valuations of shares at figures far above market prices. When the company failed in 1901 it brought down twenty-eight stock exchange firms. The deficiency of the group was estimated in 1902 to be £7·5 million. / Digested from: Aylmer Vallance, *Very Private Enterprise*, 1955 /

☐ Gerard Lee Bevan was the son of a wealthy and respected bank director. His early and successful career in the substantial stockbroking firm of Ellis & Co. earned him a senior partnership by 1912. By 1916 Ellis & Co. had acquired a large holding in City Equitable Fire Insurance Company, a firm doing business in re-insurance. Bevan became chairman of the board. 'From then until the collapse [of City Equitable], five years later, Bevan's ascendancy over his fellow directors seems to have been as complete as was his dictatorship in the affairs of Ellis & Co.' The business of City Equitable expanded; gross income and profits soared during the post-war boom. Then between 1919 and 1921 City Equitable loaned to Ellis & Co. over £900,000, more than half of which was unsecured; and other funds of City Equitable were invested in speculations that wilted as the stock market turned downwards. From 1919 the drift in the affairs of City Equitable was concealed in the accounts: by arranging to buy Treasury Bills just before balancing dates and to sell them immediately afterwards, and by other means. To help out its deteriorating cash position, City Equitable in 1920 and 1921 acquired three small insurance companies 'with respectable assets', sold off some of their assets and turned over the proceeds to Ellis/City Equitable. Finally, as all this did not provide enough to keep the group afloat, Bevan launched a new company to acquire the three smaller insurance companies and by prospectus invited the public to subscribe £250,000. The prospectus showed the assets of the companies at the end of 1920 but without any indication of the change in their affairs during 1921. By late 1921 it was rumoured that City Equitable was in trouble. In less than three weeks its preference shares fell from 55s. to 15s. At last the other directors were prompted to look more closely. In the upshot, City Equitable filed a petition in bankruptcy: Ellis & Co. was 'hammered'; the deficiency of the Bevan group was nearly £3 million. / Aylmer Vallance, *Very Private Enterprise* /

In the light of experiences such as these, it might be expected that the possibilities of 'window-dressing' the annual accounts of companies would have been eliminated in the ensuing fifty years. Also it might be thought that the potential dangers of reliance on the reports of dominant officers would have become apparent, and guarded against. Not so.

☐ Reid Murray, as we have already noted, failed in 1962. In 1972 the losses of investors and creditors, still undetermined, were expected to be of the order of $100 million. The board of directors had been dominated by its chairman for years. It had borrowed short-term money for long-term projects; interest charges and the repayment of maturing debt imposed severe strains on its solvency, requiring a constant inflow from new borrowing. The catalyst was a tightening of credit, as a governmental policy. The group took no special steps to trim its credit business in the light of this. Inter-company transactions, inflated asset values and understatement of annual expenses enabled it to sustain reported profits—until inability to raise new loans forced it into default. (Fuller details have been given on pp. 206–07 above.)

☐ Substantially the same elements contributed to the failure of Atlantic Acceptance Corporation in 1965. The assets of the group grew one hundred fold in the ten years ended in 1964. The group had been substantially under the domination of its creator and president, C P Morgan. By training he was an accountant. By disposition he was secretive and devious, and in relation to his co-directors overbearing. 'Inventive, ingenious, incompetent and corrupt, Morgan and Morgan alone drove Atlantic forward to catastrophe', said the Royal Commissioner. From the early years of Atlantic, Morgan's principal concern, according to one of the officers of the company, had been to produce balance sheets that would encourage investors, particularly in long- and short-term notes. Reported profit must therefore be sufficiently large to justify dividend payments and to show growth in earnings per share. So Morgan made very modest provisions for bad debts (by comparison with other finance companies) and brought into current revenues each year an unusually large proportion of the service charges written into loan contracts. It was shown before the Royal Commission that the aggregate results of 1963 and 1964 had been overstated by $26 million. Among the proximate causes of the company's default were 'the rising disinclination of American lenders to "roll-over" or renew their short-term loans at maturity because of the [US] presidential "guide-lines" [enjoining reduced foreign and increased domestic lending], coupled with their requirements of liquidity on tax dates'. The deficiency of the group was estimated in 1969 to be $65 million. The *Report of the Royal Commission* deals at length with the whole affair.

In all these cases, some external factor (a fall in security prices, tightening of credit) was the proximate cause of failure. This in itself is good reason why financial statements should always represent the *factual* relationships of a company with the external community. For, if those relationships are masked or misrepresented, the directors are in no position to take the necessary, even if unpalatable, steps to rehabilitate the company. But the principal point which emerges is that, as long as discretion may be exercised by management or a dominant director, the board of directors may have no 'grounds for suspicion' even in the case of quite deliberate manipulation.

FACT AND EXPECTATION

It is part of the business of directors, managers and other officers to dream, and to weigh the prospects of present operations and their alternatives. But it is dangerous to confuse expectations with facts. In the interest of judging and advancing the efficiency of a company, directors need financial facts from time to time, just as do outsiders. However, present financial facts about a company may become so confused with present expectations of its management that financial statements are poor guides to the present states and past results of companies.

The confusion arises, we suggest, from the fact that for all assets there are simultaneously two kinds of value—a present value in exchange, or market price, and what may be called a user-value. The user-value of an asset is, roughly speaking, what its owner thinks it is worth to him, or what he expects to get out of it if he continues or is allowed to continue to hold it and use it through some future interval. When accountants speak of original cost or cost less depreciation as a 'going-concern value', they seem to allude to user-value in some sense akin to the above. This seems to be the (dubious) ground on which reliance is placed on the historical cost rule whether the market values of assets have risen or fallen. An estimate of user-value is useful when the owner is considering whether to go on using it in one way or another, or to sell it and do something else. But it has no bearing on the financial position of the owner at a given date.

Suppose I buy a car for $4,000 and drive it 5 miles. I then have a second-hand car, for which I could get, say, $3,600, if I were to sell it. The user-value of the car will not have fallen by 10 per cent, however. If I expect to get 40,000 miles of service from it, its user-value to me will have fallen scarcely at all. But my financial position, my capacity to pay debts and buy other things, has declined. I am certainly less well-off financially by $400.

This is a commonplace and undeniable experience; and as we contended in Chapter 4, its elements occur just as much in corporate business as in personal affairs. Even to directors unskilled in accounting and fancy finance, the distinction between the facts of financial position and the expectations that prompt action should be clear. But apparently it is one of those commonplaces that are rejected because they are commonplace.

□ The market value of the security investments of a group of Australian companies fell heavily in 1970–71. A weakness of the group was said to be its large holdings in member companies, the prices of whose shares fell in the general market downturn. The directors of all the various companies said that they regarded the holdings as having far greater values than market values, since the market prices of the shares did not reflect the true value of the assets of the companies.

It is not unusual to find such allusions to 'true values' of assets, or to assets having greater values than market values. In all these cases the allusion appears to be to user-value or expectations. The clearest example of confusion of this kind is the retention of items such as formation costs, security-issue costs, developmental costs and payments for goodwill, as assets in balance sheets. The amounts laid out in these directions were presumably laid out in the expectation of future income, and the expectation may persist. But none of them has a market value in the ordinary course of business which can be realized to pay debts or to buy other things. Whatever user-values may have been or may be assigned to them, they do not constitute part of the financial position of a company.

That dominant directors have misled other directors, and that the financial statements of companies have misled outsiders through the use of *expected* values instead of *financially* pertinent values, is tolerably certain. It is equally certain that no action against directors could be grounded on the mere confusion of the two in reporting on financial position, even though in the *City Equitable* case it was held that 'directors ought not to be satisfied as to the value of their company's assets merely by the assurances of their chairman'.

Fine points apart, company directors do need to know what a company has accomplished if they are to judge its efficiency by comparison with other companies, or to assess the efficiency of its executive. The more so, the more complex the operations of business. It would have been impossible to put men on the moon without first developing highly sophisticated and exacting instruments for ascertaining the present magnitudes from time to time of a host of variables. The complicated exercises of modern manufacturing, distribution, transportation and so on are all equally dependent on technical instrumentation of great reliability. The financial instrumentation of business—its financial statements and records—is unlikely to match the complexity of business as long as expectations and expected values are mixed with factual statements in representations of the states and results of companies from time to time.

ACCOUNTABILITY OF DIRECTORS

Allusion was made in an earlier chapter (pp. 41–3) to the notion of the stewardship of directors. As a matter of law, the obligations of directors run to the company; the law does not link the interest of the company with the interest of its members. On the other hand, as a matter of practice, directors may be said to be accountable to members of the company by virtue of the requirement that they shall report annually on results and position. However, in the light of the vagueness of the law and the power of directors to determine or influence what is reported, this is a tenuous notion. There is seldom any serious examination, in general meetings, of the policies of directors and the power of shareholders to remove and replace directors is seldom used; it is not an adequate sanction against ineffectual directors.

Some hold that the transferability of securities enables investors to 'cast votes' for or against an incumbent management or board of directors of a company—by the prices at which they trade in its securities. Surges and drifts in the prices of a company's ordinary shares are readily observable: prices, and often turnovers, are reported daily. These movements are of continuous interest to directors since they may influence the confidence of creditors and of shareholders and speculators other than those whose transactions were reported. Buoyancy and sluggishness in the market are infectious, but it is open to serious doubt whether movements in prices and turnovers express the approval or disapproval, on adequate grounds, of a company or its management. They may often be based on rumour; and often they may be expressive of a shift of confidence in the prospects of an industry generally or a class of securities generally.

This apart, if we were seeking causes of shifts in share prices, reported profits must be counted as one of the more important. Net profit, or earnings per share, is easy to grasp and, presumably, is related to success and dividend prospects. Often it is the principal statistic noticed in comments on performance. But, as the examples of Chapter 8 have shown, directors may 'improve' reported profits by such simple steps as bookkeeping entries. Ineffectual, in any real sense, as this may be, the easy acceptance of 'bookkeeping solutions' to company difficulties is evidenced by the bland references to *increases* in earnings (as if they were substantive increases) found in company reports and comments on them (see the examples cited on pp. 128–30).

We cannot hold directors responsible for the concentration of others on one simple indicator, but this concentration makes manipulation easier. Directors have only to offer a plausible explanation of the change in one figure, if they feel obliged to explain. Any explanation that runs in terms such as 'a better indication of results' or 'a profit more readily comparable with the profits of other companies' is likely to be accepted as plausible.

The share market may be a means by which directors are held accountable, if the information that circulates in it is indicative of substantive performance. However if companies may resort to bookkeeping tricks, the market is no better than a 'rigged election'.

INSIDE INFORMATION

The ability of insiders (managers, directors, majority shareholders and others) to regulate the release of information about company affairs has long been used to their advantage. The stock exchanges and regulatory authorities have given much care to the matter. They have tried to secure that company 'news' is released promptly, so that there is no time lag during which insiders or outside contacts may take advantage of privileged knowledge, to the detriment of the uninformed. The SEC compiles and publishes the dealings of insiders in securities of their companies; these reports have been said to be among the most widely used information produced by the Commission. Both in the United States and elsewhere, when insiders seem to have acted on privileged information, inquiries have been undertaken to establish whether or not the facts were as they seemed and action has been taken to eliminate the practice. These measures have no doubt served to make the market a fairer market than it could otherwise have been. But they have not been sufficient to remove all possibility of privileged benefit; or all uncertainty about the propriety of insiders' actions.

☐ In early November 1963, Texas Gulf Sulphur Company drilled a test core on a site 350 miles northwest of Toronto which suggested that it would be worthwhile to do further exploratory drilling. Over the following four months further drilling gave rise to an estimate of an ore body of more than 25 million tons, rich in zinc, copper and silver. The directors had tried to avoid misleading investors and speculators before confirmation of the results of the early drilling but they reported the find as soon as possible afterwards. Meanwhile a number of those associated with the operations and friends and relatives had bought parcels of Texas Gulf shares; certain others had bought shares on the day the find was announced, but before the announcement appeared on the Dow Jones ticker tape service.

The SEC interpreted the buying as acting on inside information and therefore in contravention of Rule 10b-5 under the Securities Exchange Act of 1934. (The relevant part of the rule is cited on p. 179 above.) The SEC brought an action against a number of corporate insiders and those who had acted on tips from insiders, seeking among other things that the court order them to make restitution to the sellers of stock that they had bought on the basis of inside information. The US District Court dismissed the complaints against all but two of the defendants. The case against two others turned on the question 'how long must an insider wait, after the release of new information, before he himself may buy without fear of violating Rule 10b-5?' The SEC argued that 'even after corporate information has been published in the news media, insiders are still under a duty to refrain from securities transactions until there has elapsed a reasonable amount of time in which the securities industry, the shareholders, and the investing public can evaluate the development and make informed investment decisions'. The court declined to accept this argument; what was 'a reasonable amount of time' would be difficult to say, and it was not the court's business to make such a rule as the SEC implied, certainly not to make it and apply it retroactively.

The SEC appealed and won its case on all points in the Court of Appeal. In effect all share buying done from the first transaction after the November 1963 test drill was held to be in violation of Rule 10b-5.

The issue in the case was the *delayed* release of information. It seems to be quite proper to consider the decision as bearing on the delayed release of information in a much wider range of circumstances than those of prospecting or mining ventures. The discovery of a workable body of ore is regarded as a sign of the prospect of future increases in the net equity of shareholders, increases that will be accompanied by increases in cash and by distributions of cash by way of dividends. The discovery of an ore body is never a reliable basis of prospects of shareholders' income. Many mines that are profitable at a given level of technology or in a given state of the supply of minerals cease to be profitable when circumstances change. Some of them later become profitable again, when new techniques or new demands arise.

Now if it is required by law or by the securities exchanges that such signs of prospects shall be disclosed, it seems even more reasonable to require disclosure of less questionable signs of companies' and shareholders' prospects. Whether the discovery of an ore body will *subsequently* bring in earnings and in what amount and at what rate, may for a long time remain speculative. However *observed* rises in the prices of any other class of assets of industrial and commercial companies are not at all speculative. They are more reliable than prospectors' discoveries as a sign of future increases in cash holdings or cash payments to shareholders. Because they are suggestive either of increased operating income, or of the possibility of gearing up earnings by borrowing, or of the possibility of realizing in cash the increase in observed market value, reported rises in the prices of assets may directly and quite properly influence the evaluation by the market of a company's shares. But such rises in prices are not required to be, and are not, reported.

In the Texas Gulf Sulphur case it was held that violation of Rule 10b-5 arose through delaying the disclosure of 'speculative' information *for as little as four months*. However, in effect, the SEC's administrative rule, requiring the general use of original costs in the preparation of periodical accounts, enforces non-disclosure, *for indefinitely long periods*, of rises in the prices of company assets. The rule creates and enforces conditions under which violation of Rule 10b-5 is inevitable!

It cannot be said in defence of the cost rule that it gives true statements of material facts and does not omit to state material facts. Facts about the financial position of a company at a specified date are the facts which a balance sheet is expected to disclose. For this purpose and for all analytical and decision-making purposes, up-to-date prices of assets are material facts.

Nor can it be said in defence of the cost rule that the differences between book values and market prices of assets are immaterial. The UK and Australian examples we have used show that the differences may amount to millions and tens of millions of dollars. The rate of urban, commercial and industrial development has been no less rapid in the United States than in other developed countries. It seems quite likely therefore that the undisclosed increments in asset values would amount to multiples of the disclosed values, as we found in Chapter 6 to be the case for UK and Australian companies.

There seems to be no line of argument or justification for this. Inside information about rises and falls in asset prices is no less useful than inside information about other events. The ability of directors to withhold information about rises and falls in asset prices makes possible manipulation of the responses of the securities market just as surely as the engineered withholding and release of other information. The benefit may accrue to insiders directly, through dealings in securities to make gains or to avoid losses on personal shareholdings. Or the benefit may be indirect, through dealings that give directors control over other companies or greater assets (as in the cases of *Speed* and *Gerstle*, pp. 180–82 above), or that enable insiders to evade scrutiny and criticism of their management. In either case, outsiders are deprived of knowledgeable dealing in securities.

It is a matter for speculation how long it will be before a shareholder brings an action against a director or directors, in circumstances free of the special features of fraud or mismanagement, charging violation of Rule 10b-5 by virtue of what is disclosed or concealed in financial statements. If the proper function of a balance sheet is to represent financial position, and if 'material' is interpreted in the manner discussed on pp. 149–50 above, it is incontestable that many, if not most, balance sheets presently contain 'untrue statements of material facts' and omit to state material facts the statement of which would make balance sheets 'not misleading'. Such an action may be hazardous, for directors, in following the prescriptions of the SEC, might be held to have acted under duress or pressure of conventional practice. It may be foolish to draw inferences from other cases and circumstances. But after the judgments in the *Yale Express* and *Continental Vending* cases, the possibility of success in an action of the above kind may not be remote.

THE UNEASINESS OF DIRECTORS

From the law and judicial decisions so far discussed, directors appear to be under no great pressure to report on the financial affairs of companies uniformly and in the up-to-date terms we have claimed to be necessary. What then is the source of the uneasiness evident in the first caption quotation of this chapter?

In the United States, over the past decade at least, there has been a dramatic increase in the number of actions brought by stockholders and others on the grounds that they were misinformed of the financial affairs of companies in which they had acquired securities.

☐ When BarChris Construction Corporation went into bankruptcy in 1962, purchasers of debentures brought an action against certain directors, the underwriters and the auditors of the company, alleging that the registration statement filed with the SEC contained material false statements and that there were material omissions. The action was brought not on the ground that the defendants had intended to deceive the buyers of securities but on the ground that they had not exercised due diligence in respect of the contents of the registration statement. The 'due diligence defence' may be raised by any person who had, 'after reasonable investigation, reasonable ground to believe and did believe' that the statements made in the registration statement were true and that there was no omission to state a material fact required to be stated or necessary to make the statements not misleading. 'The standard of reasonableness [with reference to "reasonable investigation"] shall be that required of a prudent man in the management of his own property', says the Securities Act of 1933. None of the defendants established, in the opinion of the Court, that they had exercised due diligence. / *Escott* v. *BarChris Construction Corporation* /

☐ Law Research Service had made a public offering of shares, drawing attention to certain arrangements with Sperry Rand, but omitting to state these arrangements had been terminated by Sperry Rand through non-payment of an amount owed to it by Law Research. A group of shareholders brought an action against the officers, directors and underwriters alleging failure to state a material fact. The court found for the plaintiffs and awarded *punitive* damages against the president and underwriters. This was the first case in which punitive damages were imposed under the securities laws. / *Globus* v. *Law Research Service*, 1968 /

These cases relate to new issues of securities. The law has always taken a more stringent line on false statements in prospectuses and other new issue information than on misleading information in annual financial statements. It is not clear why this should be so. Annual reports are properly regarded as bringing up to date the information published earlier in prospectuses or otherwise. To investors and creditors up-to-date periodical accounts are of no less consequence than prospectuses are to buyers of new securities. The *Yale Express* and *Westec* cases (see p. 254 below) related to annual financial statements but, like most litigated cases, they threw no light on the ideal general style of financial information.

Beyond the United States the situation is no different. The English case of *Hedley Byrne* v. *Heller & Partners* (1963) goes no further than imposing a duty of care on those who give advice or information to one person knowing that it will be passed on to and relied upon by another person for a specific purpose. Certainly it extended the law as it then was. But there is still an unbridgeable gap between this circumstance and the case where buyers and sellers in the open securities market act upon incomplete and misleading information published by a company or its directors, when the latter do not know anything of the specific purposes of individual shareholders or share buyers. There is no way in which an aggrieved buyer or seller can have his day in court. It has yet to be recognized that financial statements may be used for *many* purposes and that, for that very reason, the damage to their users may be greater than the damage to particular classes of persons having restricted and specified purposes.

The gradual tightening of the rules affecting directors, and the gradual extension of the penalties for infringement are illustrated by some further features of the cases we have mentioned. In the *BarChris* case, an outside director had joined the board during the course of the debenture flotation. He did not sign the original statement filed with the SEC but had signed material subsequently filed. He was held to be responsible for errors in the registration statement. The *Texas Gulf Sulphur* case extended those actionable as insiders—previously the company itself, major shareholders, directors and key officers—to anyone who may acquire inside information. In the last decade there has been a notable increase in directors and officers liability insurance. But in the *Law Research Service* case, the court ruled that the underwriting firm, which had been found guilty of including misleading information in the prospectus, could not collect under its underwriters indemnification policy. In some future case the ruling may be extended to directors and officers liability insurance. Further, these rulings, though made in the courts of the United States, may come to be applied in other jurisdictions when similar cases arise.

THE PROTECTION OF DIRECTORS

The increasing obligations that the statutes lay on directors and the increasing severity of the judicial decisions in company cases are understandable. The repercussions of misfeasance, misdirection and even misfortune are wider than they once were. They fall not only on direct investors but also on secured and unsecured creditors and, indirectly, on countless individuals through their interests in unit trusts, mutual funds, insurance companies and other financial intermediaries.

When General Motors Corporation was created in 1908, its capitalization was $10 million. In the following year its gross sales were $34 million and its net profit $10·5 million. In 1970 its sales were $18,752 million; its assets, $14,174 million; its net income $609 million. Royal Dutch Shell has grown, over a longer period, to a similar size. In 1970 its sales were $10,797 million; its assets $16,977 million; its net income $938 million (all $US), according to *Fortune*. There are other companies like them. Yet in the last 70 years there has been relatively little improvement in the quality of the financial information on which the performance of companies is judged—by directors or others.

We pointed out at the beginning of Chapter 4 that the manner in which private persons consider and manage their financial affairs is no different *in principle* from the consideration and management of corporate financial affairs. Any director might therefore be supposed to know what kinds of figures properly represent a company's financial position at a given time, and by inference, its results for a preceding interval. This being the case, it seems at least feasible that failure to give such figures in financial statements may, at some time, be held to be failure to exercise due care, skill and diligence—even in the absence of a debacle of the kind that has hitherto provoked litigation against directors.

It seems to be unfair to directors to expose them to increasing penalties and disclosure obligations and to the increasing threat of damage suits while leaving obscure, in the legislation and regulations, what is expected of them in financial reporting. It seems also to be unfair to expect them to be able to exercise proper care and diligence as long as company officers may choose the rules for deriving reported positions and results and may vary them at their discretion. It is equally unfair—to investors and creditors—to allow to persist a situation in which, for plausible but questionable reasons, directors may of their volition influence the key figures used by others.

We reach the same conclusion as when dealing with auditors. It is possible to be fair—as between the company, its officers, its directors and its financial supporters—only if the financial information descriptive of a company's position and results is free of bias that favours any one of them to the detriment of others. This may be disputed by many who have become accustomed to believe that the contents of financial statements are inevitably matters of opinion. But this customary belief has been the rock on which many companies have foundered and many innocent but careless directors have come to grief. The positions of directors would be far more secure if the law were more specific about what they should disclose. So, of course, would be the positions of others.

13

THE FAILED AND THE FOOLED

'In a laboratory men follow truth wherever it may lead. In human relations men have a supreme talent for ignoring truth and denying facts they do not like.'
/ Bernard M Baruch /

'Commerce is like war. Its result is patent. Do you make money or do you not make it? There is as little appeal from figures as from battle.' / Walter Bagehot, *The English Constitution*, 1867 /

Most of the examples of variant, divergent and misleading accounting we have cited are drawn from the financial statements of companies that are still in business and still apparently successful. Why turn to failures? Firstly, because outright failure is the most common cause of investigations that uncover facts long ignored or undisclosed. Secondly, because failure is but the extreme example of 'the day of reckoning', of which every periodical balance date is a typical example.

We hope to show that insiders and outsiders alike have been seriously deluded by reports and forecasts of progress; that the delusion has its roots in the 'respectability' of rules that lead to irrelevant information; that losses and imminent insolvency have been concealed through the use of these rules; and that millions have been advanced to companies that were insolvent or in breach of loan contracts at the time, though they did not *appear* to be so.

There is little appeal from the figures in a liquidator's statement of affairs.

A statement of affairs is a financial statement, a statement of assets and liabilities in which the assets are shown at prices that they are expected to realize if sold. A statement of affairs is made up when a company has become unable to meet its debts and is about to be put in the hands of a liquidator. Generally the amount of the assets on a selling price basis falls short of the amount of the liabilities. The job of a liquidator is to dispose of the assets and to pay off the creditors in the manner and order provided by law. He starts with figures which assets are expected to realize because that is the only basis relevant to the satisfaction of creditors.

In the ordinary course of business, companies are expected to meet debts when they fall due. However as idle cash earns no income, its amount tends to be kept to a minimum. Any cutback in cash inflow may therefore imperil a company's solvency. If it can sell new securities, fine. If it cannot, due to low earnings or already existing debt, it may stave off insolvency by selling assets—potentially, any of them. In order *to avoid insolvency*, therefore, it seems reasonable that a company should keep its accounts of assets on a similar footing to a statement of affairs; not because it intends to sell any given asset, but to know the margin between its present state and the point at which it may have to sell assets other than its trading inventory. If accounts are not kept continually on a market price basis, neither management nor creditors will have a ready index of its solvency.

ARE MANAGERS FOOLED?

The conventional style of accounting does not provide such an index. It may cause no harm, as far as solvency is concerned, if the accounts are kept on a cost basis and if the market prices of a company's assets rise and stay above book value. But the very assignment of significance to book value in that circumstance may lead to dependence on book value as a guide when the market prices of a company's assets (or some of them) fll below book value.

It is comforting to think, when market values of assets have *fallen below* book values, that the prices of things fluctuate. Some prices do; some don't. Even if some prices do, depressed prices may not recover in time to save a company from insolvency. There is no appeal from market prices. If, and insofar as, managers suppose that book values are 'inherent' values, more reliable than market values, they are fooled. Creditors will not wait till the dreamboats of managers come home.

☐ Latec Investments was a finance company; much of its business involved the financing of purchases of motor vehicles. Making no provision for doubtful debts and inadequate provision for bad debts, it reported profits in the first seven years of its existence. In 1961 it announced that £1·9 million of bad debts had been written off in that year—an amount almost double the reported net profits

of the previous seven years! It reported a net loss for the year of
£1·5 million. In the following year it reported a further loss of £3·5
million. A receiver was appointed on behalf of debenture-holders
in 1962 and the affairs of the company were put under official
investigation.

Meanwhile, what had happened to investors in the company?

Between June 1958 and August 1961, the company had issued
£1·15 million in shares to shareholders for cash, and £1·2 million in
shares and £600,000 in debentures in eight takeovers. By 1962 the
company's debt to secured and unsecured creditors totalled £10·5
million.

The company's 5s. shares reached a peak price of 17s. in 1960,
making the capital value of the outstanding shares some £6 million.
In 1961 a further £1 million in shares was issued—before the 1961
loss was reported; after the reported loss the shares fell to 3s., a
fall of 78 per cent from the peak price. In mid 1964 they were
quoted at 4d., about 2 per cent of the peak price three years before;
and even that was speculative since it then appeared that the assets
were deficient by some £3·2 million in respect of creditors, leaving
nothing for shareholders.

Who had been fooled? Had the directors been deluded by the book
values of receivables for years? Perhaps; but it seems quite strange
that no disclosed provision had been made for doubtful debts up
to 1960, notwithstanding that much of the company's business
involved financing of vehicles of old makes and models. Had the
directors, then, intentionally engaged in a style of reporting that
for long had fooled shareholders, creditors and offerees? There is
no way of knowing whether the issues and bids made in 1958–61
would have been successful, or whether creditors would have
tolerated the rise in debt to £10·5 million in 1962, if profits and
shareholders' equity had not been bolstered by failure to provide
for doubtful debts. But it seems that the directors were in no doubt
about one of the facts of life—the market's reaction to a good
profit record—even though they may have ignored another—the
market exacts tribute of those who disregard the relevance of
realizable values.

It seems no less likely that managers have been fooled when
the market values of assets have *risen above* book values. Could
the directors and managers of J Sears, Scottish Drapery, Jones

and Higgins, and of many of the other companies mentioned in Chapter 10 which were the subject of takeover bids, really have believed that the book values of assets were significant values? From the viewpoint of the directors, book values were 'tactically' significant, since they bolstered rates of return and relieved directors and managers of criticism and the need for explanation. However, for the sake of this advantage an incumbent management has frequently, though perhaps unwittingly, put its own future in jeopardy by giving bidders such a lever against it as the margin between book values of assets and their discoverable market values. We can only conclude that directors and managers have been fooled—lulled falsely into a sense of security by conservative book values, or secure in the (mistaken) belief that concealment from shareholders is concealment from everyone. As before, however, there is no appeal from market prices. Which is the fact on which many bidders have successfully relied.

ARE INVESTORS FOOLED?

There are cases, notably those involving fraud or coming perilously close to it, in which investors have been deliberately misled by the financial statements of companies. It is almost certain that none of the cases of long-running fraud or mismanagement could have continued but for lax accounting practices and disregard of the pertinence of market prices of assets.

□ The name of the Liberator Permanent Benefit Building Society does not suggest that it could be a risky venture. Its ostensible object, in fact, was to encourage thrift, personal saving and individual home ownership. However under the hands of Jabez Balfour and his collaborators, the company and its subsidiaries engaged in a variety of speculative and other projects. One after another failed. For years the company's 'position' was sustained by taking credit in advance for interest payable by debtors, by arbitrarily writing up the values of assets, and by taking credit for profits on sales between companies in the group. Twenty years of dissipation of the company's assets ended in failure in 1892. 'Most of the £6 million which humble folk had placed in Jabez Balfour's hands for his various gambles had vanished into thin air; the net value of all the assets surviving the crash was put at less than £500,000; 23,000 shareholders and 28,000 depositors bewailed the loss of their little nest eggs.' / Aylmer Vallance, *Very Private Enterprise*, p. 49 /

Such an old case may be of little interest were it not that devices similar to those used by Balfour to 'window-dress' his companies still crop up in cases of failure.

☐ Reid Murray Developments (WA) was put under official investigation in 1963, consequent upon difficulties of the Reid Murray group. The joint managing directors informed the inspectors that the company had been under direction by Reid Murray Holdings to prepare the 1961 accounts on a less conservative basis than previously. The inspectors found that asset values and income had been boosted by adding interest charges to the value of land under development; that profits on sales of houses had been brought into account before the houses were built; that a change in the method of accounting for interest receivable on debts due to the company resulted in excessive amounts being brought into account in 1961; that inadequate provision had been made for bad and doubtful debts; and that a change in the method of accounting for land sales had accounted for two-thirds of the 'gross profits' on land sold in 1961.

This company was a subsidiary of Reid Murray Holdings. It seems to be a case of Reid Murray directors as directors deluding Reid Murray directors as investors (agents of Reid Murray Holdings). The company could not be made into a better company simply by changes in its accounting methods. It (and consequently also Reid Murray Holdings) could only be made to 'look' better—and that is clearly a matter of fooling investors.

☐ Ivar Kreuger, son of a Swedish match manufacturer, was by training an engineer. His first venture as an entrepreneur was a partnership with another engineer, which they formed into a limited liability company, Kreuger & Toll, in 1911. Between 1912 and 1917 Kreuger amalgamated his family's match business with the business of some of its competitors to form the Swedish Match Company. Kreuger & Toll became an investment company associated with Swedish Match. By this time Kreuger had set his sights on a world monopoly in match manufacturing. In 1923 he formed International Match Corporation of New York: by 1932 it had raised $148 million in shares and debentures from American investors. Similarly Swedish Match and Kreuger & Toll had placed substantial quantities of shares and debentures on American and European stock exchanges.

From 1925 Kreuger proceeded to make loans to cash-hungry European countries in exchange for match monopolies, lending a total of $180 million up to 1929. In that year through its American bankers, Kreuger & Toll placed an issue of $50 million in bonds on the security of the obligations of 'sovereign Governments'. Under the agreement with its bankers the company could switch its collateral provided that at all times its face value was not less than 120 per cent of the face value of debentures outstanding. The switching provision, and the reference to face value of the collateral, enabled Kreuger to sell off collateral with a high market value and replace it with poor securities of equivalent face value. (This would have been impossible if the debenture agreement had tied borrowings to the *market value* of the collateral.)

Heedless of the Wall Street crash in 1929, Kreuger arranged nearly $200 million in loans for other countries in 1930. But money was no longer easy to get—for debenture interest, dividends, and stock market operations to keep up the prices of Kreuger company shares for the sake of the company's credit rating. An uneasy two years of unsuccessful attempts to borrow odd millions when he was accustomed to deal in tens of millions, of shuffling securities among his companies, and of forgery and fraud, ended with Kreuger's suicide in March 1932. It was not until some weeks later that the first clues of the deceptive and fraudulent character of Kreuger's operations emerged. The Kreuger empire collapsed. Lee, Higginson & Company, bankers for Kreuger, was ruined; its partners and their families lost $9 million. The trustee in bankruptcy of International Match Corporation into which American investors had put $150 million was able to pay out only $37 million. Shares in Kreuger & Toll which had sold for $46 in 1929 sank to 3 cents. On secured debentures, two-thirds was paid on liquidation; unsecured creditors received about 43 per cent of their claims. / Vallance, *Very Private Enterprise*, and Robert Shaplen, *Kreuger, Genius and Swindler*, London, 1961 /

Kreuger's secret was to keep his affairs secret. He had been trusted by American bankers, Scandinavian bankers, finance houses, investment advisers and investors. So frequent and extensive were his financial operations that it seems unlikely they could have continued without the wholesale falsification of accounts which subsequent investigation revealed. Between 1917 and 1932, Kreuger had inflated earnings on the books of his various real and unreal companies by more than a quarter of a billion dollars. He had received about $650 million from security issues and bank loans; in 1932 his companies' net assets were $200 million, about half what their financial statements indicated.

In case it appears unlikely that such a debacle should recur, let it be remembered that it is still possible for companies to report asset holdings at values in excess of market values and to employ speculatively, or at least without scrutiny, the undisclosed amounts by which market values of assets exceed reported book values.

☐ In June 1970 a Federal court ordered Penn Central Transportation Co., the largest railroad company in the United States, into a bankruptcy reorganization. It was described as 'the biggest bankruptcy ever' by *Time* (6 July 1970). The immediate cause was that the company could not repay approximately $10 million in commercial notes and $22 million in debt and rental charges on some of its equipment, all due on 1 July 1970. The company arose from the merger of the Pennsylvania and New York Central railroads. Its chairman and chief executive officer pursued a policy of maintaining dividends and the confidence of investors, even though the company was committed to heavy costs of reorganization and modernization. The company's assets amounted to $4·6 billion but it was perilously short of liquid funds. In 1969 it reported a loss of $182 million and a loss of about $150 million was expected in 1970. To maintain its liquidity almost all the assets of the company had been mortgaged, and almost $200 million in unsecured commercial paper had been issued. None of these desperate measures could stave off creditors.

Like many other companies, the railroad company had issued commercial paper (promissory notes) to raise short-term loans from other companies with surplus cash. If the proceeds of such loans are used in ways that are not self-liquidating in the period of the loans, they must be continually renewed; and a drop in the credit rating (as when losses are reported) can be disastrous to the borrower when renewal is sought. Penn Central was caught in just such a situation.

Lenders on commercial paper tend to rely on the reputation of borrowers without careful scrutiny of their capacity to pay on maturity. The borrower is not obliged to register such note issues with the SEC, nor to give the lender a prospectus, nor to back the notes with collateral. His word is his bond. The company he keeps may help. The railroad's holding company had assets of $7 billion but the bulk of its saleable holdings of real estate, securities and other property was already pledged to secure about $2·6 billion of debt, of which $700 million would fall due in 1970.

The size of a company or of a group is no necessary assurance against failure. Dividend policies, borrowing short for long-term use, the necessity of heavy cash outlays for repairs and modernization, all contribute to liquidity crises. Perhaps judgments of the company were confused by the many unusual items that entered the statement of its results in its last few years. But it seems to have been over-optimistic to declare nearly $100 million in dividends in 1968 and 1969—a declaration of confidence that no doubt had much to do with the attitude of lenders, but that only served to worsen their position in the end. This is 'playing the market' in a sense rather different from the usual sense.

As for the stockholders, Penn Central shares were reported to have sold as high as $86.50 shortly after the merger, and as high as $71.75 in 1969; by August 1970 they were down to $6—a loss on market capitalization of the 24 million shares of no less than $1,500 million. Some stockholders averted the full loss, of course, but the Philadelphia Museum of Art and the Presbyterian-University of Pennsylvania Medical Center sustained six-figure losses, and the University of Pennsylvania lost $3 million on selling its holding. And for creditors—the railroad's current liabilities exceeded its current assets by $286 million; it owed $222 million in current charges for services supplied. Banks, other railroads and other business firms would have to await the processes of litigation and reorganization to 'unfreeze' such money as they could recover. There were suggestions that the propriety of bank activities in the company's collapse should be investigated. In 1968, 17 of the 38 largest holders of Penn Central stock were commercial banks. Whatever the outcome of the reorganization proceedings the consequences of the collapse would be widespread, bitter and lasting.

ARE PROFESSIONAL INVESTORS FOOLED?

It has been strongly held by some that the securities market is sufficiently well informed to be able to take account of shifts in a company's affairs, regardless of what it reports in its financial statements and other releases. It is sometimes said, for example, that investors make some allowance, in the prices they offer or bid for shares, for the difference between book (or balance sheet) values and market values of assets. How the market can take into account the undisclosed features of a company has never been explained, but there are indications that even professional investors and advisers, who might be expected to be better informed than rank and file investors, are unable to do it. We have seen that bankers and financiers were heavily involved in the Kreuger and Penn Central affairs. We add a few more cases similar in kind.

☐ *Allied Crude Vegetable Oil.* American Express Company is known to travellers around the world. In 1944, its 103rd year, it decided to go into field warehousing. Field warehousing is a custodial service intended to assure lenders that goods pledged as security for loans are not lost or improperly diverted by borrowers. American Express formed a subsidiary, American Express Field Warehousing Corporation (AEFW). It was not a success. In its first 14 years it lost nearly $500,000. In 1957 it acquired a new customer, Allied Crude Vegetable Oil Refining Corporation, under president Anthony De Angelis. This was the most profitable—and ultimately the most disastrous—account AEFW ever had. Six years later, American Express sold all of its field warehousing business with the exception of De Angelis business, which it conducted under the name American Express Warehousing Ltd (AEW).

From the beginning of the Allied account, the president of AEFW knew that an earlier venture of De Angelis was still in bankruptcy proceedings. However AEFW needed business, and given that its officers were reliable, there seemed to be no danger in the field warehousing operation. However, from September 1958 onwards there were signs—rumours of shortages and errors—that Allied was less reliable than it might have been. Some of these prompted investigations, but the inspectors were bluffed or diverted from too close an examination of the huge quantities of vegetable oils represented to be in Allied's extensive Bayonne (NJ) tank farm. In 1963 the auditors of American Express were directed to review the operations of AEW at Bayonne. They concentrated on the paper work, the formal division of duties, and the internal controls of AEW; they found nothing amiss.

Only two months later Allied was found to be a gigantic swindle. An enormous speculative exercise to corner the oil futures market prompted investigation by the Commodity Exchange Authority; completely out of ready cash, Allied could not sustain the dizzy level to which its own operations had forced the prices of futures contracts: the price plummeted; margin calls on Allied's holdings could not be met. Allied and three other De Angelis companies filed bankruptcy petitions. Ira Haupt & Co., the respected brokerage house that had financed De Angelis' margin buying, failed. The Members of the New York Stock Exchange contributed $10 million to make good the losses of Haupt clients. As for Allied Crude, 1,854 million pounds of oil with a stated value of $175 million, was missing. One tank, supposed to contain $3·6 million worth of soybean oil, poured out salt water for twelve days after it was tapped. Fifty-one companies which had loaned money to or deposited oil with Allied were caught: banks, merchant banks and trading companies right across the United States and some as distant as London, Bremen and Zurich. American Express was saddled with a liability of $60 million or more. / The story is told in Norman C Miller, *The Great Salad Oil Swindle*, 1965 /

The point of the case, as of many others, is that unreliable information on, and risky financing of, one company may have unpredictably wide and serious consequences. Financiers, however skilled, must rely on what they can learn from those closest to a company's affairs; but the latter should not rely on assurances when they have the means of discovery. American Express trusted the officers of its subsidiary, who in turn trusted the officers of Allied; the auditors trusted the systems they found 'in force'; bankers and traders trusted the documents issued by AEW and Allied; but at the end of the line there had to be adequate assets—not trust. At that point, AEW and the auditors were fooled, notwithstanding hints received over several years that all was not above board at Allied. 'Presumed existence' and 'asserted values' of assets were not good enough for the safety of creditors; but they are always potentially good for fraud.

☐ *Atlantic Acceptance Corporation.* On 14 June 1965 a cheque drawn by Atlantic Acceptance Corporation of Oakville, Ontario, to discharge a short-term note payable for $5 million was dishonoured. As a consequence, the notes in all categories of outstanding debt—some $130 million in all—became due and payable forthwith. The Supreme Court of Ontario in June 1965 appointed a receiver and manager, whose report in August estimated that the realizable value of the assets available to creditors was deficient of their claims by some $32 million. Meanwhile a Royal Commission was appointed, in August 1965; the Commissioner issued his report on 12 September 1969.

Atlantic Acceptance had grown from a group having assets of $1·2 million in 1954 to $133 million at the end of 1964. By mid 1965, with stated assets of over $150 million, it was the sixth-largest sales finance company in Canada.

'For a Canadian company of this size doing business in the field of finance in times of unexampled affluence, in respect of which no sign of instability had been previously detected, and which had debt then outstanding in excess of $130,000,000 owing to lenders which included institutions regarded as the most shrewd and experienced investors in North America, suddenly to default on a routine obligation was an event which astonished the financial world. From it flowed the collapse of Atlantic Acceptance and all its subsidiaries, the bankruptcy of many companies dependent upon it, the ruin of many lives and the searching re-examination of financial practices and legislation of long standing.' /Royal Commission, *Report*, 1969, pp. 1–2 /

The reported group net incomes for 1963 and 1964 had been $814,403 and $1,100,004. After making 'appropriate' additional allowances for doubtful debts, it was shown that these figures should have been: 1963, *loss* $7,516,708; 1964, *loss* $16,629,794. Although the group never failed to report a profit, in the light of these figures it seems likely that losses should also have been reported in years prior to 1963. Had the company reported a loss of $7·5 million in 1963, it would have been in breach of the loan indenture, for the shareholders' equity (consolidated net worth) would have been $1·8 million, whereas the indenture stipulated that it should at all times be not less than $2·5 million. Apart from this, as the borrowing power of Atlantic was tied in other ways to the consolidated net worth, growth in net worth was a condition of growth in borrowing power. In fact, one secured creditor brought an action against the trustee for noteholders, on the ground of a breach of covenant, to invalidate all senior notes issued after 30 June 1964. It appears that some $70 million of the senior debt in June 1965 was incurred after the terms of the indenture would have been breached but for the artificial inflation of income.

The deficiency of the group was estimated at the time of writing the Report to be of the order of $65,000,000. The equities of shareholders and of the holders of $4·5 million of subordinated notes were wiped out. British Mortgage and Trust Company 'escaped insolvency by a hair's breadth' by the intervention and support of the Ontario government, 'but lost its identity and the reputation of eighty years in the process'. It was holder of 30,588 common and 24,100 preference shares and $3·4 million of notes of Atlantic. Its losses from involvement with the Atlantic complex were of the order of $6·8 million, whereas the total equity of the company at 30 June 1965 was $6·3 million. Its shares had been traded at $32 before the collapse of Atlantic; the price fell to $2.50 afterwards.

It was expected that senior noteholders in Atlantic would lose something like 20c to 25c in the dollar. And who were the creditors?

'Sophisticated investors from all parts of the continent': Aetna Life Insurance Company ($8,000,000), Massachusetts Mutual Life Insurance Company ($4,500,000), Connecticut General Life Insurance Company ($4,000,000), Connecticut Mutual Life Insurance Company ($4,000,000), First National City Bank ($4,000,000) and many other US insurance companies. Toronto Dominion Bank, Royal Bank of Canada, Canada Permanent Trust Company —over $8 million in all. Of industrial companies there were Atlantic Sugar Refineries Company, Campbell Soup Company (of Canada), Chesapeake & Ohio Railway Company (USA), Dow Chemical of Canada, Minnesota Mining and Manufacturing Company (USA), National Lead Company (USA), Proctor & Gamble Company of Canada—and others, for $1 million or more each. The Ford Foundation held 25,000 common and 45,000 preference shares and $2 million in notes. Lenders on a smaller scale included universities, churches, retirement funds and many 'small investors [in amounts of $1,000, $2,000 and $3,000] looking for a higher yield on a modest capital, and reassured in many cases ... by reputable dealers and bank managers'.

That these institutions and people were misled was no fault of their own. There were examples of changes in the methods of accounting of the group during the period and there were irregularities in the auditing arrangements. But the principal difficulties arose from the policy of 'borrowing short and lending long'. Any cause which threatens the flow of new funds to a company that follows such a policy threatens its solvency and its existence. For the protection of creditors it is, therefore, particularly important that asset values and the profits based on them do not contain large elements of dubious or unmatured value, such as bad debts and 'expected' recoveries of unearned interest and service charges. Maturing obligations cannot be met out of them and new obligations cannot safely be incurred on the basis of them.

One element of the Atlantic Acceptance case, it will be recalled, was that the artificial inflation of income, and hence of assets, enabled it to borrow large sums after the date at which, on a proper valuation of assets, it was in breach of earlier loan indentures. It had happened before; some of the facts of the Reid Murray collapse in 1962 are given on pp. 205–8. But for the overstatement of income and assets, it is unlikely that the Reid Murray group could have raised the £17 million that it obtained by debenture issues after May 1960.

☐ Mineral Securities Australia was an investor in mining operations and the securities of mining companies. Formed in 1965, it grew rapidly until in 1970 its aggregate reported assets were $81 million. Of this amount investments in listed securities accounted for some $24 million with a market value at that time of $28 million. Its aggregate borrowings (liabilities) were $28 million. On 25 January 1971 its directors announced that the estimated *profit* for the previous six months was $3·5 million. On 4 February this announcement was withdrawn; the company sought suspension of trading on its shares. It was disclosed that during the six months the company had sold through brokers some 6·2 million shares it had held in Robe River at current market prices; and that its investment subsidiary, Minsec Investments, had bought 6·4 million shares in Robe River through brokers at current prices. Senior counsel had advised that 5·2 million of those shares bought by Minsec Investments had to be treated as sales by the parent company to its subsidiary. Mineral Securities was therefore not entitled to take up as profit of the group $6·6 million 'earned' on the sales to Minsec Investments. The result for the previous six months was therefore a *loss* of approximately $3·3 million, not a profit of an order similar to that previously announced.

By 29 January 1971 liabilities had leaped (from $28 million in the previous June) to $75 million. The day following the announcement of 4 February, the prices of 218 mining stocks fell. The market value of the company's holdings in four such companies fell by $4·5 million; they had cost $35 million and were now worth $20 million. Two unit trusts managed by a subsidiary of Mineral Securities suspended the sale and repurchase of their stock. Creditors sought settlement, but forced sale of the company's security investments would have depressed the market further. After a week of attempts to rescue the group, the company was placed under control of a provisional liquidator. One year later the liquidator thought that all creditors could be satisfied in full if he could sell 18·6 million Robe River shares at $1.15. The price at the time was 81c. It was doubtful whether anything would be paid on the $5·8 million of preference share capital. There would be nothing for the $4·5 million ordinary share capital. Some of these shares had been placed at a premium of $13.70 in May 1970, and in February 1971 the ordinaries were said by the directors to have an equity in the assets of $4.33 per $1 share!

The first point worth noting is the treatment of the outcome of the sale of Robe River shares by Mineral Securities to Minsec Investments. Clearly there was a difference of opinion about the method of calculating 'profit'—a difference of opinion having a material effect on the reported result. It's another case of the possibility of erroneous judgment when there are no clear and firm principles for income calculation, a matter we will reconsider presently.

The second point is who lost? Of the total liabilities to creditors in February 1971—$75 million—some $49 million was secured and, as we have noted, there was a possibility that all creditors would be met. But taking the market price ($7.40) of the ordinary shares on 3 February 1971 as a base, the loss in value to the ordinary shareholders would be $33 million. An investigation of the share register in January 1971 revealed that, of the top twelve shareholders, nine were bank nominee companies (holders of securities for banks and their clients), holding between them 18 per cent of the 4·5 million shares outstanding. Pointing out that the bigger shareholders had built up their holdings through 1970 and into January 1971, a financial journalist observed: 'Big professional share traders may not have had the foresight … that many sharebrokers attributed to them' (*Australian Financial Review*, 5 February 1971). There had been grounds for optimism; the reported consolidated net profit of the group rose from $21,000 in 1966 to $12·7 million in 1970. But the index of the prices of mining stocks had slipped from 5376 in January 1970 to 4241 in December and to 3651 in February 1971. So much for the foresight of large investors and creditors; and so much for the myth of 'growth stocks'. *Sic transit gloria mundi!*

PROFITS — ACTUAL AND EXPECTED

The significance of net profit, as a source of dividends and as a guide to performance and prospects has been alluded to frequently. So important is it, and so widely used, that it should long since have been assigned a firm meaning and a prescribed method of calculation. But:

□ There were conflicting comments on the 1971 profits of EZ Industries. The company's auditors differed with the directors on the treatment of two matters. On their view, the company's profit should have been $5 million more than the directors reported. On a different view, the profit should have been $4 million less. 'You are almost reaching the position of asking "what is profit"?' said the chairman. / *Australian Financial Review*, 30 November 1971 /

If there are marginal differences in the estimates of profit by different persons there would be little cause for complaint, but the profit reported by the directors was $3·6 million. The abovementioned differences can scarcely be considered as marginal. What indeed is profit?

And how reliable is expected profit?

□ The chairman of Midland-Yorkshire Tar Distillers forecast in 1970 that the company's profit for the following year would be 'marginally higher' than the profit of 1970. The reported profit in 1971 was £684,297, compared with the 1970 profit of £966,044. / *Accountant*, 29 July 1971 /

Not marginally higher, but materially lower.

The two companies last cited were not at the time engaged in any special project, negotiation or deal to which their reports or forecasts may have been relevant.They illustrate the divergences that may appear in figures published in the ordinary course of business. Consider now some cases in which profit calculations and forecasts were much more closely related to dealings in securities.

☐ Yale Express System was a trucking and freight-forwarding company. After 20 years of steady growth, it reported a net income before tax of $2 million in 1962. In 1963 it acquired another freight-forwarding company which had earned a similar income in 1962. In 1963, instead of reporting an income of some $4 million or better, a reasonable expectation in the light of the 1962 results of the companies, it reported a profit of $1·14 million after tax. In the first nine months of 1964 it reported an (unaudited) profit after tax of $904,000; but for the whole of 1964 it reported a *loss* of $3·3 million! And it announced that the profit reported for 1963 should have been reported as a *loss* of $1·2 million. Stockholders and debentureholders subsequently brought an action against the auditors, officers and directors of the company and the underwriters for a 1963 issue of debentures, claiming damages from material errors in and omissions from three sets of financial statements.

The circumstances illustrate again the precariousness of guesses about future income, and the extraordinary variations that may occur in reports, after the event, of what was earned.

☐ Westec Corporation was a natural resources and geophysical instruments conglomerate. The price of its shares rose from $2 in 1964 to over $67 in 1966, at which price the market value of the stock was approximately $300 million. Inability of the company's president to pay for a parcel of shares ordered in his name led to suspension of trading in August 1966. The president was ousted and the directors placed the company in trusteeship under the bankruptcy laws. It was reported that over $200 million was slashed from the market value of the company's shares. In early 1967 an investigator for the Texas Securities Board claimed that whereas Westec had reported a 1965 profit of $5,192,913, it should have reported a loss from operations of $159,188. A substantial part of the difference was claimed to have been due to unconsummated 'sales' of property and to the application of 'pooling of interests' accounting to companies acquired by Westec after the close of its fiscal year. Other irregularities were alleged in respect of the unaudited financial statements for the first half of 1966. With legal action pending against over ninety persons and organizations, including the Westec auditors and eighteen brokerage houses, it seemed likely in 1968 that the 13,000 shareholders, who had not been able to trade their stock for two years, would long await knowledge of the fate of their investment.

☐ Early in 1965 a paper submitted by the management committee of the board of directors of Associated Electrical Industries suggested that, 'if management acts vigorously', pre-tax profits of 1967 should not be less than £20 million. The company reported profits of £11·5 million in 1964 and £13·5 million in 1965. In the 1965 report the chairman looked forward to another increase in profits, but the profit reported for 1966 was £9·2 million. In November 1966, when considering proposals and prospects for 1967, the board expected a profit of £10 million for 1967. In September 1967, General Electric Company announced its intention to bid for the stock of AEI. At the time AEI forecast profits of £10 million in 1967 and £15 million in 1968. During October the management re-examined its profit forecasts, held to £10 million for 1967, but expected £16 million in 1968 and in excess of £20 million in 1969. In the upshot the GEC bid succeeded. When the result of AEI for 1967 was published (by the new management) it showed a loss of £4·5 million compared with the profit of £10 million forecast within two months of the end of the year. The auditors attributed some £5 million of the £14·5 million difference to 'matters substantially of fact rather than of judgment', and the balance to 'matters substantially of judgment'.
/ For details see Sir Joseph Latham, *Take-over*, 1969 /

Three points are illustrated. Firstly, the doubtful quality of forecasts made in the ordinary course of affairs; compare the 1966 forecast and results of AEI. Secondly, the wide margins by which matters of judgment may affect reported results. Thirdly, the magnitude of the financial operations which may turn on such a questionable figure as net profit or expected profit (questionable, that is, under traditional rules); consequent upon the AEI profit forecasts, the company's counteraction to the bid, GEC raised its offer from the initial figure of about £120 million to £160 million.

☐ Leasco Data Processing Equipment Corporation held 38 per cent of the shares in Pergamon Press. It announced its intention to acquire the whole of the issued capital. Pergamon had reported a pre-tax profit of £2,104,000 for 1968 in June 1969. Shortly afterwards the Leasco bid was withdrawn. The (London) City Panel on Takeovers and Mergers accepted Leasco's explanation of the withdrawal but raised questions about the adequacy of the information disclosed in Pergamon's report to shareholders. The Board of Trade appointed inspectors to investigate some of these matters. The Pergamon board thereupon engaged independent accountants to examine and report on the accounts. (The Pergamon auditors were a different firm.)

The report of the independent accountants proposed adjustments to the 1968 accounts which reduced the reported net trading profit, before tax, by £1,609,000 to £495,000, and the reported net assets by £2,573,000 to £4,461,000. Seventeen adjustments to figures making up the trading profit contributed to the £1·6 million reduction. The reported balance of undistributed profit at the end of 1968 was £2,685,000; the recommended adjustments reduced this to £112,000. After taking account of all trading and exceptional items to 30 September 1969, the figures of the independent accountants showed an accumulated *loss* of £2,033,000 at that date. The independent accountants had the advantage of hindsight over the company's usual auditors. The differences in the figures are nevertheless remarkable.

☐ Handley Page, Britain's oldest aircraft manufacturer (founded 1909), collapsed and was put into the hands of the Official Receiver in 1970. Its last published balance sheet (1967) showed £12·2 million in assets against which there were liabilities of £5·2 million. Since the early sixties it had been engaged in developing its new Jetstream aircraft. Up to 1965 it had charged development costs against annual revenues, but from 1966 onwards these costs were accumulated in the balance sheet as an asset, the amount of which was £549,000 in 1966, £3 million in 1967 and £6.4 million in 1968. The change obscured a marked drift in the company's affairs; thus:

	1965	1966	1967
Consolidated net profit reported (£000)	533	458	333
Consolidated net profit taking in development costs as expenses (£000)	533	92 *loss*	2,197 *loss*

During 1967 and 1968 the shareholders contributed some £4·7 million in two issues of shares and an issue of loan stock—no doubt on the strength of the repeated profit forecasts by the management and the reported profits. In 1968 the company's turnover had fallen to half the 1965 figure and it was still unable to produce the Jetstream to its promised specifications. In mid 1969 five directors were ousted and steps were taken to reorganize the management. New money was pumped in by creditors; secured debt rose from £1·8 million at the end of 1967 to £8·2 million in mid 1969. The company, its shareholders and creditors were still hanging on hopes and profit forecasts. But cancellation of orders, receivership on behalf of the company's bankers, sale of the Jetstream subsidiary to the principal (American) distributor and other luckless incidents prevented Handley Page from coming out of its nosedive. The Official Receiver found the balance-sheet values of its assets were nothing like realizable values. Stocks and work in progress, plant and machinery, and investments in subsidiaries, were written down from a total of £19·2 million to £1·2 million. The company owed some £16 million. Commented Nicolas Travers (on whose account the above is based): 'Shareholders in bankrupt companies must frequently feel betrayed. Directors gamble resources; rash decisions lead to disasters as boards pour more and more money into attempts to redeem mistakes. Often, dying companies project encouragingly rosy futures right up to the end.' / *Accountancy*, April 1972 /

'Do you make money, or do you not make it?' was Bagehot's question. In respect of many companies, the answer can only be 'Who knows?' So many companies have switched from one way to another way of calculating income (Chapter 8), and so many others have reported profits that turned out to be of no substance, that it is almost questionable whether any reported profit figure is reliable. The grounds for relying on (unverifiable) forecasts and projections are even less substantial. Neither the age nor the reputation nor the size nor the technical competence of a company provides assurance that its published results are, or will continue to be, dependable bases for the judgments of investors and creditors. Whether a change in the method of calculating profit is a forerunner of collapse, outsiders cannot know. They may throw good money after bad, for all they know, until it is too late to recover.

DOES IT MATTER?

The illustrations given in this chapter are not a fair sample of what happens in business generally, but they are a sample of what happens when some companies are faced with adversity. The possibility of disguising what has occurred or is occurring is open when financial reporting is so much a matter of opinion. Some managers and directors no doubt have the courage to face immediately the consequences of reversals of fortune. Others procrastinate in the hope that the reversal is temporary. Of these, some are driven in the end to deliberate deception and fraud.

It is not to the point to argue that these latter cases are relatively few and do not warrant tighter control over the reporting practices of companies generally. The unexpected failure of a few companies, especially if it leads to revelation of the inadequacy of the community's defences against being misinformed, may undermine confidence in the securities market and in business generally. When large investors and experienced financiers can be deluded as well as amateurs and novices, it is hard to avoid the conclusion that there is something rotten in the state of business.

We know of no attempt to compute or describe the losses suffered by individuals—managers, directors, investors, creditors, brokers, auditors—through failures or frauds exacerbated by misleading financial statements. Perhaps the task is impossible. For even in a single case the losers may number tens of thousands and loss may take forms as different as suicide, imprisonment, loss of reputation, inconvenience and penury. It would make a harrowing tale.

It is not to the point to argue that, in the trade in securities, what is one man's loss is another's gain, even though this is the case. The corporation and securities laws intend that investors shall have a chance of assessing their prospects; they were never intended to give to companies or their directors the power to effect the massive redistributions of wealth that occur when operations are continued without proper regard for the interests of investors and creditors.

Nor is it to the point to argue that the losses of which we speak would have been incurred in any case, since the companies would have failed sooner or later. The examples used are cases in which new money was introduced, in substantial amounts, on the strength of misleading reports, hopes and forecasts. If the opportunity for doing this were closed by tightening the statutes and regulations, ailing companies would have to do more than fancy bookkeeping—and sooner—to survive. And if they failed, they would fail for millions less than if they were allowed, as now, to go on fooling themselves and the financial community at large.

14

SHIFTY PRICES AND FUNNY MONEY

'The truthfulness of accounting depends largely on the truthfulness of the dollar—and the dollar is a liar! For it says one thing and means another.'
/ Henry W Sweeney, *Stabilized Accounting*, 1936 /

'One of the basic assumptions of accounting is the stability of the dollar. It just isn't so.'
/ Robert H Montgomery, *Auditing*, 7th ed., 1949 /

'An acceptance of the assumption that the monetary unit is stable ... under present conditions amounts to sticking one's head in the sand.'
/ Paton and Paton, *Corporation Accounts and Statements*, 1955 /

'She can't do Addition', the Red Queen interrupted. 'Can you do Division? Divide a loaf by a knife—what's the answer to that?'
'I suppose—' Alice was beginning, but the Red Queen answered for her. 'Bread and butter of course. Try another Subtraction sum. Take a bone from a dog: what remains?'
/ *Through the Looking Glass* /

Everyone knows that the prices of goods and the purchasing power of money change from time to time. Everyone is affected by these changes. But for over fifty years businessmen and accountants have been bothered by the fact that traditional business accounting does not systematically take account of them.

The substantive problem, as it appears to businessmen, is related to the amount of profit that is taxable and the residue that is available for dividends or for the maintenance or replacement of depreciating assets.

CHANGES IN THE COSTS OF ASSETS

Usually company taxes are levied on income calculated according to historical cost principles. Suppose that a company earned a total revenue from sales of goods of $10,000 in 1972, and that the goods were bought in 1971 for $8,000. The taxable income would be $2,000. If business income tax were at the rate of 40 per cent, $800 would be payable in taxes. However if the purchase prices of the goods had risen between 1971 and 1972 from $8,000 to $9,000, the company will have already used up $1,000 of the $2,000 taxable income, in purchasing in 1972 the same inventory in quantitative terms as it purchased in 1971. If $800 is payable in taxes only $200 of its income would be available for dividends. If the company had been accustomed to paying $500 in dividends each year, it would be unable to do so in 1972 without reducing the scale of its business. It is therefore claimed that the calculation of taxes on the above basis is inequitable or unduly severe; that it amounts in part to a tax on wealth (or capital); and that the 1972 taxable income should only be the difference between the $10,000 revenue and the $9,000 that is the 1972 cost price of the inventory.

Now suppose that the above company was a manufacturer and that the cost of goods sold in 1972 includes depreciation charges on plant and equipment bought five or ten years earlier. The amount of depreciation would be based on the costs of the plant and equipment when they were purchased. If the price of replacing them had been rising since their purchase, the depreciation allowance for tax purposes would be much less than if it were based on the 1972 costs of the plant. Taxes would bite more deeply than in the former case into the amount available to replace the inventory and the plant and to pay dividends.

Suppose however, that there were no taxes. The calculation of income according to historical cost principles would still be misleading for dividend or other purposes. If the purchase price of goods had risen, the full amount of $2,000 in the first example would not be the amount that the company could properly pay out as dividends without reducing the scale of its business.

The inflation following the first world war, the climb out of the depression in the mid thirties, and the inflation following the second world war, all gave rise to argument against the adequacy of traditional accounting, to complaints about the inequity of taxes based largely on 'accounting' income and to comments on the difficulty of replacing assets at higher prices. In the late forties and early fifties, among the companies that commented critically on the combined consequences of accounting methods and fiscal rules were: Courtaulds (1948 Report), Patons & Baldwins (1951 Report), Shell Transport and Trading Company (1952 Report), and Peninsular and Oriental Steam Navigation Company (1953 Report), in the United Kingdom; United States Steel (1947 Report) and National Steel Corporation (1949 Report), in the United States; and Broken Hill Proprietary Company (1952, 1953 Reports), in Australia. Pamphlets dealing at length with the problems of 'capital erosion' or 'capital attrition' in inflationary periods were published by Machinery and Allied Products Institute (Chicago, 1947), Colonial Sugar Refining Company (Sydney, 1950) and Federation of British Industries (London, 1951). Similar complaints have been made from time to time in the intervening period.

The hypothetical example and the criticisms of directors mentioned in this section all relate to the cost or replacement prices of specific assets, assets of the kind used by a company at a given time. It is proper enough for directors to be anxious to maintain and replace specific assets, but this is not a difficulty peculiar to inflationary periods. The replacement price of any good may rise even though prices generally do not rise (because the prices of other specific goods have fallen). Even in inflationary periods some prices may not rise, while others rise at different rates. The difficulty of replacing assets at higher prices simply becomes more pressing in inflationary periods because so many prices tend to rise.

When the prices of goods change relatively to one another, the holders of some goods become relatively better off than the holders of others. This is one consequence that is not brought into account when companies keep the book values of assets at cost prices.

INFLATION

Inflation is said to have occurred when the prices of goods in terms of money have risen generally, or on average. The measure of inflation is the rise in an index of changes in the level of prices. The index is based on movements in specific prices—the prices of a selected 'basket' of goods and services. A rise in the general level of prices means a fall in the general purchasing power of money. The dollar then is not what it used to be.

The 'devalued' dollar is the only dollar then in circulation, the only dollar whose meaning is then understandable. If any financial statement is to be understandable in the economic context to which it relates, its components should be in dollars of this understandable kind. And the loss in the purchasing power of *every* dollar expressing the money equivalent of each asset should be taken into account in calculating the income or profit of every year.

This consequence of inflation (or deflation, when it occurs) is disregarded when companies base their accounting on the cost price of assets. 'Thus the furnace built with 1961 £s, with money borrowed in 1960 £s, on land bought with 1929 £s, using coke purchased with 1969 £s produces profits expressed in 1970 £s' ('How Inflation Warps Accounts', *The Economist*, 16 January 1971). The addition and subtraction of any such numbers of £s (or dollars) is absurd, it gives financially and commercially meaningless results. It is reminiscent of the Red Queen's question: 'Take a bone from a dog; what remains?' Or of the French writer who in 1926 likened it to adding cabbages and carrots and little red radishes, an operation that 'you were taught when you were a child ... could not be done'. Or of the remark of an American writer in 1934: 'one cannot add horses and apples'. Accounting practice has survived all this lampooning. The impossible and absurd is still with us. Current ratios, debt-to-equity ratios and rates of return are calculated as if the numerators and denominators were in similar terms. In fact the numerators and denominators are in such mixed dollars and mixed prices that they can have no firm or significant meaning—no more meaning than a 'sum' of horses and apples divided by a 'sum' of cabbages and carrots and little red radishes.

PROFESSIONAL RESPONSE

Let it be emphasised that there are two effects of changes in the prices of goods which are disregarded under the strict use of the professionally endorsed historical cost rule—changes in the prices of particular assets and changes in the purchasing power of the monetary unit in which the values of assets are expressed from time to time. These two kinds of change work in opposite directions. If the prices of assets rise, those assets become worth more dollars than before; but if the purchasing power of money simultaneously falls, each of those dollars is worth less than before. The net assets of a company will only have the same purchasing power as before (the company will only be as well off as before), if the rises in the prices of its net assets exactly offset in total the fall in the purchasing power of the money unit. The likelihood of this occurring is astronomically remote. Both of the above effects must therefore be brought into account, each in its distinctive way, if financial statements are not to be misleading.

The accountancy profession has occasionally been mindful of the defects of its avowed practices, when prices and price levels rise and fall. In 1947 the American Institute of Accountants published *Accounting Research Bulletin No. 33*, 'Depreciation and High Costs'; it subsequently co-sponsored a study published in 1952 as *Changing Concepts of Business Income*. In 1952 the Institute of Chartered Accountants in England and Wales published its *Recommendation N15*, 'Accounting in Relation to Changes in the Purchasing Power of Money'. In 1952 the Institute of Cost and Works Accountants (England) published *The Accountancy of Changing Price Levels*. In 1952 the Association of Certified and Corporate Accountants published *Accounting for Inflation*. In 1956 the American Accounting Association published a study by Professor R C Jones, *Effects of Price Level Changes on Business Income, Capital and Taxes*. In 1963 the American Institute of Certified Public Accountants published Accounting Research Study No. 6, *Reporting the Financial Effects of Price-Level Changes*, and followed it up in 1969 with *Accounting Principles Board Statement No. 3*, 'Financial Statements Restated for General Price-Level Changes'. In 1968 the Research Foundation of the Institute of Chartered Accountants in England and Wales published *Accounting for Stewardship in a Period of Inflation*.

Besides these statements, a mountainous quantity of periodical literature and books have been devoted to the same problem—or problems.

The arguments and proposals of this literature have generally been partial and incomplete. Some have been in support of adjusting the cost prices of assets by use of a general price index, so that they are expressed in terms of 'up-to-date dollars'. The adjustment is in effect an adjustment for the change in the purchasing power of money, *not* for the changes in specific asset prices. Others have supported adjustment of the cost prices of assets to their current costs or replacement prices, but *without* adjustment for the change in the purchasing power of money. Each class of proposal therefore only strikes at one of the two kinds of shifts (in relative prices, and in the purchasing power of money) distinguished earlier in this chapter.

FISCAL MAKESHIFTS

While the debate has been proceeding, companies have not been entirely without relief. Governments found it necessary or desirable to ease the burdens of higher taxes or to encourage investment in industrial plant by tax concessions. The instruments of relief were new rules for calculating taxable income or tax payable. In the United States in the late thirties, LIFO was introduced for inventory valuation; accelerated depreciation and investment credits were later introduced in respect of plant investments. In other countries, investment grants and high initial depreciation charges for plant were introduced.

Most of these devices lowered taxable income or tax payable in the year in which a company availed itself of the concession. That was their intention. However most of them also entailed relatively higher taxes in later years because the total charges against revenue, for tax purposes, could not exceed the cost price of the relevant assets. The concessions were in the nature of tax-deferrals or interest-free loans, to be met or 'repaid' in higher taxes later, provided of course that taxable income was earned later.

These makeshifts had unfortunate side-effects. In some cases, the tax concessions were available only if the company used in its *published* financial statements the same methods of valuation and calculation used for tax purposes. Consequently, if the rules previously used were deemed to give a fair representation of financial results and position, the new rules could not but give a distorted representation. To benefit from the tax law, companies had to disregard the 'fair presentation' rule of the securities laws! In other cases, companies adopted the tax rules of their own volition for financial reporting. It is curious to note that these new rules, made respectable by the tax laws, created the opportunities for much of the variant and divergent accounting illustrated throughout this book. It does not seem to be pressing the matter too hard to assert that the diversity and confusion thus created have stemmed from attempts to rectify the consequences of the failure of conventional accounting to bring into account changes in prices and in the purchasing power of money.

PRICE-LEVEL ACCOUNTING

The latest publications of the professional bodies in the USA (1968) and the UK (1969) have both proposed a form of price-level accounting. Under these proposals, the original costs of non-monetary assets would be adjusted for changes in the purchasing power of money, by the use of a general index of price changes. Charges against revenues, for inventories and depreciation, would be adjusted consequentially. And gains due to the fall in the purchasing power of money owed to long term creditors would be brought into account. It is said to be an advantage of this style of accounting that it holds to the 'principle' of using original costs. But it also holds to the defects of that principle, namely its disregard of relative shifts in the prices of specific goods, and the irrelevance of purchase prices, however adjusted, as indicators of financial position.

The defects may be illustrated by a simple example. Suppose that on 1 January 19×1 a company bought a parcel of land for $100,000 and a parcel of shares for $50,000; that it held the same land and shares at 31 December 19×1; and that an index of the general level of prices rose from 120 to 126 (i.e. by 5 per cent) in the year. At 31 December, under price-level accounting, the company's balance sheet would report the land at $105,000 and the shares at $52,500. But these figures need have no relation to the *purchase price* of equivalent land and shares at that time, for prices do not move in step. And the figures have no necessary relation to the *selling prices* of the land and shares, which are the only prices indicative of the company's financial position at 31 December 19×1. The market (selling) price of the land may have risen to $120,000 or fallen to $90,000. The price of the shares may have moved in the same direction as the general level of prices, or in the opposite direction, or by more or less than 5 per cent. Price-level accounting therefore will not give figures relevant to tests of solvency, or of gearing, or of rate of return; nor will it give a proper basis for stewardship or accountability for the monetary amount at the disposal of the company and its directors from time to time.

In the light of these defects, it is pertinent to ask what evidence may have prompted the professional bodies to favour price-level accounting. There is very little. The US study, *Reporting the Financial Effects of Price Level Changes* (1963), cited some thirty companies, in eight countries, which had 'done something' about the effects of changes in prices and price levels. Only one of these, Reece Corporation, had used systematically the price-level adjustment idea. Most of the others had made occasional revaluations of assets on other footings than the change in the general level of prices. This is little evidence indeed of support, on the initiative of businessmen themselves, for price-level accounting.

REPLACEMENT-PRICE ACCOUNTING

There is much more evidence in support of revaluation of assets by reference to replacement prices. The most widely publicized example is the accounting of Philips' Gloeilampenfabrieken. Other companies in the Netherlands have adopted the same principles but the practice is by no means general in that country. In other countries, Imperial Tobacco Company of Canada, Fisons (UK, see p. 100 above) and Rocla (Australia, see p. 222 above), for example, have based asset revaluations or depreciation charges on replacement prices.

As representing the financial position of a company, replacement prices are better approximations than original costs adjusted for general price level changes. They do take cognizance of relative shifts in prices. Also depreciation based on replacement prices ensures the retention out of total revenues of a better approximation to the cost of maintaining a given physical plant.

However a replacement price is not strictly pertinent to financial position. A replacement price is what a company would have to pay to acquire a good that it does *not* have—namely the 'replacement' good. Financial position, on the other hand, relates to prices of goods and other assets which a company does have.

Replacement price, like any other purchase price, is considered when choosing *whether* to hold an old good, or to buy a 'near replacement' or to buy something else altogether. It has nothing to say about the financial capacity of a company to do any of these things. Indeed if the price of replacing particular assets has risen relatively to other prices, a company may choose to buy quite different assets when the old assets must be scrapped. The funds required may then have no relation to the replacement price of the old assets.

Furthermore, replacement price is a cost price; like all cost prices it has no logical connection with indicators of solvency, and gearing or leverage, nor with rate of return calculations. Finally replacement price accounting as it is usually practised does not deal systematically with effects of the fall or rise (if any) in the purchasing power of money.

ACCOUNTING FOR CHANGES

There is a way of dealing systematically with changes both in prices and in the purchasing power of money. We take it for granted that the relevance of the market prices of assets to financial calculation and dealing has already been established. The very act of finding the net market prices (or cash equivalents) of assets at the end of each period takes account of changes in prices. One simple calculation takes account of the effects of changes in the purchasing power of money. The procedure may be illustrated in four steps. (Readers unfamiliar with accounting should be able to have the illustrations explained by any accountant.)

A Suppose the balance sheets of Company *A* at the beginning and the end of a year were as follows:

Balance sheet at 1 January 19 x 1		$
Assets	—Cash	10,000
Equities	—Shareholders' equity	10,000

Balance sheet at 31 December 19 x 1		$
Assets	—Cash	12,000
Equities	—Shareholders' equity	12,000

If there had been no change in the purchasing power of money during the year the company would clearly be better off (better able to buy any good or service available in the market) by $2,000. Its net profit would be $2,000. But if the general level of prices had risen by 5 per cent during the year, the company would need to have $10,500 at the end of the year in order to be as well off as at the beginning. The mere change in the date of the balance sheet signifies that the two balance sheets refer to dollars of different purchasing power. In effect, the company used its 'January' dollars in the course of trade and finished the year with 'December' dollars, each of which had a lower purchasing power than the 'January' dollar.

The gross increment in dollars ($2,000) must be divided into two parts. One part is the number of dollars ($500) that together with the original number of dollars ($10,000) would have the same purchasing power in December as $10,000 had in January; we call this part a *capital maintenance reserve*. The other part of the gross increment ($1,500) is the net profit of the year in 'December' dollars, or dollars of December purchasing power. Of course all dollars at 31 December have the same general purchasing power; a dollar at a given date means nothing else than its purchasing power at that date.

We could now draw up the balance sheet at the end of the year as follows:

Balance sheet at 31 December 19 x 1		$
Assets	—Cash	12,000
Equities	—Shareholders' equity	
	Nominal, 1 January	10,000
	Capital maintenance reserve	500
	Net profit, 19 × 1	1,500
		12,000

In this simple example there are no non-cash assets and no creditors. The next example introduces non-cash assets.

B Suppose the balance sheets of Company *B* at the beginning and the end of the year were as follows:

Balance sheet at 1 January 19 × 1	$
Assets —Cash	4,000
—Non-cash assets (at market selling prices)	6,000
	10,000
Equities —Shareholders' equity	10,000

Balance sheet at 31 December 19 × 1	$
Assets —Cash	5,500
—Non-cash assets (at market selling prices)	6,500
	12,000
Equities —Shareholders' equity	12,000

Suppose that during the year the company had net revenue (cash receipts less cash payments) of $1,600; that it spent $100 on additional non-cash assets; and that the *net rise* in the market selling prices of its non-cash assets was $400. And suppose, as in the first case, that the general level of prices rose by 5 per cent.

The gross increment in dollars is the same as in the case of Company A. However, part of it arose from net revenues and part from rises in the cash equivalent (selling prices) of its non-cash assets. Both of these have the same effect; it would be improper (because it would be incomplete) to report the effect of net revenues but to disregard the effect of the net rise in the cash equivalent of non-cash assets. This net rise in market prices of *all* assets we call a *price variation adjustment.* (Where depreciation of assets has occurred, this is a price variation adjustment downwards, of course). In this case, as in the case of Company A, there must also be the division of the gross increment into the capital maintenance adjustment ($500) and the net profit ($1,500).

We would now draw up the income account of Company B for the year and its balance sheet at the end of the year thus:

Income account for 19 × 1	$
Net revenue	1,600
Price variation adjustment	400
	2,000
Less capital maintenance adjustment	500
Net profit	1,500

Balance sheet at 31 December 19 × 1		$
Assets	—Cash	5,500
	—Non-cash assets (at market selling prices)	6,500
		12,000
Equities	—Shareholders' equity	
	Nominal, 1 January	10,000
	Capital maintenance reserve	500
	Net profit, 19 × 1	1,500
		12,000

It may be noted that the charge in the income account described as the capital maintenance *adjustment* is transferred to the capital maintenance *reserve* in the balance sheet.

We have illustrated the two ways in which changes in prices affect the positions and results of companies. If the prices of assets rise, the total amounts of assets and of equities rise. If, at the same time, the general level of prices rises (and the purchasing power of money falls), this offsets in part (and it may exceed) the effects of rises in asset prices on the shareholders' equity. In the special case in which the net rise in the prices of a company's assets is equal to the fall in the purchasing power of the amount of the opening shareholders' equity, the two adjustments offset each other. The two types of change are different in effect.

Next consider a company that finances its operations, in part, by borrowing.

C Suppose that at 1 January 19×1 Company *C* held cash and other assets worth $10,000 as in the case of Company *B*. Suppose that these were financed by borrowing $3,000 and by shareholders' equity $7,000. Suppose that the other data were as for Company *B*: net revenue, $1,600; price variation adjustment, $400. In this case the amount of the *net* assets (total assets less liabilities) at 1 January 19×1 was $7,000. The capital maintenance adjustment would be 5 per cent of this figure, i.e. $350; and the net profit $1,650. This is higher than the net profit in the case of Company *B*. The reason is that the amount owed to lenders is fixed in nominal terms; the lenders carry the risk of a rise in the general level of prices (a fall in the purchasing power of money) and they have suffered a fall in purchasing power (5 per cent of $3,000 = $150) equivalent to the gain by shareholders ($1,650 net profit compared with $1,500 in the case of Company *B*).

One final example will make the case of Company *C* quite general. Most companies have, besides cash on hand, some receivables (trade debtors) and some short-term payables at the end of a year. These may be described as cash items or monetary items because, like the amount borrowed by Company *C*, the amounts of them are receivable or payable at their face value regardless of changes in the purchasing power of money. Consider a company that is like Company *C* in all respects other than in having some short-term receivables and payables.

D Suppose the balance sheet at 1 January 19×1 of Company *D* were as follows:

Balance sheet at 1 January 19 × 1		$
Assets	—Cash	5,000
	—Receivables	3,000
	—Non-cash assets (at market selling prices)	6,000
		14,000
Equities	—Short-term payables	4,000
	—Long-term loan	3,000
	—Shareholders' equity	7,000
		14,000

Suppose its operations were as for Company *C* above. Their results are summarized as follows:

Income account for 19 × 1	$
Net revenue	1,600
Price variation adjustment	400
	2,000
Less capital maintenance adjustment	350
Net profit	1,650

On the basis of these results and certain changes in receivables and payables, the company's position at the end of the year will be:

Balance sheet at 31 December 19 × 1		$
Assets	—Cash	7,000
	—Receivables	3,500
	—Non-cash assets (at market selling prices)	6,500
		17,000
Equities	—Short-term payables	5,000
	—Long-term loan	3,000
	—Shareholders' equity	
	Nominal, 1 January	7,000
	Capital maintenance reserve	350
	Net profit, 19 × 1	1,650
		17,000

In respect of the determination of net income, Company *D* is exactly the same as Company *C*. The price variation adjustment is the same, since the amount of non-monetary assets is the same. The capital maintenance adjustment is the same, since the opening shareholders' equity is the same. The only difference is the addition of like amounts to the monetary assets and the liabilities. As losses of purchasing power are made through holding money when its purchasing power falls, and as gains in purchasing power occur in respect of money owed when its purchasing power falls, the addition of like amounts to monetary assets and to liabilities does not change the net profit.

RESULTS AND POSITION

Observe now the features of the income account and balance sheet derived in the above manner.

(i)   Assets are shown at market prices or cash equivalents, and the net shareholders' equity is the aggregate of these prices less the amount of liabilities. The balance sheet is consistent with what is commonly understood as financial position.
(ii) The individual amounts of assets and equities are understandable, since they represent or depend on money equivalents at a recent specified date, in the setting of the general level of prices and the structure of prices at that date.
(iii) The net profit is the increment in general purchasing power of the company over the period it covers, expressed in dollars of the purchasing power at the balancing date. It is a genuine surplus after maintaining the purchasing power of the opening shareholders' equity. The capital maintenance adjustment is easily explicable or understandable, since everyone will have experienced the effect of the change in the purchasing power of money which it expresses.
(iv) The balance-sheet and net profit figures are all in terms of 'current' (or recent) dollars. Any calculation of the rate of return, the current ratio, the debt-to-equity ratio or subsidiary ratios will be practically significant, since all the component figures are of the same up-to-date kind. The figures give a true and fair view of results and position, since the full effects of all transactions of a company and of all changes that have affected results and position have been brought into account.

Subsequent years: The illustrations relate to one year only. The process is exactly the same for subsequent years. Suppose that a general index of changes in prices stood at the following figures at successive dates:

1	January 19 × 1	120.0
31	December 19 × 1	126.0
31	December 19 × 2	133.5

The rise during 19×1 was thus 5 per cent as in the earlier examples. The rise in 19×2 was approximately 6 per cent. All the items in the income account and balance sheet of Company D at the end of 19×2 would be obtained in the same way as in 19×1. There is one complication in respect of shareholders' equity.

The capital maintenance reserve at the end of 19×1 ($350) *together with* the opening nominal amount ($7,000) is equal in purchasing power to the shareholders' equity at 1 January in '1 January dollars'. The amount of the capital maintenance reserve is therefore not divisible as profit, if it is held that the purchasing power of the company's capital (or net assets, which is equal to shareholders' equity) is to be maintained. Only the 19×1 net profit, $1,650, is divisible.

Suppose that no dividend is paid out of the 19×1 profit. Then at the end of 19×2 it is necessary for the company to 'keep up' the purchasing power both of the 'capital amount' ($7,350 at December 19×1) and the retained profits amount ($1,650 at December 19×1) before striking its profit for 19×2. The adjustments necessary for this are:

Capital maintenance adjustment 19 × 2 7,350 × 6 per cent = 441
Retained profit adjustment   19 × 2 1,650 × 6 per cent = 99.

The result for 19×2 may then be represented thus (assuming that net revenues and price variation adjustments have been accumulated by ordinary bookkeeping processes):

Income account for 19 × 2	$
Net revenue	1,900
Price variation adjustment	300
	2,200
Less Capital maintenance adjustment	441
Retained profit adjustment	99
Net profit	1,660

The amounts of the two subtracted adjustments would be transferred to the appropriate shareholders' equity accounts. The balance sheet would be as follows (starting with the balance sheet of Company D at 31 December 19×1, and assuming that the effects of all events and transactions have been accumulated by usual bookkeeping processes):

Balance sheet at 31 December 19 × 2		$
Assets	—Cash	5,000
	—Receivables	5,000
	—Non-cash assets (at market selling prices)	9,700
		19,700
Equities	—Short-term payables	5,500
	—Long-term loan	3,000
	—Shareholders' equity	
	Nominal, 1 January	7,000
	Capital maintenance reserve	791
	Retained profit	1,749
	Net profit, 19 × 2	1,660
		19,700

The profit of 19×2 is a genuine surplus after allowing for all rises in asset prices (through the price variation adjustment) and the effect of the fall in the purchasing power of money (through the capital maintenance and retained profit adjustments). The whole of the amounts described as profit in the balance sheet could be appropriated and paid as dividends without impairing the 'capital'. The balance of the capital maintenance reserve is not divisible as profit but it may be converted into 'share capital' by bonus issues (capitalization issues in UK and stock dividends in USA).

The whole process secures the continual and complete up-dating of the information on the financial position of the company from time to time.

The question of the price index to be used is not a serious problem. What is required is an index of the changes in the general level of prices which will serve as an indicator of changes (in the opposite direction) in the purchasing power of money. Indexes are, of course, only approximations, but it is sufficient that some single index prescribed by law or regulation be used generally. It will be clear that any defect in the index would not affect any account balances other than the shareholders' equity accounts, and it would affect only the composition of these, not their aggregate.

This book is not a textbook on accounting. It was unnecessary to explore in detail the manner of dealing with each of the assets and equities that may appear in balance sheets, but it has been necessary to illustrate the process in a general way so that the suggested changes in the law, to be presented in the final chapter, may be understood.

IN SUM

The system represents 'a coherent and logical structure of accounting principles' of the kind which the English Institute in its *Recommendation N15* considered to be desirable (see p. 60 above). It would do away with the anomalies and the 'tactical' disclosure of information so copiously illustrated in this book.

The dollar may not be what it used to be; prices may not be what they used to be. Nevertheless there can be no excuse for continuing to account in terms of (fixed) cost prices when prices are always shifty. Or for continuing to account in 'funny money', which is the only way to describe the mixtures of different dollars found in financial statements at present.

15

AWAY WITH STOCK MARKET POLLUTION!

'Now, no matter how beautiful a map may be, it is useless to a traveller unless it accurately shows the relationship of places to each other, the structure of the territory... But if we are just drawing maps for fun without paying any attention to the structure of the region, there is nothing in the world to prevent us from putting in all the extra curlicues and twists we want in the lakes, rivers, and roads. No harm will be done *unless someone tries to plan a trip by such a map.*
'Similarly, by means of imaginary or false reports, or by false inferences from good reports, or by mere rhetorical exercises, we can manufacture at will, with language, "maps" which have no reference to the extensional world. Here again no harm will be done unless someone makes the mistake of regarding such "maps" as representing real territories.'
/ S I Hayakawa, *Language in Thought and Action,* 1963 /

'Ever since chemists began to manufacture substances that nature never invented, the problems of water purification have become complex and the danger to users of water has increased. As we have seen, the production of these synthetic chemicals in large volume began in the 1940s. It has now reached such proportions that an appalling deluge of chemical pollution is daily poured into the nation's waterways. When inextricably mixed with domestic and other wastes discharged into the same water, these chemicals sometimes defy detection by the methods in ordinary use by purification plants. Most of them are so stable that they cannot be broken down by ordinary processes. Often they cannot even be identified. In rivers, a really incredible variety of pollutants combine to produce deposits that the sanitary engineers can only despairingly refer to as "gunk". Professor Rolf Eliassen of the Massachusetts Institute of Technology testified before a congressional committee to the impossibility of predicting the composite effect of these chemicals, or of identifying the organic matter resulting from the mixture. "We

don't begin to know what that is", said Professor Eliassen. "What is the effect on the people? We don't know." '
/ Rachel Carson, *Silent Spring*, 1962 /

Neither do we know the effects on the fortunes of people and on the efficiency of business corporations, of the pollutants that enter the stream of financial information serving the securities market. We know some of their consequences in a general way—unexpected reversals of reported results, unexpected losses, unexpected collapses and bankruptcies, unexpected takeovers and unexpected but costly litigation. We may suspect that companies are far less efficient than they would be if they were unable to manufacture instant profits by book entries, and if their states and results were strictly comparable. But we do not know.

However, we do know some of the things that create 'gunk'.

STAGNANT INFORMATION

We know that the purchase price of a good, any good, has no necessary connection with financial position at any subsequent date. The continued representation in balance sheets, year after year, of assets at cost prices is simply throwing stale news in the way of investors. It is as useless as the newspapers of a year ago—or ten or twenty years ago—for any current purpose. It has nothing to do with the on-going processes of change, negotiation and adaptation by which companies seek to survive and grow.

No private person would, for any serious purpose, tot up the prices he paid for things years ago in order to determine his present financial position. He would list the things he possesses, find their approximate market prices and deduct what he owes. Why any manager or director of a company should act any differently it is impossible to say. How any investor or financier can depend upon and calculate upon aggregates of cost prices has never been demonstrated.

Apart from the sheer irrelevance of cost prices as such, the accumulation of stagnant information produces nonsense. Aggregations of dollar amounts, when the dollars in question had significantly different purchasing powers, are meaningless. No person or company can pay debts or buy other things with the mixture of dollars of different purchasing powers, which appear in disguise simply as dollars, in most balance sheets. In 1972 there are no 1950 or 1955 or 1960 or 1970 dollars about—except in balance sheets; there they stagnate, breeding confusion.

MEANINGLESS 'INFORMATION'

We skipped lightly over a number of so-called 'technical' terms, when dealing with the alternative rules available for valuing assets and calculating income. We might now ask whether those terms are meaningful, or whether they and the money amounts to which they lead are, to use Hayakawa's words, 'manufactured at will' and have no reference to the outside world.

Take first some of the rules for inventories.

One of the rules most commonly used is 'the lower of cost and market'. It is easy to understand the rule and to follow it. But does the rule make sense? Suppose a company has two items of inventory: A—cost price $30, market price $40; and B—cost price $30, market price $25. If it applies the rule to each item separately, it will report its inventory at $55. However, the sum of a cost price and a market price is meaningless in any financial dealing, negotiation or calculation. If the company applies the rule to the aggregate cost prices and market prices, it will report its inventory at $60. But no one will know whether this figure is the sum of cost prices, the sum of market prices, or partly one and partly the other. The phrase 'lower of cost and market' itself does not give a clue to the real nature of the reported figure. In any case, in the outside world there is no such thing as a 'lower-of-cost-and-market' price; there are only buying prices and selling prices. The phrase and the figure which results are both manufactured, and neither has reference to anything in the external world.

Another rule is the first-in, first-out rule (FIFO). Again it is easy to see what the rule says and to follow it, but does it make sense? Suppose a company has two units of inventory, both the same except that one was bought first for $100 and the other was bought later for $120. As both are the same, it is really immaterial to the company which it sells first. But the rule says: charge the price first paid against the proceeds of the sale, whichever is sold first; if one unit is left on hand at the end of the year, use the price latest paid ($120) as the value of the inventory. However, if the company was indifferent as to which unit it sold first, why discriminate in this way?

Exactly the same question could be asked of the LIFO rule, which operates in exactly the opposite fashion to the FIFO rule. There is no such thing as a LIFO price or a FIFO price in the outside world, with which a LIFO value or a FIFO value of a balance sheet inventory can be compared. And there is no such thing as a LIFO debt or a FIFO debt which could be discharged by realizing the LIFO or FIFO amount of the inventory.

These rules all give rise to fictions—figures that have no significance for any kind of financial dealing; figures that are indeed not comprehensible and not comparable with any sum of money, any debt or any price by which a company may proceed with its business. To assert in opposition to this that such figures are used in calculating net profit or income is beside the point. For if any such figure is a fiction, the result of adding it to or taking it from any other figure is also a fiction.

The traditional rules for calculating the amount of depreciation likewise lead to fictions. The rules are easy to describe and follow but this does not mean that the result is understandable or significant. Depreciation means fall in price, or loss in value in that sense. That this is its meaning is implied in the customary writing down of assets to an expected scrap value (selling price) by the end of an asset's useful life. But the routine application of the rules invariably leads to writing down asset values at a faster rate or at a slower rate than the market value falls. Indeed, the routine application of the rules often leads to writing down asset values when their market prices have gone up.

It may seem harsh to call the results of these rules fictions; more charitable to call them approximations. However, when, as we have seen, there may be 'adjustments' of the order of millions, tens of millions and hundreds of millions in the previously reported book values, the fictional character of what is reported can hardly be disputed.

UNSYSTEMATIC INFORMATION

Chapter 4 showed that certain aggregates which appear in balance sheets and income accounts may be related to discover important features of a company's position and results. We showed also that these aggregates are themselves systematically related. Current assets plus other assets equals total assets. Total assets less liabilities equals shareholders' equity. The change in shareholders' equity in a year (disregarding new receipts from shareholders and dividend payments to shareholders) is the amount of net profit.

Now observe some of the effects of incorrectly stating the amounts of some of these aggregates. If current assets are understated, the current ratio is unfavourably affected, the debt-to-equity ratio is unfavourably affected, and the rate of return is favourably affected. If the other assets are understated, the debt-to-equity ratio is unfavourably affected and the rate of return is favourably affected. If the current liabilities are understated, the current ratio is favourably affected and the debt-to-equity ratio is favourably affected. These are only some of the possibilities. The fact that the aggregates in question affect the ratio calculations—and some of them in opposite directions simultaneously—makes it imperative that *the proper values for each asset and liability should appear in the main columns of the balance sheet.*

What are proper values? The argument and evidence all point in the direction of market values of assets and face values of liabilities. (To be rather more exact we should perhaps say net market values of assets, to allow for known costs incidental to sale; and net values of liabilities, to allow for cases where settlement of liabilities at the date of the balance sheet would attract some discount.)

We have considered it a step in the right direction that some laws and regulations now require the market values of quoted or listed securities to be given, and the market values of property assets to be the subject of comment. But if these values are given only in parentheses or in footnotes or in directors' reports, their consequential effects on total gains will not appear in the main columns of the financial statements. Those who use the financial statements for the calculation of 'test' ratios will be using irrelevant figures. Only those who know how to incorporate the differences between book values and market values into calculations of total gain and who know the effects of these differences on the amount of shareholders' equity can benefit fully from the additional information.

We do not believe that it was the intention of the legislators to provide investors with a do-it-yourself kit, the pieces for which were to be found by a prior treasure hunt.

The only way of ensuring that significant figures and their effects are incorporated systematically in the published financial statements is to rule that they shall be so incorporated—not left as footnotes or parenthetical addenda.

Turning to the securities market generally, the present state of affairs is thoroughly unsystematic. Every company in jurisdictions on the UK pattern may choose whether and when to revalue its assets, which assets it will revalue and on what basis it will revalue. Comparison of the significant financial features of two or more companies, on the basis of balance-sheet information, is logically impossible. The task of trying to make comparable the figures on any two companies is also impossible, since the necessary additional information in respect of each is known only to the insiders of each.

It is common in some jurisdictions to find that companies supply, to investment analysts and stockbrokers, additional and explanatory material above or other than that published to share-holders and others directly. It may be supposed that this makes good or corrects any defects in the financial statements. But this is no solution. Firstly, the additional information is given infor-mally and is not subject to the independent verification that audit should provide. Secondly, it makes analysts and brokers 'insiders' (unless the same information is publicly released simultaneously) and properly subject to the rules against insider trading. Thirdly, the law contemplates that *all* users of financial statements shall have equal access to the same information, which entails that the financial statements shall be complete in themselves.

INCONSISTENCIES AND SUPERFLUITIES

One does not wish to doubt the good intentions of some of the recent amendments to the statutory provisions on company accounts, nor to doubt the good intentions of the companies that try to follow them out. But the consequences are more curious than informative.

We suppose, for example, that the object of published accounts is to remove doubts about what may have happened to a company's financial affairs since the last previous report. Rather than allay doubts, some of the rules create doubts. Every case in which different figures are given in respect of the same assets, in the directors' report and the appended financial statements and notes, raises the question: which of the figures should the reader rely on?

☐ The 1961 accounts of Globe Telegraph and Trust Company showed investments quoted on British stock exchanges 'at cost less amounts applied from net surplus on realizations, £9·25 million'; their market value was £32·30 million. The book value of all quoted investments was £12·22 million; the market value was £37·95 million. By contrast with this disregard in the accounts proper for known market values, in the same year the book value of an *unquoted* investment was written up from £1·34 million to £6 million. The shareholders' equity was shown as £15·65 million; using the market values of quoted investments it would have been £41·38 million. The earnings rate (using the reported net profit) was 5·4 per cent on the published net equity. It would have been 2 per cent on the net equity if market prices of quoted investments had been used in computing net equity. Which was the reader to believe?

☐ In the 1968 accounts of Conzinc Riotinto of Australia, the total assets of the *group* were shown to be $423 million, the total assets of the *company* to be $122 million. Among the investments of the *company* were shares in a subsidiary, the cost of which, $27 million, was included in the balance-sheet figures. The notes to the accounts gave to these shares a market value of $755 million. Among the assets of the *group* were listed shares in associated companies, the cost of which, $4 million, was included in the balance-sheet figures. The notes gave the market value of these shares as $69 million. A footnote to one note (!) gives the company's equity in the net tangible assets of three unlisted associate companies as $47 million, whereas the book value used in the balance sheet was $33 million. Which of these different figures is a reader expected to rely on and base his judgments on?

The addition of new requirements to the statutory provisions is quite possibly the easiest way to get some information disclosed which, as past events have shown, should be disclosed. However, mere addition without rationalization of related requirements increases confusion—not intentionally, but certainly inevitably. The 1967 amendments to the UK Companies Act increased the amount of information required on fixed assets. One result:

□ The 1968 accounts of Norcros gave a full-page note to the item 'fixed assets'. There were two six-column sets of figures, one for the group, one for the company. The columns were for five classes of assets and a total. The narrations down the page were: cost at December 1967, cost of additions, cost of inter-company transfers, cost of disposals, cost eliminated on disposal of subsidiaries, adjustments on conversion of overseas currency assets, and an aggregate of these; then under 'depreciation', there was aggregate depreciation to December 1967, amount provided in 1968, inter-company transfers, eliminations in respect of disposals, eliminations on disposal of subsidiaries, adjustments on conversion of overseas currency provisions, surplus arising on property valuations, and a net sub-total. Finally there were the net balances at December 1967 and December 1968. There were also a dozen or so lines of explanation. In all, 160 separate figures to describe a handful of balance-sheet figures.

This is full disclosure with a vengeance. However there was no indication of the dates at which the 'costs' were incurred, or how out-of-date the figures were, and no indication of an up-to-date value of the assets. Much ado about nothing relevant. Yet in superlative fashion it conformed with the statute.

NON-ASSETS AND NON-LIABILITIES

Then there is the continued inclusion of account balances representing expenditures, payments or 'losses' in years prior to the year under report; and the inclusion of balances representing liabilities that are not liabilities at the date of the report.

When a company incurs formation expenses and security flotation costs, and makes payments for goodwill, the money has gone. The company no longer has an asset which, in the ordinary course of its business, it can turn to other uses—buy other goods or discharge debts. Yet these figures may be carried in balance sheets for years afterwards as assets. No discriminating user of such balance sheets will take any notice of these figures; they would be excluded from consideration of the security for debts and in calculations made preparatory to or in the course of takeover negotiations. Undiscriminating users of the balance sheets may be misled. Much the same may be said of provisions for 'deferred taxes'. As was indicated in the previous chapter, some fiscal laws allow large charges for depreciation when an asset is first purchased but correspondingly lower charges in later years. The tax burden is thus less in the first year than it may be in later years. However, this does not mean that there already exists a liability for the taxes of later years, or any part of them. Yet some companies show, and some auditors appear to insist that clients show, the amount of this non-existent liability.

If footnotes have any special use, it could well be in respect of such items as these. A company may want to explain that its assets have been diminished by payments for intangible prospective benefits, and that it *may* incur higher taxes in later years because of some relief from tax obtained in the year of purchase of fixed assets. But to include these items in balance sheets *as if they were actual* assets or liabilities at the balance-sheet date is merely to confuse matters.

THE VIRTUE OF UNDERSTATEMENT

Legislators seem to have been particularly anxious to prevent investors and creditors from being misled by the overstatement of asset values. Accountants, on their part, have tended to go along with this, often making use of a notion of conservatism as a guiding principle. Both seem to have overlooked the possibility that investors may be misled just as much by understatement of assets as by overstatement. The cited examples of takeover bids (Chapter 10) indicate by how much outside parties may be misled. We took takeover bids as sources of evidence of understatement—not of the only occasions in which there is gross understatement.

Understatement (like overstatement, of course) may seriously distort the distribution of investible funds among companies, for it results in fictitious overstatement of the rate of return and fallacious comparisons of the actual and prospective states and performances of companies. Suppose, for example, that there were two companies, one of them forty years old and one four years old; that both kept their accounts on the basis of historical cost figures, on the ground that their assets would thus be conservatively valued; and that their accounts for the latest year showed they both earned the *same* rate of return. It would be supposed, on the basis of the figures, that both were equally efficient, financially. However, there would be a far greater element of understatement of the assets of the older company than of the younger. Other things being equal, the older company would *appear* to be equal in financial efficiency to the younger only because of this understatement of assets and consequential understatement of the shareholders' equity (the denominator in the rate of return calculation).

If, according to the legislation, a true and fair view or a fair presentation of a company's position and result is to be given, the law should be opposed equally to overstatement and understatement. By way of example, some recent amendments to Australian state Companies Acts set upper limits to the amounts at which certain assets may be shown: current assets at *not more than* expected realizable values, and any fixed asset at *not more than* 'it would be reasonable for the company to spend to acquire that asset as at the end of the financial year'. There is no rule against understatement except the general rule that a true and fair view be given. But if that rule is sufficient, additional rules against overstatement should be unnecessary. And if that rule is insufficient, both overstatement and understatement should be proscribed. In short, a firm rule should be prescribed.

THE RESULTANT

Whatever else the securities market needs, hard factual information on company positions and results is necessary as a prophylactic from time to time to flush out the accumulation of rumours, promises, hopes and fears which affect the judgments of all who operate in it. It needs a more or less clear stream of up-to-date information. What does it get? A slurry made up of stale information, commercially meaningless figures and descriptions, scattered and unsystematic bits of information, inconsistent and superfluous information, and most of it in terms of funny money. In Hayakawa's words, we have 'maps' or 'pictures' with hosts of 'extra curlicues and twists', which have no reference to the external world but which are used as if they fairly and fully represent the positions and results of companies in their dealings with the external world.

THE CAUSE?

We can blame no particular class of people for this state of affairs.

The legislation has grown in patchwork fashion as new rules have been super-imposed on old. The defects of the old are not eradicated when the old rules remain as permissible alternatives. Occasionally fiscal legislation has, in effect, forced companies to use rules that cut across the rules of the securities legislation.

Businessmen have tolerated, and in some cases actively upheld, loose and contradictory rules. They may not have intended to use those rules for tactical 'income smoothing' or otherwise to manipulate the flow of information to the securities market. Nevertheless many of them have taken advantage, in these ways, of the absence of firm rules.

The judiciary has generally lent its support to the practices adopted by businessmen and companies, partly out of respect for the legislation whatever its defects, and partly out of the belief that businessmen would not adopt rules that were technically defective.

The stock exchanges and regulatory bodies, though concerned with the maintenance of a fair market in securities, have taken no effective stand on the style of information that is usable and necessary for analytical and comparative purposes.

Accountants, under pressure from the law, the judicial decisions, the directors they serve and the stock exchanges, have no doubt found it difficult to throw over old practices, notwithstanding their absurdities. Perhaps they have been confused about what constitutes a true and fair view of results and position, by the many different kinds of information they are required to produce for special purposes from time to time. Perhaps many of them have come to believe that the curious figures and descriptions which emerge from the folk-lore do have some real-world significance.

The financial affairs of companies have engaged the special skills of lawyers, businessmen, financiers, brokers, analysts, regulators and accountants—each in their special way. However, each such way is technically limited, and the 'languages' of each in respect of the same matters are often at odds. Further each such group of specialists has shown a rather tender regard or courtesy towards the expertise of the other: to such effect that the intention of the legislation—to secure reasonably well-informed dealing between companies and those who have or deal in financial interests in them—is lost to sight. Diverse views, opinions, arguments, tactics, compromises and makeshifts have interacted to produce the unanalyzable residue that flows as 'information' to the securities market. In its own way it is no less dangerous than the product of the pollutants of which Rachel Carson's experts complained. Like other environmental pollution, it can, and should, be stopped at its source.

THE REMEDY

The argument and evidence throughout this book points clearly to the rules that should supplant the present widely accepted rules. The evidence shows that financial statements based on market prices of assets are necessary in principle, and that, for large categories of assets, market prices of assets are discoverable. The market does not have to put up with figures that by their nature have no connection with a present financial position, and that are so remote, as they have been shown to be, from figures relevant to financial decisions and negotiations.

It is possible to do away with stock market pollution.

16

RX: IN THE PUBLIC INTEREST AND FOR THE PROTECTION OF INVESTORS

'Besides the general principles of justice, the law must be so clear and reproducible that the individual citizen can assess his rights and duties in advance, even where they appear to conflict with those of others. He must be able to ascertain with a reasonable certainty what view a judge or a jury will take of his position. If he cannot do this, the legal code, no matter how well intended, will not enable him to lead a life free from litigation and confusion.'
/ Norbert Wiener, *The Human Use of Human Beings*, 1950 /

The existing laws on corporate financial publicity, on the patterns of the United Kingdom and of the United States, express a firm and wise principle. It is epitomized in the phrases 'a true and fair view', 'fair presentation' and 'full and fair disclosure'. The laws do not interfere with the liberty of investors and others to run risks in the pursuit of gain. They intend only that those who deal with companies shall have reliable financial information on the past performance and present condition from time to time of each company to which the statutes apply. Given this information, investors, creditors, financiers and other parties of interest may form such judgments of past results and such opinions of future prospects as seem fit to them.

The present auxiliaries to the primary principle do not amplify that principle. The 'accounts' schedule to acts on the UK pattern permit companies to use cost prices for some assets, replacement prices for others, market prices for others, and various hybrid rules. Administrative regulation under the US acts generally enforces the use of cost prices as basic figures, but in practice various hybrids are used. We have shown that none of these mixtures of 'prices' or valuations can yield figures of the kind that are informative to outsiders on the matters of which they must be informed if they are to choose knowledgeably between securities, or between security investments and other kinds of investments.

Reform lies in the direction of specifying in the acts, or in the auxiliary schedules or regulations, rules by which the practices of companies may be consistent with the principle of full and fair disclosure.

The recommendations and suggestions which follow relate only to those parts of the acts and regulations that need to be modified in the light of the arguments and evidence already presented. No stipulation is made in respect of the items of income and expense, or the particular assets and equities, which shall be shown in financial statements. Most modern statutes and regulations provide a full list of these. Our suggestions are directed almost entirely to the kinds of figures that shall be used in those statements.

While no pretence is made of expertise in legal drafting, it has seemed desirable to cast the suggestions in the form of sections of statutes or regulations, for that is the form through which, if at all, they will be introduced.

For the sake of simplification, the framework of an act having an 'accounts' schedule in the manner of the UK Act will be adopted. But the particular sections or sets of sections may be readily introduced into any other framework. Throughout we have used 'year' to refer to the 'period of accounting', the latter more general term could be used.

A TRUE AND FAIR VIEW OR PRESENTATION

'The law must be clear and reproducible', said Wiener. 'Reproducibility is prior to equity, for without it there can be no equity'. If directors and others are to be held accountable for giving 'a true and fair view' of a company's affairs, the meaning of the phrase must be made clear. What kinds of figures will yield a true and fair view must be indicated. Following the evidence, arguments and opinions cited, we have concluded that the appropriate figures are or are based on up-to-date market selling prices of assets.

It is presumed that the statute specifies that a balance sheet and profit and loss (or income) account shall be drawn up and published periodically and that these statements shall give, respectively, a true and fair view of the financial position (or state of affairs) of a company as at the end of its accounting period and a true and fair view of its results for that period. By way of definition or amplification, there should be *added to the statute* the following sections or sub-sections:

> No balance sheet shall be deemed to give or declared to give a true and fair view of the state of affairs of a company unless the amounts shown for the several assets are the best possible approximation to the net selling prices in the ordinary course of business of those assets in their then condition as at the date of the balance sheet, and in the case of debts receivable the best possible approximation to the amounts expected at the date of the balance sheet to be receivable or recoverable.

> No profit and loss account shall be deemed to give or declared to give a true and fair view of the profit or loss of a company unless that profit or loss is calculated so as to include changes during the year in the net selling prices of assets and the effects during the year of changes in the purchasing power of the unit of account as specified in the Schedule to this Act.

Comment: The rule for asset valuation explicitly recognizes that net selling prices may be approximations but it directs that the best possible approximation be obtained. This does not entail that each company shall, at its balancing date, actively seek out a buyer. It entails only that a genuine attempt be made to obtain an up-to-date price, whether by observation of sales of similar goods or property, by reference to valuations for rating or taxing purposes, or by reference to the catalogues of resellers or the estimates of valuers. Some of these are specified below in the suggested additions to the Schedule to the Act. It would be sufficient if the prices or valuations on which the reported figures are based were obtained at some date as close to the end of the period of accounting as was reasonably convenient.

The adoption of one guiding rule for asset valuation would greatly simplify acts and schedules on the English pattern. It would reduce the scope for understatement and overstatement of asset values, eliminate the need for reference to alternative methods of valuation by eliminating optional rules altogether, remove the need for complicated footnotes 'explaining' methods of valuation, and remove the possibility of 'engineered' changes in accounting principles. The specific simplifications are too numerous to deal with here.

The rule in respect of the profit and loss account is intended to ensure that *all* changes by which a company becomes financially better off or worse off are reported in the year in which they occur. It would remove the optional treatment, available under some statutes, of gains and losses on sales and revaluations of so-called fixed assets. It would eliminate the possibility of deferring the reporting of such gains and losses for 'tactical' reasons. It would not prevent the separate reporting, within the account, of gains and losses of different kinds. But it would prevent the reporting of net profits and omitting to report in the same place, as is now possible, offsetting declines in the values of fixed assets. Further comments are given when dealing below with suggested changes in the Schedule to the Act.

For the purpose of giving effect to the rule in respect of the profit and loss account and the subsidiary rules to be suggested below, it is necessary that there be prescribed an index of changes in the general level of prices which shall be used uniformly by companies to bring into account the effects of changes (in the opposite direction) of the purchasing power of the unit of account. There should, therefore, be a section or a definition, somewhat as follows:

> 'Prescribed index' where used in this Act or in the Schedules thereto shall have reference to an index of changes in the general level of prices prescribed by (the appropriate authority).

Comment: The index is to be used solely for the purpose of making certain adjustments consequent upon changes in the general purchasing power of money. The kind of index generally used and recommended for this purpose is an index of changes in the level of the retail prices of consumer goods. Every index number series may be said to have some defects but shifts in the purchasing power of money do occur and it is better to make some approximation to their effects than to disregard them. The advice of an official statistician should be sought on the appropriate index.

INCOME CALCULATION

It is presumed that there will be, in the Schedule to the Act, an indication of the contents of the profit and loss account. The common stipulations relate to the separate showing of amounts received and due and receivable in respect of dividends and inter-est from stated classes of security investments, amounts of interest paid or due and payable in respect of the company's outstanding securities, amounts paid or due and payable to auditors and to directors, and the amount provided for payment of income tax in respect of the income of the period. We shall present here only the additional clauses necessary to specify the manner in which certain charges or credits shall be calculated. These clauses may become sub-clauses of a main clause of a re-drafted schedule but for convenience we shall simply number them PL1, PL2 ... to signify that they relate to profit and loss account items.

> **PL1** There shall be shown separately in the profit and loss account the amount of the price variation adjustment which amount shall be obtained by taking the sum of all adjustments to the book values of assets made during the year or at the end of the year to make those values equal to the amounts at which under this Act the assets are required to be shown in the balance sheet.

Comment: The function of the price variation adjustment is to bring into account at the end of a period the effects of appreciation and depreciation of plant, machinery, land and buildings, security investments, inventories and other assets. The several assets will have been written up or down to the amounts required to be shown in the balance sheet. The amount of the price variation adjustment will be the net aggregate of these separate adjustments. If it is deemed to be desirable, an additional clause could require that the net adjustment in respect of each main class of assets be given either in the profit and loss account itself or in an explanatory footnote.

The clause allows any company to keep its accounts in any way it pleases during the year, provided it makes the appropriate adjustments at the end of the year. If a company wishes to keep its accounts in such a way that they continuously represent current market selling prices, it may accumulate adjustments to book values during the year in the price variation adjustment account.

Some may object to the inclusion of all rises and falls in asset prices in the determination of income or profit. However, every rise or fall has exactly the same effect on the company's financial position as a gain or loss on trading, and all such gains and losses are part of the result of the year's operations. There is therefore no ground whatever for treating rises or falls in the prices of some assets in a manner different from the treatment of others.

PL2 There shall be shown separately in the profit and loss account the amount for the year of the capital maintenance adjustment, which amount shall be obtained by applying the proportionate change during the year in the prescribed index to the sum of the paid up ordinary share capital, share premium reserve, other capital reserves and the balance of the capital maintenance reserve, all as at the beginning of the year.

PL3 There shall be shown separately in the profit and loss account the amount for the year of the undistributed profits adjustment which amount shall be obtained by applying the proportionate change in the prescribed index to the sum of all amounts of undistributed profits, however described, as at the beginning of the year.

Comment: Under the general asset valuation rule all assets are to be reported at approximate prices at the end of the year. They will be in terms of units of 'end-of-the-year purchasing power'. A net surplus of the nature of profit for the year will only arise if the ordinary shareholders' equity accounts (such as paid-in capital, capital maintenance reserve and undistributed profits) have first been made up to the amounts at the end of the year which are the equivalent in purchasing power of the amounts reported at the end of the previous period. The object of the two adjustments PL2 and PL3 is to deduct from the gross surplus a sufficient number of dollars to 'make up' the opening balances to equivalents in end-of-the-year dollars. In effect, net profit is calculated by making a definite provision for the maintenance, in purchasing power, of the ordinary shareholders' equity at the beginning of the year. It is a true distributable surplus.

When prices are rising, the price variation adjustment will include appreciation in asset values which some may not regard as properly distributable. But the object of charging the adjustments PL2 and PL3 against the gross surplus is to take account of the loss in purchasing power (when the general price level has risen) of the opening net assets *as if* the net assets were wholly in cash. It is therefore only proper to add back the appreciation of any non-cash assets whose prices have risen, as part of the price variation adjustment. The net effect of the price variation adjustment and the adjustments PL2 and PL3 may be a gain or a loss, but whatever it is, it represents a genuine gain or loss.

Though the adjustments PL2 and PL3 are calculated in the same way, they are kept separate so that a proper distinction shall be made in the balance sheet between what is 'in the nature of capital' and what is divisible surplus (undistributed profit).

> **PL4** If in any year a new issue of ordinary shares is made, the amount of the capital maintenance adjustment in that year in respect of that issue shall be obtained by applying to the total consideration received (in respect of share capital and share premiums, if any) the proportionate change in the prescribed index between the nearest subsequent date of the index number series and the end of the year.

Comment: This auxiliary rule relates to new issues only. If the law were amended to allow the issue of shares of no par value, the references here, and in PL2 and elsewhere, to paid up capital and share premiums would be replaced by a reference to the 'total consideration paid by subscribers'.

Certain specific rules would be necessary for the year in which the change from the present form of reporting to the suggested form is made. To make retrospective calculations in respect of movements in share capital and reserve accounts and changes in the purchasing power of money would be cumbersome and perhaps complicated. When, previously, changes in the law have required new bases of valuation to be adopted, the short-cut of 'deeming' the most recent values to be the required values has been adopted. A similar short-cut could be adopted in the present case.

> **PL5** In respect of the year for which these provisions shall first become effective
>
> (a) there shall be annexed to the accounts a reconciliation statement which shall show
>
> > (i)   the total amount as at the beginning of the year by which the valuations of the assets made in accordance with the provisions of this Act exceed the amounts shown in the balance sheet as at the end of the preceding year;
> >
> > (ii) the division of the total amount referred to in the last preceding sub-clause in the same proportion as the total of ordinary paid up share capital, share premium reserves and other capital reserves bears to the total of undistributed profits and reserves in the nature of undistributed profits;

(b) the amounts determined in accordance with sub-clause PL5 (a)
     (ii) shall be treated, as to the first part, as the opening balance of
     the capital maintenance reserve, and, as to the second part, as a
     separately stated undistributed profits adjustment;

(c) where the above rule shall, in the special circumstances of any
     company, result in amounts which do not give a true and fair
     view of the respective proportions of amounts in the nature of
     capital and amounts in the nature of undivided profits, and
     where an alternative distribution is adopted, the reasons for that
     distribution shall be stated.

BALANCE SHEET

It is presumed that the Schedule to the Act specifies the principal
items of assets and equities which are to be separately stated. We
shall present here only the additional clauses necessary to amplify
or clarify the intention that a true and fair view be given. They
relate principally to the methods of obtaining the amounts to be
shown in the balance sheet. As in the case of the profit and loss
account, these provisions may be added to the existing Schedule
wherever appropriate. For convenience they are simply designated
BS1, BS2 ...

BS1 The methods of obtaining the amounts to be shown in respect
of any investment or asset at the end of any year shall be as
follows:

(a) in respect of any asset for which there is a readily ascertainable
     market resale price at the end of the year for such asset in its then
     condition, the amount shall be that price; provided that

     (i)   in respect of any land or other real property, the amount
            may be or be based upon the valuations of the Valuer
            General or any expert valuer, but so that the best possible
            approximation to a current market resale price is obtained;
     (ii)   in respect of any stock in trade, the amount shall be the
            net price at which the goods are sold in the ordinary course
            of business of the company, and in respect of any work in
            progress, the amount shall be the price (if any) at which it
            could be sold in its then state and condition;
     (iii) in respect of any trade or other debtors, the amount shall
            be the amount which on due consideration or inquiry is

        expected at the end of the year to be recoverable, provided that the amount of any debt payable with interest in instalments shall not be shown at a greater sum than the company would accept in full settlement of the account at the end of the year;

(iv) in respect of any investment in any class of securities of a subsidiary company or of any other company the securities of which are not quoted on a stock exchange, the amount shall be that proportion of the equity of that class of securities in the assets of that subsidiary or other company which the company's holding bears to the total securities of that class issued by that subsidiary or other company;

(b) where it is known that any commission or rebate or allowance would have to be paid or made on sale in respect of the approximate resale prices referred to in sub-clause (a) of this clause, the amounts to be shown shall be reduced by the amounts of such commission, rebate or allowance;

(c) where any resale price or valuation has been obtained at a date prior to the end of the year, and upon due inquiry there is no reasonable ground for believing that that price or valuation has changed, that price or valuation may be shown as the amount of any investment or asset as at the end of the year;

(d) where the company has made any outlays on or in respect of assets for which there is no resale price in the ordinary course of business at the end of the year, and in respect of any other assets, the company may at the option of the directors show the cost of any such assets in parenthesis or footnote, but no such cost shall be included in the main columns or figures of any balance sheet.

Comment: These provisions are consistent with the suggested section of the Act which states what shall be considered to give a true and fair view of results and position. They are intended to make clear that different sources of information may be relied upon for different kinds of asset, provided always that the amounts shown are reasonable approximations to the current market resale prices of assets, or their monetary equivalents. On the introduction of these provisions, of course, all other references to methods of valuation would be removed from the Act and the Schedule.

BS2 There shall be shown separately in the balance sheet

(a) the amount paid up or deemed to be paid up on all ordinary shares issued by the company;

(b) the amount of any share premiums and other reserves of a capital nature the residuary interests in which run to the holders of ordinary shares;

(c) the amount of the capital maintenance reserve;

(d) the amount of undistributed profits, however described, the residuary interests in which run to the holders of ordinary shares, inclusive of the amount of any undistributed profits adjustment made in respect of the year.

Comment: These provisions are designed to distinguish amounts which are not available for division as dividends—items (a), (b) and (c)—from divisible surpluses. Where shares have a specific par value, it seems desirable to keep separate the nominal amount of paid up share capital; the procedure is illustrated in Chapter 14. The capital maintenance reserve is a cumulative account, as is the profit and loss appropriation account but it is in the nature of capital. Its amount does not represent divisible profit but, like share premium reserves, it may be appropriated for the purpose of making bonus issues of shares, and for other purposes for which the balance of a share premium account may be used. An appropriate section or subsection should be added to the Act indicating the restricted character of the capital maintenance reserve. The amount of undistributed profit, however described, is of course available for dividends and other purposes, since it is a genuine surplus and is represented by assets having a money equivalent.

The effects of these provisions on the contents of the profit and loss account and balance sheet may be seen, in simplified form, in the examples given in the latter part of Chapter 14.

HOLDING AND SUBSIDIARY COMPANIES; GROUPS

We have not directed a great deal of attention in this book to the financial statements of groups of companies. We have, of course, noticed that inter-company shareholdings and transactions have given cover to fraudulent dealing and to legally less serious but financially no less deceptive mis-statements of results and position. All this has been possible because assets could be shown at values determined at the discretion of company officers and having no relation to their current money's worth or resale prices. The possibility would be removed by enforcement of the asset valuation rules we have suggested. For no matter what prices were agreed upon between related companies on the transfer of assets from one to another, valuation at an external market price at the end of the year would squeeze all the 'water' out of the 'agreed price' when the balance sheet and profit and loss account of the buyer company was made up.

There is one respect however in which the present law and practice under it seem to be of questionable validity. Consolidated accounting or group accounting is a device by which the various assets and equities of each company in a group of companies are 'consolidated' *as if* they were the assets and equities of one entity—the group. In fact, of course, there is no such legal entity as 'the group'. Each company is in its own right a limited liability company; and the rights of creditors are restricted by the limited liability of the members of their debtor companies. The group is a fiction, and, as far as creditors are concerned, not even a legal fiction.

Further, the provisions on consolidated or group accounts in the acts and their schedules permit groups to make complete consolidations or several partial consolidations or to give the separate accounts of all companies in a group, at the discretion of the directors. This introduces diversity into the reporting of groups which may interfere with the possibility of comparing any group figures in successive years, or of comparing the figures of any two or more groups.

These defects of consolidation accounting would be removed if groups were required to give not consolidated accounts but 'supplementary financial statistics'. The following provisions are therefore suggested in lieu of the provisions relating to the accounts of groups in the present statutes. The clauses are numbered GS1, GS2 . . . to signify that they relate to group statistics.

GS1 There shall be annexed to the financial statements of every holding company a statement in the same form as the profit and loss account of the company stating in particular the aggregates for all subsidiary companies (except as provided in clause GS3) of the amounts of the several items required by this Act to be shown in profit and loss accounts and indicating the extent to which the profits or losses of the group of subsidiary companies have been brought into the accounts of the holding company by way of dividends or by way of increases or decreases in the valuations of interests in subsidiary companies as required by clause BS1 (a)(iv) of this Schedule.

GS2 There shall be annexed to the financial statements of every holding company a statement in the same form as the balance sheet of the company stating in particular the aggregates for all subsidiary companies (except as provided in clause GS3) of the amounts of the several assets required by this Act to be shown in balance sheets and indicating the extent of the equities in those assets of the holding company and of minority shareholders and of creditors.

GS3 In respect of any subsidiary company or companies which is or are incorporated in or operating in any jurisdiction subject to material constraints on the repatriation to this jurisdiction of dividends or of the amounts of the investment in or debts of such company or companies, there shall be shown, in parallel with the information required by clauses GS1 and GS2 to be shown, the amounts for that subsidiary or the aggregates for those subsidiary companies of the several items required by this Schedule to be shown in profit and loss accounts and balance sheets; and there shall be stated the reasons why there is a difference, if any, between the amount of the investment of the holding company in such company or companies shown in the balance sheet of the holding company and the amount shown in the annexure, and why there is a difference, if any, between the amount of the profits from such company or companies shown in the profit and loss account of the holding company and the amount shown in the annexure as paid or attributable to the holding company.

Comment: Clause BS1(a)(iv) requires that the interests of companies in other companies whose shares are not quoted on a stock exchange shall be shown in the amount of the investor company's proportionate interest in the assets of the other company. This amount is thus genuinely represented by assets (of the other company) having market prices or monetary equivalents, under the suggested rules. In respect of subsidiary companies other than those referred to in GS3, the holding company's equity as shown in the holding company's balance sheet should be equal to the holding company's equity as shown in the supplementary statistics. There is no need under the above rules to 'consolidate' accounts in order to eliminate inter-company profits, since the market selling price rule for assets cuts out all fictitious or intra-group profits. Inter-company transactions will determine which of the companies in a group makes profits but will not affect the aggregate profit of the group.

The aggregations required by the group statistics provisions will be straight aggregations; there will be no set-offs as between companies in the group. Thus, for example, the aggregate debts of companies in the group to other companies in the group would be shown; the aggregate profits of those companies making profits, and the aggregate losses of those companies making losses, would be shown, each in its proper place in the summaries required by these clauses.

Finally, these suggested provisions are not an essential element of the reforms to which the evidence and argument of this book point. They are directed against the possibility of misdirection of investors and creditors who may believe that group 'accounts' represent the legal interests of one entity—the group—in the assets there shown and that the several classes of equityholder have clear equities in those assets. The group is not a legal entity, as we have said; to imply, by any provision of the statute, that 'group accounts' are similar in significance to the accounts of a legal entity may be misleading.

IMPLEMENTATION

The proposals may seem radical but they are quite practicable. They may require some modest time and effort on the part of companies to make the conversions they entail. It may therefore be reasonable to provide, in the amending act by which they are introduced, that they shall become effective not later than, say, two years after the date of enactment.

CAVEAT

We have sought to present only those changes in the acts, schedules or regulation which are necessary to specify the style of the financial statements which follow from the evidence and argument presented. Consequential changes may be necessary in other parts of the acts, schedules or regulations to make the whole of their provisions consistent. However the nature of these changes will depend on the particular provisions of the legislation of each individual jurisdiction.

A JUST AND FAIR LAW

Those who prepare financial information on companies, those who publish it, those who authenticate it, those who rely on it as investors and creditors, those who analyze it and give advice on the basis of it—all are entitled to promote and to protect their interests. But within the law.

Accountants, directors and auditors are by law put on notice of their general duty to provide dependable information. The present law is insufficiently precise in some respects to secure this; in other respects it is in demonstrable conflict with the general duty it enunciates. While this is the case, 'the legal code, no matter how well intended, will not enable [accountants, directors and auditors] to lead a life free from litigation and confusion', to use Wiener's words.

On their part, investors, creditors, financiers and dealers in securities are entitled to expect that they can depend on the information which the law requires to be backed, as to its quality, by declarations of directors and auditors. Too often, and often too late, they find the information they received to be unreliable. 'The slings and arrows of outrageous fortune' are trial enough in the commercial world. Their effects are compounded by the unpredictable release and the unwitting or deliberate suppression of information that the securities market needs for the fair evaluation of the results and prospects of companies.

The mechanism of the market has its defects in spite of the heavy concentration of attention on it. However a perfect mechanism will only result in more errors more quickly made if the information that should be both stimulus and stabilizer to the market is irrelevant, out-of-date, incomplete and non-comparable. The generation of information is a costly process. No one can guess the cost of generating and publishing *irrelevant* information.

Much of it is concealed, since the inefficiency that flows from its use is not traceable and the personal misfortunes of the many who suffer its consequences are not reported.

The complexities of corporate business and the securities market deserve a form of financial instrumentation which, because it is comprehensive and not readily manipulable in the interest of any one class of persons, is fair to all. The variations from present practice which this chapter sketches would greatly enhance the 'fairness' of the market. They would bring about the publication of information of the style clearly intended by the law—in the public interest and for the protection of investors.

LIST OF REFERENCES

Accounting Research Division, Staff of, American Institute of Certified Public Accountants. *Reporting the Financial Effects of Price-Level Changes.* New York, 1936.

American Accounting Association. *A Tentative Statement of Accounting Principles.* 1963.

American Institute of Certified Public Accountants.

—*Accounting Research Bulletins.* (1939 to 1961).

—*Accounting Research Studies.* See Accounting Research Division, Staff of, Grady, Wyatt.

—*Accounting Trends and Techniques.* (annual).

—*Approved Methods for the Preparation of Balance Sheet Statements.* New York, 1917.

—*Examination of Financial Statements by Independent Public Accountants.* New York, 1936.

APB Hearing on Accounting for Investments in Equity Securities Not Qualifying for the Equity Method: Cases in Public Accounting Practice No. 8. Arthur Andersen & Co., Chicago, 1971.

Archibald, T Ross. 'The Return to Straight Line Depreciation: An Analysis of a Change in Accounting Method'. *Empirical Research in Accounting: Selected Studies 1967.* The Institute of Professional Accounting, University of Chicago.

Association of Certified and Corporate Accountants. *Accounting for Inflation.* Gee & Company (Publishers), London, 1952.

Ballantine, Henry Winthrop. *Ballantine on Corporations.* Revised edn. Callaghan, Chicago, 1946.

Berle, A A, Jr., & Fisher, Frederick S. 'Elements of the Law of Business Accounting'. *Columbia Law Review,* vol. xxxii, no. 4, April 1932.

Blaine, Earl. *Reported Accounting Changes and Financial Statement Manipulation.* University of British Columbia, Vancouver, 1970.

Briloff, Abraham J. 'Distortions Arising from Pooling of Interests Accounting'. *Financial Analysts Journal,* vol. xxiv, no. 2, March-April 1968.

—'Much Abused Goodwill'. *Barron's,* 28 April 1969.

Brooks, Collin (ed.). *The Royal Mail Case.* William Hodge & Company, Edinburgh and London, 1933.

Bull, George & Vice, Anthony. *Bid for Power.* 3rd edn. Elek Books, London, 1961.

Canadian Institute of Chartered Accountants. *Financial Reporting in Canada, 1959.* Toronto.

Chambers, R J. 'Financial Information and the Securities Market'. *Abacus,* vol. 1, no. 1, September 1965.

—'A Matter of Principle'. *Accounting Review,* vol. xli, no. 3, July 1966.

City Working Party. *The City Code on Takeovers and Mergers.* London, 1968.

Clendenin, John C. *Introduction to Investments.* 4th edn. McGraw-Hill, New York, 1964.

Cohen, Milton H. ' "Truth in Securities" Revisited'. *Harvard Law Review,* vol. 79, no. 3, January 1966.

Cole, William Morse. *Accounts, Their Construction and Interpretation.* Houghton Mifflin, Boston, 1915.

Dicksee, L R. *Auditing.* 8th edn. Gee & Company, London, 1910.

Duke University Symposium on 'Uniformity in Financial Accounting'. *Law and Contemporary Problems,* vol. xxx, no. 4, Autumn 1965.

Federal Trade Commission, Staff of. *Economic Report on Corporate Mergers.* US Government Printing Office, Washington, 1969.

Fisher, Irving. *The Nature of Capital and Income* (1906). Reprint. Augustus M Kelley, New York, 1965.

Foulke, R A. *Practical Financial Statement Analysis.* 6th edn. McGraw-Hill, New York, 1968.

Fulton, J W. *British-Indian Book-keeping.* G Auld, Bengal, 1800.

Gilbert, Lewis D & John J. *Twenty-Eighth Annual Report on Stockholder Activities at Corporation Meetings during 1967.* New York.

Gower, L C B. *The Principles of Modern Company Law* 3rd edn. Stevens & Sons, London, 1969.

Grady, Paul. *Inventory of Generally Accepted Accounting Principles for Business Enterprises.* American Institute of Certified Public Accountants, New York, 1965.

Graham, Benjamin, Dodd, David L & Cottle, Sidney. *Security Analysis.* 4th edn. McGraw-Hill, New York, 1962.

Greer, Howard C. 'What are Accepted Principles of Accounting?'. *Accounting Review,* vol. xiii, no. 1, March 1938.

Hamilton, Robert. *An Introduction to Merchandise.* For Elliot, Edinburgh, 1788.

Hatfield, Henry Rand. *Modern Accounting.* Appleton-Century, New York, 1909.

Hayakawa, S I. *Language in Thought and Action.* 2nd edn. George Allen & Unwin, London, 1965.

Hayes, Douglas A. 'Accounting Principles and Investment Analysis'. *Law and Contemporary Problems,* vol. xxx, no. 4, Autumn 1965.

Hayes, Richard. *The Gentleman's Complete Book-keeper.* J Noon, London, 1741.

Hicks, J R. *Value and Capital.* 2nd edn. Oxford University Press, London, 1946.

Hobson, Sir Oscar. 'As I See It...'. *The Banker,* vol. cxi, no. 424, June 1961.

'How Inflation Warps Accounts'. *Economist,* 16 January 1971.

Hunt, Bishop Carleton. *The Development of the Business Corporation in England 1800–1867.* Harvard University Press, Cambridge, Mass., 1936.

Institute of Chartered Accountants in England and Wales. *Accounting for Stewardship in a Period of Inflation.* 1968.

—*Recommendation N15.* 'Accounting in relation to changes in the purchasing power of money'. 1952.

—*Recommendation N18.* 'Presentation of balance sheet and profit and loss account'. 1958.

—*Survey of Published Accounts, 1969–70.*

—*Technical Statement S8.* 'Accountants' liability to third parties—The Hedley Byrne decision'. 1965.

Institute of Cost and Works Accountants. *The Accountancy of Changing Price Levels.* London, 1952.

Jobson's Financial Services. *Jobson's Year Book of Public Companies of Australia and New Zealand.* Sydney, 1970.

Jones, Ralph Coughenour. *Effects of Price Level Changes on Business Income, Capital and Taxes.* American Accounting Association, 1956.

Kelly, P. *The Elements of Book-keeping.* J Whiting, London, 1801.

Kohler, Marcel F & Matz, Adolph. 'Swiss Financial Reporting and Auditing Practices'. *Abacus,* vol. 4, no. 1, August 1968.

Kripke, Homer. 'The SEC, The Accountants, Some Myths and Some Realities'. *New York University Law Review,* vol. 45, no. 6, December 1970.

Laeri, J Howard. 'The Audit Gap.' *Journal of Accountancy*, vol. 121, no. 3, March 1966.

Landman, Allan. 'What's Wrong with Appraisal Values?' *Journal of Accountancy*, vol. 131, no. 3, March 1971.

Lindon, J B, assisted by Parker, G Brian & Williams, Hugh R. *Buckley on the Companies Acts*. 13th edn. Butterworths, London, 1957.

Lipsey, Richard G & Steiner, Peter O. *Economics*. Harper & Row, New York, 1966.

Loss, Louis. *Securities Regulation*. 2d edn. Little, Brown & Company, Boston, 1961.

MacNeal, Kenneth. *Truth in Accounting*. University of Pennsylvania Press, Philadelphia, 1939.

Mair, John. *Book-keeping Moderniz'd*. Bell & Bradfrute and W. Creech, Edinburgh, 1800.

Manne, Henry G (ed). *Economic Policy and the Regulation of Corporate Securities*. American Enterprise Institute for Public Policy Research, Washington, D.C., 1969.

Marriott, Oliver. *The Property Boom* (1967). References to Pan Books edn, London, 1969. Reprinted with permission of A D Peters & Co.

Mill, John Stuart. *Principles of Political Economy* (1848). Longmans Green & Co., London, 1940 edn.

Montgomery, Robert H. *Auditing*. 7th edn. Ronald Press Company, New York, 1949.

Morrison, James. *The Elements of Book Keeping*. For Longman, Rees, Orme, Brown & Green, London, 1825.

Myers, John H. 'Depreciation Manipulation for Fun and Profits'. *Financial Analysts Journal*, vol. 23, no. 6, November-December 1967.

National Bureau of Economic Research. *Measuring the Nation's Wealth*. Papers from the Wealth Inventory Planning Study, George Washington University, Columbia University Press, New York, 1964.

Newbould, Gerald D. *Management and Merger Activity*. Guthstead, Liverpool, 1970.

Paton, William Andrew. *Accounting Theory*. Ronald Press Company, New York, 1922.

Paton, William A & Paton, William A, Jr., *Corporation Accounts and Statements*. Macmillan Company, New York, 1955.

Pixley, F W. *Auditors: Their Duties and Responsibilities.* 5th edn. Henry Good & Son, London, 1889.

Plum, Lester V, Humphrey, Joseph H & Bowyer, John W, Jr. *Investment Analysis and Management.* Richard D. Irwin, Homewood, Ill., 1961.

Rappoport, Louis H. *SEC Accounting Practice and Procedure.* Ronald Press Company, New York, 1959.

Reiling, Henry B & Taussig, Russell A. 'Recent Liability Cases—Implications for Accountants'. *Journal of Accountancy,* vol. 130, no. 3, September 1970.

Reports, Official

Report of the Committee on Company Law Amendment, Cmd.6659 (Cohen Committee Report). HMSO, London, June 1945.

Report of the Company Law Committee, Cmnd.1749 (Jenkins Committee Report). H.M.S.O., London, June 1962.

Interim Report of Inspectors H C Stewart and B L Murray, QC, on the Affairs of Reid Murray Holdings Limited . . . Reid Murray Developments (WA) Pty Ltd [and certain other companies]. Mimeograph, 1963.

Interim Report of an Investigation . . . into the Affairs of Reid Murray Holdings Limited and . . . Reid Murray Acceptance Limited. Government Printer, Melbourne, 1963.

Interim Report of an Investigation . . . into the Affairs of Reid Murray Holdings Limited . . . and Final Report of an Investigation . . . into the Affairs of Payne's Properties Pty Ltd, and Certain Subsidiary and Associated Companies. Government Printer, Melbourne, 1965.

Final Report of an Investigation . . . into the Affairs of Reid Murray Holdings . . . and Certain Other Companies. Government Printer, Melbourne, 1966.

Report of the Inspectors appointed . . . to Investigate the Affairs of Sydney Guarantee Corporation Limited. Government Printer, Sydney, 1964.

Report of the Royal Commission appointed to inquire into the Failure of Atlantic Acceptance Corporation Limited. The Queen's Printer, Ontario, 1969.

Ripley, William Z. *Main Street and Wall Street.* Little, Brown & Company, Boston, 1927.

Robert Morris Associates, Staff of. *Annual Statement Studies.* Robert Morris Associates, Philadelphia, 1968.

Sanders, Thomas Henry, Hatfield, Henry Rand & Moore, Underhill. *A Statement of Accounting Principles.* American Institute of Accountants, New York, 1938.

Savoie, Leonard M. 'Accounting Improvement: How Fast, How Far?' *Harvard Business Review,* vol. 41, no. 4, July-August 1963.

'SBA Revises Reporting Requirements for SBICs'. *Journal of Accountancy,* vol. 127, no. 6, June 1969.

Securities and Exchange Commission (USA). *Report of the Special Study of Securities Markets* (available only in SEC offices). 1963.

—*Accounting Series Release* No. 4. 25 April 1938.

—*Accounting Series Release* No. 53. 16 November 1945.

—*Regulation S-X.*

Shackle, G L S. *Expectation, Enterprise and Profit.* George Allen & Unwin, London, 1970.

Shaplen, Robert. *Kreuger, Genius and Swindler.* André Deutsch, London, 1961.

Simon, Sidney I. *Accounting and the Law.* Bureau of Economic Research, Rutgers—The State University, New Brunswick, NJ, 1965.

Simons, H C. *Personal Income Taxation.* University of Chicago Press, Chicago, 1938.

Spicer, E E & Pegler, E. C. *Practical Auditing.* H Foulks Lynch & Co., London, 1911.

Stephens, Hustcraft. *Italian Book-keeping.* W Mears, London, 1735.

Sterling, Robert R. 'In Defence of Accounting in the United States'. *Abacus,* vol. 2, no. 2, December 1966.

Stigler, George J. *The Theory of Price.* Macmillan Company, New York, 1946.

Study Group on Business Income. *Changing Concepts of Business Income.* Macmillan Company, New York, 1952.

Sweeney, Henry W. *Stabilized Accounting.* Harper & Brothers, New York, 1936.

Thompson, Wardhaugh. *The Accomptant's Oracle.* N Nickson, York, 1777.

Vallance, Aylmer. *Very Private Enterprise.* Thames & Hudson, London, 1955.

Wechsberg, Joseph. *The Merchant Bankers.* Little, Brown & Company, Boston, 1966.

Wilcox, E B & Hassler, R H. 'A Foundation for Accounting Principles'. *Journal of Accountancy,* vol. 72, no. 4, October 1941.

Wise, T A. *The Insiders.* Doubleday & Company, Garden City, NY, 1962.

Wyatt, Arthur R. *A Critical Study of Accounting for Business Combinations.* American Institute of Certified Public Accountants, New York, 1963.

INDEX OF COMPANIES

GENERAL INDEX

www.ingramcontent.com/pod-product-compliance
Lightning Source LLC
Chambersburg PA
CBHW082348230326
41599CB00058BA/7150